THE LIBRARY OF HOLOCAUST TESTIMONIES

The Children Accuse

The Library of Holocaust Testimonies

Editors: Antony Polonsky, Martin Gilbert CBE, Aubrey Newman,
Raphael F. Scharf, Ben Helfgott

Under the auspices of the Yad Vashem Committee of the Board of
Deputies of British Jews and the Centre for Holocaust Studies,
University of Leicester

My Lost World by Sara Rosen
From Dachau to Dunkirk by Fred Pelican
Breathe Deeply, My Son by Henry Wermuth
My Private War by Jacob Gerstenfeld-Maltiel
A Cat Called Adolf by Trude Levi
An End to Childhood by Miriam Akavia
A Child Alone by Martha Blend
I Light a Candle by Gena Turgel
My Heart in a Suitcase by Anne L. Fox
The Children Accuse edited by Maria Hochberg-Mariańska
and Noe Grüss

The Children Accuse

Edited by
Maria Hochberg-Mariańska
and
Noe Grüss

Translated by
Bill Johnston

VALLENTINE MITCHELL
LONDON · PORTLAND, OR

First published in 1996 in Great Britain by
VALLENTINE MITCHELL & CO. LTD
Newbury House, 900 Eastern Avenue, London IG2 7HH

and in the United States of America by
VALLENTINE MITCHELL
c/o ISBS, 5804 N.E. Hassalo Street, Portland, Oregon 97213-3644

British Library Cataloguing in Publication Data
The children accuse. - (The library of Holocaust
testimonies)
1. World War, 1939–1945 - Children - Poland 2. World War,
1939–1945 - Poland - Participation, Juvenile 3. World War,
1939–1945 - Personal narratives, Polish
I. Hochberg-Mariańska, Maria II. Grüss, Noe
940.5'3161'09438

ISBN 0 85303 312 9

Library of Congress Cataloging-in-Publication Data
Dzieci Żydowskie oskarżaja.   English
   The children accuse / edited by Maria Hochberg-Mariańska and Noe
Grüss; translated by Bill Johnston.
      p.   cm. — (The library of Holocaust testimonies)
   ISBN 0-85303-312-9 (pbk.)
   1. Jewish children—Poland—Biography.   2. Holocaust, Jewish
(1939–1945)—Poland—Personal narratives.   3. Jews—Persecutions–
–Poland.   I. Hochberg-Mariańska, Maria.   I. Gris, Noah.
III. Title.   IV. Series
DS135.P63D95   1996
940.53'18—dc20   96-2522
                                                       CIP

This book was originally published in Polish by the Jewish
Historical Commission, Cracow, in 1946.

Typeset by Regent Typesetting, London
Printed in Great Britain by
Watkiss Studios Ltd., Biggleswade, Beds.

Thanks are due to the Barnet and Sylvia Shine Foundation for its help with the publication of this book.

Contents

Contents

Glossary

Aktion: An organised operation in the ghetto, often lasting a number of days, in which Jews were rounded up and 'evacuated' to the camps

Arbeitsamt: Labour exchange

Arbeitseinsatz: The compulsory supply of a contingent of people for a particular job

Arbeitskarten: Work card

Aryan: Living 'on the Aryan side' or 'on Aryan papers' meant staying in the non-Jewish community and passing oneself off as a non-Jew.

Ausweis: Identity card

Bahnschutz: Railway police

Banderists: Members of a Ukrainian nationalist terrorist organisation under the leadership of Stepan Bandera (1908–59)

Capo/Kapo: Prison foreman in the concentration camps

Centos: An organisation uniting charitable societies caring for Jewish orphans

'Dark blue' police: The Polish police

Joint: International Jewish Aid Organisation

Judenrat: Jewish council in the ghetto

Kapo: see *Capo*

Kennkarte: Identity card

Kripo: The criminal police

Lagerälteste: The senior prisoner in a camp

Meldekarte: Residence card

Montelupich: The main prison in Kraków

Ordnungsdienst, OD; Ordners: The Jewish police

RGO: Rada Glowna Opiekuncza – the Central Welfare Council – an institution for social care under the occupation

SA: Sturm Abteilung – the army of the Nazi party

Schoppen: Places of work in the ghetto

Schutzpolizei, Schupo: The security police

Sonderdienst (SD): The Special Service

TOZ: Towarzystwo Ochrony Zdrowia Ludności Żydowskiej – a society for Jewish health care

Umschlagplatz: The square in Warsaw where Jews were assembled during the *Aktions*, before being put onto transports

Volksdeutsch: Those who lived outside the borders of Germany but claimed German nationality

The Library of Holocaust Testimonies

It is greatly to the credit of Frank Cass that this series of survivors' testimonies is being published in Britain. The need for such a series has long been apparent here, where many survivors made their homes.

Since the end of the war in 1945 the terrible events of the Nazi destruction of European Jewry have cast a pall over our time. Six million Jews were murdered within a short period; the few survivors have had to carry in their memories whatever remains of the knowledge of Jewish life in more than a dozen countries, in several thousand towns, in tens of thousands of villages, and in innumerable families. The precious gift of recollection has been the sole memorial for millions of people whose lives were suddenly and brutally cut off.

For many years, individual survivors have published their testimonies. But many more have been reluctant to do so, often because they could not believe that they would find a publisher for their efforts.

In my own work over the past two decades, I have been approached by many survivors who had set down their memories in writing, but who did not know how to have them published. I realized what a considerable emotional strain the writing down of such hellish memories had been. I also realized, as I read many dozens of such accounts, how important each account was, in its own way, in recounting aspects of the story that had not been told before, and adding to our understanding of the wide range of human suffering, struggle and aspiration.

With so many people and so many places involved, including many hundreds of camps, it was inevitable that the historians and students of the Holocaust should find it difficult at times to grasp the scale and range of the events. The publication of memoirs is therefore an indispensable part of the extension of knowledge, and of public awareness of the crimes that had been committed against a whole people.

Martin Gilbert
Merton College
Oxford

MAP OF WARTIME POLAND

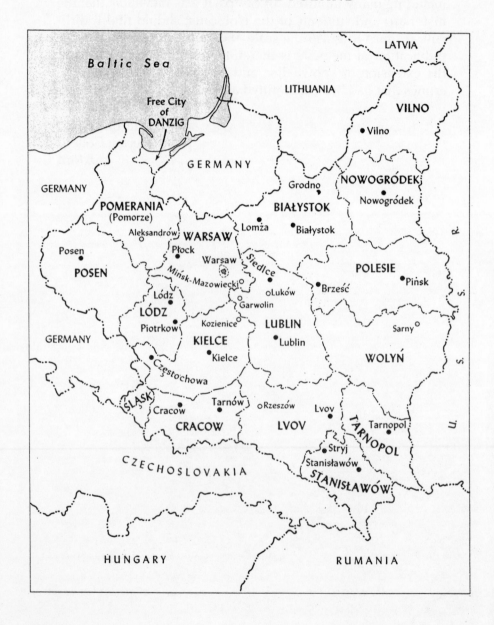

Introduction

It is a powerful and pitiless fact of nature that thick grass is growing over the mounds, ditches and pits that are the common graves of the murdered Jewish children.

It is an established and immutable fact of humankind that those who have remained alive, caught up in everyday cares, cover up their memories and their feelings with a thousand concerns which now are once again of most importance to them.

The task of history is to stand above the laws of nature and above human weakness and pass on the truth to the future.

The truth contained in this book about children is naked and terrible. It will open many a wound, deliver many a sudden blow, fill the reader with bitterness, arouse mixed feelings. The children accuse ...: those who survived, escaping death by a thousand devious pathways; those from beyond the grave; those who reached maturity in life before they could read or write; and those whose mouths were covered with earth before they could utter their first words.

This accusation will not be made before an international court of law, recorded in hundreds of volumes, roundly phrased in accordance with the regulations, following the letter of the law in its lifeless clauses. This will be a judgement among people. Sentence will be passed by Jewish children and their mothers. Mothers who were told in the death camps that 'your children have already been roasted'; mothers whose children were torn forcibly from their arms; mothers who were scandalously deceived, denied the mercy of a shared death, and condemned to live out their lives in the smoke from the bodies of their children being burned alive.

Sentence will be passed by children deprived of all of the sacred, timeless rights of childhood, children who were humiliated, whose privileges, respected the world over, were trampled upon, and who were finally put to death by a thousand means unknown to the most savage peoples on earth, or condemned to live in fear, despair and deceit.

May this book about the Jewish children go out into the world. Into a world where high-ranking judges relax their vigilance with a thousand laws protecting human rights – on paper. Into a world where mothers have known no fearful anxiety beyond the ordinary suffering of the mother sitting by the child's sick bed. Into a world where the children of the Nazi thugs, deprived of the calories they need, arouse pity for their plight. Into a world which so quickly and so willingly seeks to forget about the greatest crime of history.

The task of this book is to translate inhuman things into human language.

In June 1945 I spent a few hours with some children in a Jewish hostel in Zatrzebie outside Warsaw. The boys in the oldest group told me about their experiences. One of them, whose story I did not write down and whose name I have forgotten, recounted how in the death camp at Birkenau there were no bowls for the soup from the cauldron that everyone wanted so much, how bread was thrown at their feet and jam flung in their faces; then how, an hour later, they were given bowls which under threat of torture they had to scrub till they shone, only to go for the next meal with bare hands once again. A young man who was present at the conversation and who had survived the war on 'Aryan papers', expressed his opinion about such camp experiences, the judgement of a person of honour and dignity. Something to the effect that he would never accept such a situation, and would rather die than ... and so forth.

The boy, that 14-year-old inmate of Birkenau, answered: 'But before that, I was in the ghetto; I'd lived through *everything*.'

A rather indirect response, perhaps even amusing for one who has not followed the dark meanderings of the German crimes from their source. For at the source were the first, second, third *Bekanntmachung* (decree) ...

The future inmate of a death camp learns one day, in the first phase of the occupation, that starting from tomorrow he can no longer attend Polish school. So he gathers his books and, walking through the classroom door and out of the gates of the school, he moves off the path of a simple, bright childhood; he loses the right to live with other children, and is already on the wrong side of life.

Then another *Bekanntmachung* appears on the walls of the cities and towns, and children of ten or 12, and in some towns even younger, put on an armband with the Star of David on it, so that there should no longer be any doubt. There are still the youngest children, who have not yet been marked by the criminals' laws. Their contribution is in the domestic conspiracy; their privilege is a freedom that the older ones no longer have. A pernicious atmosphere begins to form around the child; he will continue to live in this atmosphere till the very end – if he survives.

Lying, which in the first few years of life was punished and in every way reviled, now becomes obligatory. For failing to lie you are not sent to the corner, as you were before for failing to tell the truth. Telling the truth for the moment leads to losing one's property and one's freedom, and to various dangerous conflicts with the authorities in whatever uniform – that of the ghetto policemen, the 'dark blue' (Polish) or the 'green' (German military) policemen. In time, the truth will lead to death.

But at this time the future death camp inmates, the future denizens of a cave in the woods, a dark bunker or a sewer, the future young partisans and condemned prisoners transported out to die in the gas chambers, in their worst moments of doubt do not anticipate their fate. Slowly, day after day, step by step, the time is inexorably drawing close when all false appearances and hopes will be abandoned, and the German invader will no longer be worthy even of the name of an animal or beast.

The whole period from the entry of the Germans into Poland up to 1942, though not treated in this book in a separate chapter, is described in all the various sections of the book. It is a period of preparation for hell. The Jewish children are alive, and breathe air which, though already infected with the venom of hatred, is not yet mortally poisonous. Jewish children are born. The day that greets them is clouded over with a foreboding of terrible things. But between foreboding and reality there is a huge gap, not of time but of conception and imagination.

At this time, Jewish communities from the smaller towns and villages are drawn in as with a fisherman's net, to larger centres, into a well-planned trap. The children of these communities, especially those from the villages, are tougher and more resourceful and have better personal circumstances, enabling them to lay down pathways that will be of use to them in the near future. These include elements of fundamental importance – a mastery of the Polish language, often in the form of a distinctive dialect; a knowledge of customs and experience of certain religious practices gleaned from living closely with Polish children; a good knowledge of the area. Aside from this, the harder the life and the more primitive the living conditions, the greater will be the physical resilience, quick-wittedness and self-assurance – all qualities that will constitute advantages in the fight ahead.

The life of the Jewish children in this period can still be called abnormal; later such a human term will be out of place. The children do not attend school; they move house frequently, see incomprehensible things, learn forbidden practices. Nothing holds any secrets for them. The life that is beginning for them shows them its worst stinking courtyards. The competition in the struggle to make a living, in this struggle that from day to day turns into a battle for life itself, contains within it a terrible cruelty, the unfeeling selfishness of someone driving a path at any cost through the weak and the defeated. The children look and they see bribery and treachery, humiliation and fear. They learn to recognise the hierarchies that have sprung up and which are nourished by the evil that the invaders have diligently sown and carefully nurtured. They learn to recognise enemies among their own brothers. Fed each day on new German rules and orders, restricted in their natural freedom and deprived of the care-free delights of childhood, they become suspicious and mis-trustful, and even before the wall or the barbed wire is put up around their ghetto, they will already have understood that they are different, and on their weak children's backs they will take a share of the responsibility for the imagined terrible sins of all the Jews of the world.

Now certain streets of the city are closed to Jews; in the trams they have separate compartments; they are not allowed to wear fur collars on their overcoats. Father has to bow to every German he meets, brother hides from round-ups for the work camps, from which most people never return. The child's eyes see a burning synagogue, and a man beaten till he bleeds. The child lives through dozens of daytime and night-time searches; he sees that from his home, which had seemed to be untouchable, anything of any value can be taken away; his mother can with impunity be struck in the back with a rifle butt, and his father's face bloodied; that on the stairs a man taken from his flat a moment before can be shot dead. And his friends, the Polish children who had seemed to be the same kind of children as him, call out on the street: '*Jude! Jude! Jude!*' For this is an easy word, the easiest of all German words. So in the end he has to believe in his own guilt, believe he is different, inferior.

It is difficult to resist personal reflections when one is writing not just the introduction to a book but the most deeply experienced tragedy of the Jewish children, their path of torment from beginning to end. In 1941, when the Kraków Jews had dispersed into the various outlying villages, I visited my cousin's children in the village of Tonie. Even then, for the children, I was a being from another, better world. I did not wear an armband, I was allowed to live in Kraków, I was not afraid of Germans or of 'people'. And at that time the children could still call me aunt, though we told the landlord that I was not a real aunt, but an Aryan one. The house stood among luscious meadows; there were few people. The children could still shout out loud for joy when they saw me, greet me freely and wish me goodbye without a care. When, a few months later in spring and summer 1942, I visited the children in the Jewish quarter in Bochnia, which at that time had not yet been closed off, the same two girls ran out to meet me. But they did not shout, and they did not fling their arms around me. They ran past me, greeted me with a flash of their eyes, turned round and again ran past. Not a single word was uttered. On the street, where someone's unfriendly eyes could notice us, we did not know each other. A stranger from Kraków had come; she had brought us some soap and was going to buy some of Mama's wardrobe ... That was how it looked. But once inside that Jewish flat, two pairs of arms hugged the 'lady' who was a free woman, and two pairs of young eyes searched my eyes for hope, and for a reflection of those days, not years but months ago, when on the meadows outside Kraków they could laugh and greet me aloud. This, then, was the beginning of that 'everything'; this was the sequence of things to which the young prisoner of Birkenau had referred. Sinking lower and lower, and before each turning, beyond which lay unknown danger, thinking with regret of the previous stage, when things had not been so bad after all.

All the experiences of the first year of the war – the German banditry, the bare-faced robbery, the petty, underhand stealing, and the crimes committed by the Germans – could never have prepared the Jews for the fact that in the case of the children, the murderers would commit a slaughter that was so brutal, so hideous, so cold-blooded and carried out with such clinical heartlessness that all their previous crimes would pale in comparison.

And yet what was the child, the Jewish child, compared to the vast German war machine, to the superb administration, to the victories and conquests on every front? What tiny thing was the life of a Jewish child compared to the ambitions of the 'masters of the world', compared to the plan that guaranteed certain victory? Who would have suspected that this child, along with the elderly, the sick and the infirm, would be the principal enemy of German power and the first to be condemned; that against this child there would be sent hordes of heavily armed soldiers?

The murderous wave spreads from the east. In the territories occupied by the Germans after the withdrawal of the Soviet army, at once there begins the systematic killing of Jewish communities. From here comes the first news of the terrible deaths of Jewish children, of their being exterminated *en masse*. But hope, mother of the blind and the deaf, forces people to look for a hundred reasons and arguments with which Jewish parents reassure themselves when the appalling news reaches them. They do not, will not and cannot believe the stories.

For try to make a mother believe, as she looks at her tiny, beautiful child, that that child will die before her eyes at the hands of a soldier – a soldier in uniform and helmet, armed, a large, strong man who will come to smash the little one's head against the wall, to run it through with a bayonet, to throw it alive into a grave. Try to make parents believe that their children, who are barely able to read or write, are the enemies of mighty Germany, and must die not by virtue of the merciless laws of war, that bring the misfortunes of famine, sickness and fire, but through the terrible abuses of cynical beasts and the bloody henchmen of crime.

The first summer months of 1942 shatter these feeble illusions. The 'evacuations' from the small towns, where ghettos had never even been set up, or where they had only been in existence for a few weeks, open the eyes of those who have hitherto been blind. More and more trains take people from the southern and eastern regions to Bełżec and Sobibór, and from the west and north to Treblinka and Majdanek. These are the 'transports'; in them are children. In cattle wagons spread with quicklime, barred and sealed, without a drop of water in the sweltering hot summer.

Those who remain, gathered once again in the ghettos, for no more than a few weeks, are desperate to believe in the possibility of them and their children surviving. Behind the walls, barbed-wire and fences, the children who have survived the first massacre begin their lives.

The ghetto is only one of the phases on the Jews' road of death. From here there lead branches, like the tentacles of a polyp, rapaciously devouring the living flesh of the nation. In the children's recollections, then, their experiences in the ghetto cannot constitute a separate finished whole. The children who did not perish in the ghetto continued their wanderings – to a camp, on Aryan papers, in hiding.

The interviews in the first part of the book speak of life in the ghettos in various places and communities. The picture of these experiences is simple and clear. The children, confined within walls and barbed-wire fences, together with their parents live through the hell of perpetual anxiety, the constant fight to survive, the battle with hunger, the struggle within the trap, where waiting meant death, escape brought the danger of death, and going into hiding often ended in death. This fearful companion accompanied the children step by step; his constant presence turned these children into different beings, unknown to experienced psychologists and the shrewdest experts on the mind of the child.

And yet the children who after a number of years recall their life in the ghetto remember it as somewhere that was still connected with the idea of home, with the awareness of belonging to someone, with a sense of ownership. You had your flat in the ghetto. It was more and more crowded and dangerous; every *Aktion* tore someone from the family organism who had previously seemed to be a permanent, secure part of the child's life. But even in the fight for life, the struggle to buy food and to build shelters, in the lull between one *Aktion* and the next, in all these jobs and cares there was a faint glimmer of hope. Here father has obtained a valuable stamp that gives him the right to live and to keep his family; here brother and sister succeed in getting the jobs they wanted; and it seems that the heavens are smiling upon this family. After all, the war will not last forever, the hiding-place built in the cellar, in the attic, in the cupboard, in the pantry will allow them to survive the next couple of *Aktions*, and then – maybe things will calm down, maybe it will all come to an end …

In the larger towns and cities, famine and typhus begin their own *Aktion* in the ghettos. There is terrible poverty everywhere, especially among those who, hounded from place to place, robbed mercilessly at every step, materially ruined, at last find their place in the worst hovels of the ghetto. The Łódź ghetto, the Warsaw ghetto, the Wilno (now Vilnius) ghetto, the Białystok ghetto and those of the smaller towns in the east, where famine was rife in 1941–42: each of these accursed places forms a separate chapter in the martyrology of the Jewish children. As early as the beginning of 1942, in the Jewish quarter of Kielce, which was still open then, I saw a little girl who had been brought out of the Łódź ghetto with great difficulty and at great cost by her parents. The child, whose outward appearance I shall not even attempt to describe, rubbed her eyes in astonishment when she saw bread and butter: 'Do you get things like that to eat here?' she asked. Fed for months on potato and cabbage peelings, she could not believe that in a ghetto one could eat something other than what the Germans provided, that Jews were allowed to eat such things as bread, eggs or vegetables. And that was only the very beginning.

Few children are left who survived the hell of that poverty. Those whose testimonies from the ghetto are included in this book are not children; they are spectres, begging in their hundreds on the streets of the city ghettos, dying of starvation and disease, without a roof over their heads, or material help, or moral care. These children, their life and their slow death, are the subject of the testimonies in the final chapter of this book. The recollections of people who survived, charity workers, teachers and doctors, depict the heroic efforts of individuals whose purpose in the face of inescapable death was to labour and to struggle against poverty, famine and the abandoning of Jewish children. This struggle was as desperate and as heroic as all the armed uprisings of the dying nation. Doomed to failure from the beginning, among children who were fated to die, yet dictated by a lofty sense of social responsibility, love and self-sacrifice, it will leave an indelible mark in the history of those years. Alongside the Janusz Korczaks, in the Warsaw ghetto and the ghettos of other Polish cities, dozens of devoted teachers fight for the children and often accompany those children voluntarily when they are sent to their deaths. The recollections of those who remained alive, and the memory of those murdered, will suffice for a memorial and an indictment.

The *Aktions* and the evacuations from the ghetto led the children to their deaths. It was not a merciful death. A lethal bullet was a rare luxury; gas was not wasted on children. Why was it that it was the children who had to die in the most monstrous ways – burned alive, buried alive, smashed by rifle butts, beaten against a wall, drowned in sewers? The murderers evidently believed that the faint cry, the feeble moaning of the Jewish children would disappear without a trace in space and time. And in dealing with these utterly defenceless creatures, the criminals' worst, unfettered instincts were unleashed: the true face of German 'heroism' revealed itself.

In the death camps the Jewish children died in their thousands. Hundreds remained, ordered by a whim of the criminals to be condemned for the moment to live, constantly subject to 'selections', held in a permanent, tangible sense of threat.

Along the road in the camp that leads to the crematoria, trucks are driving, full of the naked bodies of children; those who remain alive, locked into wooden cages, watch, and they know: those children are being taken to be burned; they went today, and we – maybe – will be taken tomorrow ... .

The first children I met immediately after the liberation were in fact prisoners from the camp at Birkenau (Auschwitz), boys and girls from the age of four. As I sat among them, listening to their stories, all my own experiences in the resistance, all the years of working and fighting, seemed insignificant and feeble, something unworthy of being mentioned in comparison with their terror and their quiet children's suffering and heroism.

For Jewish children not only died, stayed in hiding or ran away from their executioners; they fought for their lives on all fronts in this uneven battle.

In the ghettos, they are usually the sole providers for the whole family. In places where a big strong adult cannot pass, a frail child can slip through, in order to smuggle food into the ghetto by ways that would seem to be accessible only to an agile little animal. Sometimes it is only a handful of potatoes concealed in their coat, or a small loaf of bread; but who could understand the importance of these treasures to a group of destitute people, and understand that they were worth risking one's life for? For beyond the wall lurked perpetual danger. The German thug and the dark-blue policeman, the blackmailer and the Gestapo informer – all of these were the mortal enemies of the little Jew from the ghetto. But they had to go, because there, in the hovel where they lived, their mother, sick with typhus, their brother and their sister were waiting for a handful of flour, a slice of bread, an onion or a carrot.

In the camps, the struggle for life and for survival is conducted on the very threshold of death. The children learn to 'organise' things, to obtain extra bread, soup or clothing. They take on jobs that are beyond their strength, anything to avoid being 'sent to scrap'; they fight for every day of their existence, with an undying hope in their hearts. There are some who escape three times from a locked barracks, from a group of people condemned to die.

It is rare that these efforts actually saved their life. Usually there comes a moment when their courage, quick wits, strength and will to live are to no avail. The might of the criminals is incomparably greater. The child, fighting to the very last, goes to his death, sent by a slight gesture, a single movement of the finger of the German doctor and murderer.

The last cry of the dying is the column of smoke rising into the sky from the oven at the crematorium. The glow from the burning bodies of the children lighting up the sky over the camps shines as an omen and as a warning to the world.

The battlefield of the Jewish child is not restricted to the ghetto and the camp. Indeed, it is beyond the bounds of the places where the condemned are allowed to be that a quiet, stubborn fight unparalleled in its intensity is fought with the enemy. And 'enemy' is a broadly conceived term here. It is precisely here that the tentacles of the monster are spread, and here that poison courses through the veins of crime and infects the air of this land, which is after all the children's homeland. In this battle, ranged against the Jewish child is all that is low in humanity, all that is ruthless in nature, and all that is predatory in life.

Children also escape from the trains taking the Jews to be executed. It is not difficult to escape from the ghettos; there are camps which it is not impossible to get out of. But the child's escape from these places is nothing compared to the task of surviving the first day of 'freedom'.

Two long chapters of this book give a rich picture of the life of children 'on the Aryan side' – in hiding or on 'Aryan papers'.

What are these 'papers' like? In most cases they do not exist, because to get them you need to have contacts, acquaintances, money. And the escape of a Jewish family, or of the children alone, usually takes place at the last minute; the decision is taken when there is no time left for searching and securing for oneself some kind of legal document. So 'papers' remains just a term. The principal factor in the new life is 'the right appearance'. This is also a term which the Jews started using under the German occupation. The 'right appearance' is everything that on the outside signifies so-called 'race'. This is a very complicated concept for people who, living in their own skin, have never reflected on the shape of their nose, mouth or eyes, or the colour of their hair, from the point of view of life and death.

'Do I look like one?' This is one of those concepts that do not require further explanation. It is obvious what it means; the word 'Jew' is superfluous. For the children who flee the ghetto just before an *Aktion*, or jump from a death transport, their credentials are, above all, their appearance. If that appearance is 'wrong', they usually die at the first stage. Taken to the German or Polish police at the nearest police station, they are usually shot on the spot. At this last terrifying moment they stand in the face of death, all alone. The death of these abandoned children, killed one by one, is a silent one, but so much the weightier and more bloody will be their final accusation.

Much has already been written about how diligently and professionally the Germans prepared the ground for the murder of the Jews. Written, graphic and spoken propaganda addressed the mass of the Polish population, particularly those classes with whom, by the nature of things, the Jewish child seeking salvation first came into contact. In the moment of escape, urgently in need of support if only for a brief initial period, it was hard to find people (according to some indefinable index) worthy of the name. Among Polish passengers who in the summer of 1942, in the period of the most frequent 'evacuations', travelled on various railway journeys, there were without doubt many who were horrified and ashamed to see escaping Jews being caught and handed over to the police. But few of them had the courage to speak out at this time – nothing more than speak out. I know from my own experience that a few simple, down-to-earth words are enough to make a person think twice and back down after standing on the very brink of wrongdoing.

Nor did the depravation of human morality spare the Polish children, who denied their Jewish friends entry to their hearts, to fellowship and sympathy. I have before me an article by Irena Chmieleńska, Commissioner for Children's

Affairs at the Ministry of Social Security, printed in the occasional newspaper *The Child*, published in Kraków as part of the 'Week of the Child'. I should like to quote a passage from that article:

> There were two principal sources that led to the corruption of a certain group of children in Warsaw: the Jewish question, and practices such as trading, smuggling, looting, theft and fraud, all of which it was impossible fully to eradicate.
>
> Boys from the age of six, but mostly aged 10–15, would spend whole nights keeping watch by the walls of the ghetto and blackmailing Jews who were trying to cross the walls. In the daytime, those same boys would slip under the same wall to sell the Jews bread and potatoes at extortionate prices, and to buy clothing from them for paltry sums. No one could have made them understand that they were acting immorally.
>
> The Germans accustomed our children to brutality, and made a game of it; and they accustomed them to the notion of the *Untermensch*: a Jew belongs to a different class of being.
>
> A child is not critical; and for the uncritical mind, a suggestively presented opinion becomes his own opinion. I have met children who explained to me that the Germans were absolutely right to exterminate the Jews, because 'Jews have got too many lice'. [The posters read: 'Jews – Lice – Typhus'.] They themselves would not want to die if they became infected with lice; but Jews, that was something else …

The author mentions the children of Warsaw in particular probably because she knows them best and it was there that she had the experiences she writes about. But these were not localised problems. The posters reading 'Jews – Lice – Typhus' were put up everywhere, in every corner of occupied Poland, just as the German virus of hatred and baseness reached everywhere in the country.

Introduction

The children give their testimonies simply and frankly. In their recollections, mostly gathered as early as 1945, there is a tone of freshly experienced pain or hope. In preparing these testimonies for publication, we took pains to preserve those impressions – the authenticity of the children's experiences.

Wherever the children encountered good people, help or encouragement, they express their appreciation in words full of the warmest feelings. Every human gesture, even just the offering of a slice of bread or words of genuine sympathy, these heartfelt reactions in the terrible days of the holocaust – none of this has been forgotten by these persecuted children, and in this book it is preserved in words of the warmest gratitude.

Here is how the Jewish children write about the worthy people who were their benefactors:

> He guessed who I was but he did not say anything to me. Then the whole village found out. But the farmer did not fire me and no one gave me away ... ['On the Aryan Side': Josek Mansdorf]

> It was not bad in the hide-out. Mr Łopatyński or his wife brought me food a few times a day. I ate the same things as they did. Sometimes they gave me a bath, but only when their children were not at home ...
> While I was at Mr Łopatyński's sister's I played with her son Ryś. Ryś loved me and never did me any harm ... ['In Hiding': Eryk Holder]

> Then father went into town to look for somewhere for us, and he visited the family of one of his patients, the famous artist, Mr W., whose daughter Wicula was happy to take care of us. She found us a flat for a few days, and since we could not go out she brought us food, and cakes for me ... ['In Hiding': Jerzy Aleksandrowicz]

> I stayed at the Albertine Brothers and Mrs Thiel, the teacher, guessed that I was Jewish, and the Brother

Superior did too, and they helped me a lot. They did not say anything to me, but the Brother told me to bathe in bathing trunks like the older boys ... ['On the Aryan Side': Zygmunt Weinreb]

We went to Mr Łuczyński's, where there was a bunker. Our lady took us there late at night, after the curfew, risking her own life ... That lady was our good angel, and she helped us many times ... ['In Hiding': Dawid Wulf]

Every Sunday Mrs Jaśkowa came to visit us. She would get up at three in the morning, come to us in the morning and leave in the afternoon ... When she was with us I felt completely safe. It seemed to me that if she, our dear guardian angel, was with us, nothing bad could happen to me ... ['In Hiding': Franciszka Guter]

Every day, from the first day, the Polish sewer workers brought us food – black bread and margarine. They were very good to us. ['In Hiding': Krystyna Chiger]

All these quotations are not rhetorical turns of phrase. They contain not just the gratitude and emotion of a child's heart, but the true, moral worth of a person prepared to make sacrifices in the interest of that greatest human possession: the life of an innocent child, and the person's own dignity. This struggle almost always results in a life being saved. From the testimonies of the Jewish children it emerges quite clearly that where will-power directed to a conscious goal, courage and rectitude join hands, the Nazi thug is defeated in his desire to murder.

In the same frank and straightforward way the children describe evil deeds and base people. And in the same way, uncorrected and unexpurgated, these descriptions are included here.

Bitterness and pain fill the children's recollections of those Poles who hunted them, betrayed them and handed them over to the common enemy; of cruelties perpetrated by other children, and of every human ignominy. To be accurate, there are few such testimonies, but the reason for this is simple yet painful: the children who encountered treachery and deceit are not here to record their stories.

The moment of liberation is in the majority of the testimonies marked with joy and a warm sense of gratitude to the Red Army: the children saw the Soviet soldiers come and open the door for them to a free world. The shots which once again shook the earth were aimed this time at the mortal enemy in open battle. The soldiers' weapons regained their dignity once more.

The interviews gathered in this volume were transcribed in the various branches of the Central Jewish Historical Commission (CJHC) in Poland. The first were conducted at the beginning of 1945, almost immediately after the liberation. Certain inaccuracies in the personal details of those testifying come from this period, when the methodological principles had not been worked out with the same precision as later on.

At this point, one might add up the bloody account and produce a balance of the crimes. But this is a task for the statistician, who deals with silent rows of figures; he counts up the living children and the murdered children and presents his final reckoning as a document of the crimes to the tribunal of history.

Yet for me, it is difficult to lay down my pen. I am not a statistician. During the Nazi occupation I would meet Jewish mothers and children living in hiding. Listening to the mothers' stories, and seeing the children's lives, my heart often stirred as I thought about the moment when, saved and liberated, they would step out of their hiding-places into a good, bright, free world. As soon as that moment came, I began to work on the provision of care for the Jewish children as they returned, abandoned and homeless. It was at this time that the next chapter of the children's suffering began.

The world, a broad and vague concept, was not quick to offer help in that most difficult period. The reality of the children's first months of freedom was far from my grand dreams. The children slept on the floor, ate horsemeat, and were dressed in rags. Arranging suitable accommodation for them, organising schooling, and securing food and clothing all constitutes a separate chapter.

First there came the children from the camps; then they began to emerge from the bunkers and hiding-places, joined by those who had been on Aryan papers. The older ones, and those who had no one, arrived alone. There were boys and girls – cowherds from the country, farm-hands, nannies and washer-girls. Most of them were strong and healthy, and some of them had the 'right appearance' to such an extent that it was difficult to believe they were of Jewish origin. They were mostly in good mental and physical health.

The children who emerged like moles from their dens and hiding-places looked at the world with new eyes. They were at once like old men and women and like new-born babies. The youngest especially, who had spent the first years of their lives in hiding, were born again at this time. At the age of five, six or seven they were seeing many everyday objects for the first time, and learning to use them, recognise them and name them. Some of them were afraid of a bed, a cupboard, a chair, a plate or a spoon. It was difficult to find words to explain the change that so terrified them. Deafened and blinded by their new surroundings, they often cried helplessly and pulled away from the arms that brought them caresses. They did not understand all this, they wanted to go back to their hiding-places. There were some who could only walk around the edge of the room, clinging onto the wall with their little hands; the open space of even the smallest room was something perilous to them, an abyss or an ocean. For a long time some of them continued to talk in a whisper; their tendons were stiff from spending long hours in one position; they found it hard to bear the sunlight.

Gradually, as nature and the child's organic recovery began to prevail, other problems arose. It transpired that not all those who had come in on their own were orphans. Mothers began returning from the camps and seeking out their children. There were moments that were indescribably moving. But other children were standing by who already knew beyond a doubt that no one would come for them. Hope died anew in the eyes of those children. More and more frequently, in bouts of depression one would hear: 'Why couldn't I have died with Mama?'

All these things took place as it were on the inside, in the closed circle of our care, in the four walls of our sympathy. But the children were not in captivity. The streets of the city were open to them; there were no separate compartments in the trams for them, or signs forbidding entry to Jews, or armbands.

How then did freedom greet the children, who had been returned to life, pulled from the bottom of the abyss, the depths of hell?

It soon became clear that some of the Polish population had not yet come to terms with the fact that a handful of Jews had survived. For so many years these people had witnessed the unpunished murder, the daily death and the persecution of the defenceless Jews that their will to live was simply seen as one more offence to add to the long list of Jewish 'crimes'. The smoke of those times still hung in the air. The children coming back from school, from a walk, from the cinema or the shop would speak bitterly of their everyday experiences. It was difficult to explain to them the background to these matters, and to convince them of the need to continue the struggle, which must go on for a long while yet. They were already mortally weary and wounded. In the end they no longer wished to speak of the distress they experienced; they kept it inside. The most typical reaction of a child who has been wronged I saw in the Jewish orphans' home in Zakopane, where one nine-year-old boy, who had always been of a mild disposition and full of life, spent a whole afternoon crying desperately; nothing could be done to calm him down. In the end, deeply upset, his nerves shattered, he began to speak about the death of all his loved ones as if it was a completely new story. As he sobbed, he repeated that his father and mother and his little sister had been murdered, that he was all alone in the world, that he had no one – no one – no one ... We were all astonished at this sudden outburst of despair, now, after the boy had been at the home for several months. But the next day everything became clear. At school, a group of the boy's friends had picked on him, bullying him and making fun of him, and the teacher had listened indifferently as they mocked him and called him names. The boy did not want to tell tales to the director of the home; yet the wrong he had suffered had to provoke some reaction – in an atmosphere of animosity and injustice he felt so terribly abandoned.

All these incidents led to a state of affairs which, despite all our efforts, could not be avoided – the isolation of the Jewish children. It was hard, but it was necessary to consider the children's need to relax and to breathe freely. If at school or at play they shout at a child 'Jew! Jew! Jew!', we know that this name-calling is older than Nazism; but the child who remembers little or nothing from before the war will always find in this name the echo of another: '*Jude – Jude – Jude.*' And this the child should be allowed to forget.

The next painful matter which I encounter constantly and about which it is difficult to remain silent is the moral attitude of certain of the guardians of those Jewish children who survived by staying with families or in hiding-places. I shall pass over here the so-called 'child trade', this time a post-war expression, though no less monstrous than all the expressions from the occupation. This far-reaching and deep-seated problem needs to be discussed elsewhere. Here something else is at stake: the difference between merit and shame, the consciousness of, and pride in, fulfilling one's duty as a person and as a citizen. In this book, in many of the testimonies, the names of the people who saved the Jewish children are given; in others, only initials are used. Why is this, if their names are known? I do not know if anyone outside Poland can understand the fact that saving the life of a defenceless child being hunted by a criminal can bring shame and disgrace upon someone, and can expose them to harassment.

In the face of all these problems stands the child. This is the Jewish child who survived that fearful Gehenna, and the shade of the child who perished on every inch of the bloody soil of Poland.

The words with which history is written must be permanent. This book about the Jewish children is written in blood, and blood washes away easily – it leaves behind only faint, rust-coloured stains. We who have remained alive must remember this, so that the blood, and the wrongs done to the children, should never, ever be washed from the foreheads of the murderers, from their hands or from their consciences.

Maria Hochberg-Mariańska

1946

Chapter One
THE GHETTOS

1. MIECZYSŁAW EICHEL

(Written account – excerpts)

On 1 September 1939 war broke out between Poland and
Germany. In October 1939 the German army entered Warsaw.
As soon as they arrived they began to persecute the Jews. My
eldest brother Jankiel escaped to Russia. At the beginning of
1940 the Germans began stealing from the Jews. When they
could not tell who was a Jew and who was a Pole, they took
bad Poles with them who showed them who was a Jew; they
took goods from Jewish traders, broke the windows of Jewish
shops, and made pogroms in the streets. The Germans
rounded up Jews with beards, shaved off their beards and
sent them to camps, where they died of hunger. Jewish men
could not go out on the streets, because they rounded them up
and sent them to do forced labour in Okęcie or Sejm, where
they were beaten and punished and given nothing to eat.

In the winter of 1940, one Saturday, we were all at home; we
lived on the ground floor. In the afternoon, a group of Poles
burst in with some Germans. They began beating up my
father. They left the flat. In the courtyard outside they
smashed all the windows, and when they caught Jews they
beat them till they bled. After they went away my mother
cleared up the flat and found that my father's suit was
missing, along with her overcoat and some leather that she
was going to have some boots made from.

Then the Germans ordered the Jews to wear armbands with
the star of David. When a German was walking along the
street, a Jew had to bow to him. In 1941 the Germans set apart
some of the streets in Warsaw especially for the Jews. All the
Jews of Warsaw and the surrounding district had to move to
this area, the so-called 'ghetto'. A short time later the Germans
built high walls around these streets.

To begin with, everything was cheap in the ghetto. Then
food prices shot up, as there was no legal supply. There was
famine in the ghetto, and people died on the streets. In the

3

winter people had no fuel to burn, and they took floorboards, furniture, stairs, even window-frames from the outside staircases, and chopped them up for firewood.

More and more frequently people were dying on the streets. When the snow fell it covered them. There was an undertakers' firm that cleared the bodies away every day, but they could not keep up with the work, as every day hundreds of Jews died, mostly from starvation and cold. Then typhus broke out. The Germans organised anti-typhus steam baths by locking the gates of a whole apartment block, not letting anyone in, and hanging a sign on the gate that said 'Typhus' – 'Fleckfieber'. Everyone was taken to be disinfected; mattresses were burned and bedding was taken to be disinfected and was often also burned. The sick were taken to hospital, and the family of the sick person and anyone who lived in the same flat were sent into quarantine for 14 days, where they usually died of starvation. In our family, too, my mother, father and sister fell ill at the same time. My brothers and I looked after our parents. When the doctor came or we bought medicine, it was in secret, so that the neighbours would not find out that there were sick people in our flat.

After a short while the supplies ran out, as no one at home was earning any money. My brother and I took our parents' last few złotys and left the ghetto to buy food, for in the ghetto it was 50 per cent more expensive than in the Aryan district. It was not so easy to leave the ghetto, since it was surrounded by high walls patrolled by the Polish police and the Jewish militia. And at certain points there were gates with German sentries: for example, at the corner of Żelazna Street and Grzybowska Street, the corner of Żelazna and Leszno, in Grzybowska, Chłodna and Graniczna Streets and at the corner of Nalewki Street and Dzika Street. With difficulty we managed to climb over the high walled fence. Then, when we had bought food, we went up to the Wache [guardhouse] to go back into the ghetto. Here there were two German military policemen, two Polish policemen and three Jewish militiamen. I was not afraid of the [Polish] policemen as much as I

4

The Ghettos

was of the German military police, because when the military police would not let someone into the ghetto, there was nothing that the Polish or Jewish police could do. I hid near the guardhouse so that the Germans would not see me. After a few hours a large number of carts arrived at the checkpoint, and the Germans began searching them. While they were busy with the search, I slipped into the ghetto. In the ghetto there were lots of people willing to buy what we had. The Jews sold clothes and bedding for next to nothing, because they needed the money to stay alive. So every day my brother and I left the ghetto. Sometimes the Germans or the Polish police caught me outside the ghetto and confiscated the goods I had. Every day I had to fight with Polish boys who tried to take what I had from me. Often I bribed them to leave me alone. On one occasion, a few weeks later, I went to the market hall in Koszykowa Street, because everything was cheaper there than in the Mirowska market hall. Unfortunately some officers caught me in Koszykowa Street and took me to Police Station 11 at 13 Poznańska Street; there, one officer took a policeman's truncheon and began to beat me. When he had beaten me severely he gave the policeman back his truncheon and left the station. Forty-eight hours later a policeman took me to the checkpoint at the corner of Grzybowska and Żelazna. Luckily, there was a good military policeman there, who the smugglers had paid off, as a car carrying goods arrived without a pass. The policeman who had brought me left me with the one on duty; he struck me on the back a few times with his truncheon and let me into the ghetto. When I reached home my brother was not there. I asked mother where he was, and she replied that a card had come from the police station to say that my brother was in prison for leaving the ghetto. Two days later we were sent word that my brother had been transferred to the ghetto, to the police station in Śliska Street. Here my mother paid for him to be released. When he was supposed to come home, he could not walk, as his feet had been frozen. My mother hired a cart to take him home. He was howling with pain. He told us

5

that when they arrested him his stockings had been wet; there was a frost that night and, because he did not take his shoes off for the night, his feet got frozen. In a few weeks he was well again.

On 21 July my brother and I left the ghetto to buy food. Later, we tried to get back in. Unfortunately we were unable to, as there were very strict guards on duty. We went to Mokotów for the night, to a lady we knew. People advised us not to go back because the Germans had cordoned off the ghetto, and whenever they caught a Jew outside the ghetto they shot him on the spot. So we stayed in Mokotów. A few days later, on the street I saw some carts with several dozen Jews riding on them. I went up to the carts and asked what was happening in the ghetto, but they did not know anything either. A dozen or so boys escaped from the ghetto during one of the *Aktions*. When they did not have anywhere to sleep they slept on a building site. One of them, my friend Heniek Bursztyn, brought us the news that on 25 July my whole family had been sent to Treblinka. The caretaker at 10 Szarotki Street was called Piorun; he was the one who had informed on them. At night, agents surrounded the building site where the Jewish children were and arrested all of them. I do not know what happened to them after that. But there were also a few boys who were sleeping on a different building site. In the Aryan part of the city there were round-ups of Jews every day. They captured all the children. Only Heniek Bursztyn and my brother and I were left in Mokotów. A few weeks later we went back to the ghetto, as the *Aktions* had finished. There we met a man who took us in. The man was called Kohen.

In January 1943 the Germans organised another *Aktion* to finish off the Jews. In the morning the neighbour knocked on the door; we were still asleep. After knocking for several minutes the neighbour shouted that there was an *Aktion*. There was confusion in the flat. Half-dressed, we all got into the hiding-place. It was under the window; before, it had been a food cupboard. A few minutes later we heard the Germans come in and start shouting. Somehow we managed to get through the day without them finding us. In the evening our friend Bursztyn came to see us and stayed the night. The next day, first thing in the morning we got into the hiding-place. At seven o'clock in the morning we again heard loud German voices. The Germans came and searched right by our hiding-place. Fortunately they did not find anything. When the *Aktion* was over and people were already out on the streets of the ghetto Heniek Bursztyn went out to the Aryan part. My brother and I stayed in the ghetto. In March 1943, I left the ghetto and went to Mokotów to the lady we knew because I felt that things were getting bad in the ghetto. At the beginning of April my brother also left and came to join me in Mokotów. Two weeks later, during the night of 19 April 1943 we heard the powerful cracks of rifle fire.

The uprising had begun in the ghetto.

(Archive of the CJHC, statement no. 174)

---

2. NINA BONIÓWNA

Born 20 July 1930, in Warsaw

(*Written account*)

I was born in Warsaw, and was fortunate enough to live in comfortable circumstances. Till the time I went to school my life was like that of many other children. It was only when I was at school that all my troubles began. It was my ambition to be a good pupil. After five years I had to end my education. In 1939 the world was shaken by a bloody war. The Germans launched victorious attacks on several European countries. Before they occupied Poland, they bombed Warsaw mercilessly. It was a very difficult period for the capital. There were shortages of food and water. Sirens constantly gave warnings of air raids; more and more buildings were burned and destroyed. After four weeks of uninterrupted bombing,

7

during which people lived in the cellars, the Germans entered the city. The principal aim they set themselves was to exterminate the Jews. According to them, we were the cause of the war. In Poland, as everywhere else, there began the brutal *Aktions* against the Jews. After numerous round-ups, and the establishment of the ghetto, the Germans began to eliminate the Jews. For seven months, my whole family and I survived all the round-ups and transports to places of extermination. Three months before the final liquidation my father died. Then each of us independently had to try and cross to the Aryan part of the city. We kept putting off our separation until, in the end, the final *Aktion* began. This time, however, we Jews showed the whole world that not only are we able to do business, but that, when necessary, we can take up arms. We all realised that this was a lost cause, offering resistance to a motorised army that had already conquered so many countries. But we refused to fall into line at their order like defenceless cattle; we preferred to die in arms. On 19 April 1943 the furious *Aktion* began. The inhabitants of our apartment building took to their hiding-places. My brother and his friend took up an observation post in the attic. At first they let me stay with them. The windows of our blocks looked out onto the Umschlagplatz, from which the trains loaded with our brothers and sisters set off for various places of execution. At 7.15 a detachment of the executioners moved in. Grenades, called 'bottles', rained down on their heads. There arose an incredible uproar and panic in the detachment. Masses of Germans lay dead, and the rest withdrew hurriedly and in a cowardly fashion.

A deathly silence hung over the ghetto. It lasted for only half an hour. There was something threatening in the air. And, sure enough, after this time not only the building but the whole street began to quake. Tanks and flame-throwers moved in, and observation planes appeared, flying low over the rooftops. A red glow appeared. At this time our insurgents stayed off the streets. The battle was fought in camouflaged shelters and on the Umschlagplatz. The brave rebels led people to safety through the sewers. As far as possible they provided food and water, the shortage of which had very much begun to make itself felt. Three days passed as the various *Schoppen* [work places] and factories were liquidated. Everyone was taken to the Umschlag under heavy escort. The ranks of the doomed passed before our eyes. We could tell which 'shop' they were from by the numbers they wore. First of all the brush-makers ran past, their hands in the air. They had put up a stubborn defence when their bunker was discovered by the Germans, and large numbers of them had committed mass suicide. This was the punishment that awaited those who were captured. I comforted myself with the thought that we lived close to the Umschlag and that the journey there would at least not be a tiring one. Exhausted, I strained my eyes and could hear suspicious-sounding voices. A short while later the Germans moved in and cordoned off the building. I was terrified, and rushed into the hiding-place. We sat there, holding our breath. The Germans came in and turned the flat upside down, but fortunately they did not find the hiding-place. Half an hour later the next cordon was organised. They gassed the shelter next door, and set about two tiny children, leaving parts of their bodies scattered all around. Two more days passed; there was nothing to eat, but no one gave this a thought. The ghetto was ablaze. We sat among the red flames, the stinging smoke and the rags blowing in the air. There was no hope of getting out. We waited our turn in resignation. The news coming in was worse and worse.

On 25 April the organisers' bunker fell. The majority of them, including the commander-in-chief Anielewicz, committed suicide, and the rest were burned in the fire. Anielewicz's second-in-command, Botman, shot his mother and then himself. The same day a handful of Jews were driven out on five carts, to the smaller ghetto as it later turned out. For some reason these carts were standing outside our building. At the same time a fire broke out at the back of the building. In a split second we had the idea of getting onto those carts. We bribed

9

a military policeman and he let us on. My brother and I jumped onto the first cart and my mother onto the second. Ten minutes later Konrad, one of the leaders of the ruthless *Aktion*, came up. And the same policeman who had let us join the group on the cart told his superior about this. The order was given for a second selection. Everyone got off the carts. Some of the people were allowed back on, others not. My brother was one of the lucky ones, while my mother was put in line to be marched to the Umschlag; I was to be shot. It happened so quickly that my brother, who wanted to join my mother, was unable to. I stood against the wall. I felt no fear at all. Everyone was flashing before my eyes, and I realised that I would not see anybody ever again.

When the man in front of me fell, I felt afraid. They shot him twice and in the end they had to finish him off with a bayonet. I was not afraid of such suffering so much as aware of the fact that none of my loved ones were with me. At the last moment a woman friend of ours shoved me onto the cart and pinned the necessary number on me, fooling the guard with her quick and unexpected action.

The cart was escorted on both sides by ten Ukrainians armed with cocked pistols. I was so dazed that at first I did not notice my brother sitting next to me. We rode through the burning streets. We could see what were clearly charred human bodies.

We drove into the Aryan streets. On many faces one could not see the flicker of sympathy or pity that might be expected. Quite the opposite; from time to time we heard 'There are still too many of them'. Looking at us, a small group of people, half-dead and wild-eyed, one should only burst out crying and not utter such cruel words.

We rode for an hour in this sorry state. Finally we arrived. Our compatriots received us with open arms. The ghetto was still burning, district after district. In the meantime, we were being sent to the camps. Only very few individuals managed to cross to the Aryan side. I was one of them. It was a hard time for me.

Without anyone to look after me, I struggled with my lot; after two months I found my sister. I had to part with her a short while later for reasons connected with the resistance. Once again I experienced a period of painful hunger and of bombing, as the Russians approached the Vistula. I was glad that they already were so close but at the same time I was afraid that I might not survive.

I was living in a village right on the Vistula. I was exhausted. I felt my situation all the more because I had lost contact with my friends. At the same time the uprising broke out in Warsaw.

On 15 January 1945 the victorious Red Army entered Warsaw. It was only then that I began to cry. A few days later I realised that my morale had been greater during the occupation than it was now that I was free. It was only now that I felt the absence of those dear to me, the lack of schooling and education. During the occupation my mind had been fixed on not being caught, on seeing the end of the German crimes and on avenging the blood of our loved ones.

(Archive of the CJHC, statement no. 659)

3. RENATA TRAU

Born 1934 in Przemyśl; daughter of Leon and Golda
(Statement taken by Dr Dawid Haupt, Przemyśl)

We lived in our own little house in Dworski Street in Przemyśl. When the Germans occupied Przemyśl in 1941, my father had a shop selling miscellaneous goods; we had a source of livelihood and did not go short of anything. My sister Tosia was four years older than me.

I remember that the Germans ordered the Jews to wear armbands. For three months my father did not wear one, but he had to put one on in the end because Jews were shot for not

11

wearing an armband. In 1942 we had to move from our house to the ghetto; here my father continued his business for just two more weeks, as there was an *Aktion* in the ghetto. We did not get the stamp we needed on our papers and we had to go to be 'resettled'. My parents went to the assembly point, and we went with them to see them off. My sister and I cried because we did not want to be separated from our parents, but my father calmed us down by saying that he would be back, and my uncle, who was an officer with the *Ordner* [Jewish police], took us to our aunt's flat in the ghetto. Aunt had permission to stay in the ghetto, but she had to have her papers checked. After a few hours a Gestapo officer came. Aunt showed him one paper, pointed at me and my sister and said that we were her children. My father and mother did not come back and we kept crying. At last my parents came back from the assembly point, where thousands of Jews had been lined up and had been afraid to move. Our uncle, Marek Trau, who was in charge of the *Ordners*, saved our parents by saying my father was a locksmith, though my father never had been and knew nothing about such work.

This was the end of July 1942; in November there was another *Aktion*. In the meantime we had to move twice, as the ghetto was made smaller. During the second *Aktion* we hid in a small pantry which father had hidden by pulling a wardrobe across the door with a rope so that the door could not be seen. The Gestapo used to come round to check that no Jews were hiding, and they came into our flat. They broke the door down with an axe and searched the flat. They took the axe and smashed the dresser and the wardrobe that hid the door to the pantry. Fortunately for us, however, they did not move the wardrobe, and they went away. I was terrified when the Gestapo were smashing up the wardrobe, but I stood still and did not cry. There was not much room in the pantry and we had to spend a whole day and night there. We had bread and water with us. There was a bucket to the side we could go to. It was only in the evening of the next day that our uncle came to us and told us that the *Aktion* was over.

After the *Aktion*, the ghetto was divided into two parts: one for those with jobs and one for those without. We stayed in the district for those in work, though father did not have a job. He had to hide there so that the commandant of the ghetto work-camp did not see us. This was a German SS officer. Children were not allowed in the workers' district, so we only went out onto the street when the commandant was not there.

In the workers' district there was a Jewish orchestra, a small choir and a Jewish ballet. They performed for the Germans, and when the commandant was away they rehearsed and played for the Jews who administered the ghetto. They had their own theatre; sometimes I would steal out of the house and go there to listen to the music and the singing. Janka Haubenówna sang with them, and Stegmanówna was one of the dancers.

On 2 and 3 September 1942 there was a third *Aktion* in the ghetto. Father knew beforehand that there was to be an *Aktion*, and he hid us in a hiding-place. This was over the attic; you entered the hiding-place through an opening in the roof, then you slid a metal plate across to conceal the opening. There were 18 of us hiding there, including Samuel Hauben, who was shot a few days later by a sentry patrolling the ghetto boundary fence. Hauben used to steal things from flats abandoned by Jews during the *Aktions*, and exchange these things for food with Christian traders at the boundary fence. For this, each time, he would give the sentry (who had previously been a Russian soldier) 50 złotys. On that occasion he had only given him ten złotys, and the sentry shot him, stuck the ten złotys in his mouth and robbed his body.

After this *Aktion* we learnt that the ghetto was going to be closed down, and that all the Jews would be transported out. My parents decided that we would hide in the city, in the flat of a Polish lady who had made an agreement with my father.

My mother and sister left earlier, and father and I were to leave the next day. However, we were too late, as the next day the *Aktion* began. Father and I hid again in the same hiding-place. This time there were 20 people there. Some other

13

people wanted to come in as well, but father did not let them, because there was no room and there was a danger that the ceiling of the attic would collapse under us.

The next day the German soldiers came; they took ladders and climbed up onto the roof. They began hammering on our hiding-place with axes and shouting '*heraus!*'. Everyone climbed out; only father, me and a Jewish lady, Mrs Feuerowa, stayed. We hid under some quilts that were there, but one of the Germans looked through the opening of the roof, saw father's legs poking out from under the quilt and shot him in both legs. The wounds began to bleed.

I got frightened by the Germans' shouting and I told my father to climb out, and father and I climbed out onto the roof. From here we went down to the ground. The Germans pushed my father and kicked him. As we were leaving the building, father saw a group of Jews standing in the courtyard with their hands up, and he turned into the cellars. At this time the Germans were on the first floor and in the courtyard. We hid in one of the cellars, covering ourselves with some plywood that was there. Father threw the overcoat he had been carrying into the neighbouring cellar.

The Germans searched the whole house for us; they came down to the cellars, but did not move the plywood. In the other cellar, though, where they found the overcoat, they made a thorough search and even dug up the floor.

We stayed in the cellar till night-time, and then my father, wounded in both legs, crawled on all fours to our flat and washed the wounds with water. In the night our uncle came and called Dr Schattner, who bandaged father's legs.

Uncle told us to hide, saying that the Germans were going from house to house blowing up the bunkers, but father was unable to stand so he stayed in bed. The next day the Germans came and blew up bunkers in the cellar and attic of the building where we lived, but they did not come into our flat, and in this way we were saved. At this time I hid under the wardrobe and father hid under the quilt. This was in the apartment building at 26 Iwaszkiewicza Street.

The next night father and I crept out of the ghetto and hid at the house of a Polish lady from Przemyśl; mother was supposed to be waiting for us. However, mother was not there, as she had gone back to the ghetto to find out what had happened to us. On the way to the ghetto she had been stopped by a secret policeman, a Pole, who had taken all her money and jewellery. When she was coming back from the ghetto, she was stopped by a group of Ukrainian policemen and taken to the commandant of the ghetto, SS officer Schwamberger; he had my mother and my sister shot. My father and I hid at the Polish lady's until the Red Army arrived.

(Archive of the CHJC, statement no. 884/II)

4. ESTERA ZALCBERG

On 12 August 1942 a *punkt* or assembly was organised in Będzin, on the pretext of having our cards stamped. The whole population of Będzin had to gather on two playing-fields, where there was barely enough room for so many thousands of people. Previously, football matches had been held on these fields; now, terrible things were happening there. As early as five o'clock in the morning my family and I set off, not knowing what awaited us. There were crowds of people and children walking the same way; the elderly and the sick also had to go. There were cases of people hiding, but I did not envy them, because if they were found they were in danger of being shot on the spot. When we arrived at the playing-field we were led round it several times, and then we were ordered to wait. We waited like this till the afternoon; the sun was impossibly hot, and my head ached terribly. From far off you could see more and more of the barbarians driving in. There were sentries everywhere, watching over the crowd of people. The afternoon passed; it began to rain. Evening came and the rain continued to fall. It was dark; there were only two lamps on, in the light of which nothing could be made out. You could hear the shouting and crying of children who had never found themselves in such darkness, never stood in such rain, never seen such barbarians. And the raindrops fell mercilessly and without a break on the backs of the people, who were standing with shoulders hunched, already soaked to the skin. Then Kucyński arrived, the man in charge of the *Arbeitseinsatz* [labour supply] operation in the Zagłębie region. Now our fates were going to be decided. Segregation. Children began to be torn from their parents, families divided, people beaten mercilessly and so on.

Kucyński was the one who decided who would be sent where. Following his orders, three groups were formed, numbered 1, 2 and 3. Group 1 was for those who had a job, and so they were allowed to go home. Group 2 was for reconsideration, and group 3 for resettlement. Those of the third group faced a terrible fate. Surrounded by guards, they were already doomed. Often there were brave people who tried to escape from group 3 to group 1, but they never succeeded, since for such an attempt the guards would shoot them on the spot. My turn came. I walked up with my father, brothers, sister and sister-in-law. Kucyński pointed at me and at father. I was gripped by despair as I saw that I was being separated from my family. Father and I were assigned to group 2, and the others were sent home. In group 2 there was a huge crowd, people were crying and wailing. I was terrified. I stood with my father, clutching his hand tightly. No complaints, no pleas to God were of any use. The rain was falling more and more heavily; but fortunately it had already begun to grow light. I stayed by the fence of the playing-field the whole day; I thought someone would come and get me, that someone would reconsider us. Unfortunately, however, there was obviously no one, everything had stopped. You could only see the field, and the half-crazed people, some of whom were fainting from hunger and from what they had suffered there. Night was coming again, and we were still waiting on the playing-field. After one hour had passed we were ordered to form fives, and we were forced to drill. Then, with our heads hung low, we walked down the street.

Things were noisy and cheerful on the street, but our hearts were heavy. A train was approaching from far off. Our hearts sank, our legs were unsteady, and great pain showed on our faces. The train pulled up, and we were also ordered to halt. We were breathless. I held on tight to my father; I gave him a pitiful look and thought to myself that these were our last moments. But fortunately the train moved on, and we too were ordered to march on. This was done deliberately, to unsettle us. After walking for a long time, we arrived at the community administration building, where we were separated and sent to different rooms. Again I spent the whole night on my feet, but at least it was not in the open air. Morning came again. I had been in the hands of the murderers since Wednesday morning, and it had not been till Friday that someone began to deal with me. Father jumped across the roof, twisting his ankle as he did so, and later I also escaped. I began to feel afraid when I went out onto the street; it was sad and deserted, there were orphans wandering about crying and looking like corpses. My aunt had also been resettled, and when I met her children I did not recognise them, they had changed so much in the course of the last few days.

When I arrived home, I did not know what was happening to me. The room was full of people, everyone had been waiting for me impatiently. I walked up to the window; tears poured from my eyes. In the distance there were trains heading away; you could hear the cries of those being transported far away to Auschwitz, where so many people were burned. I shall never forget the twelfth of August; it was a day of tragedy.

(Archive of the CJHC, statement no. 659a)

17

5. LIDKA STERN

Born 1930 in Lwów

(Statement taken by Iza Lauer, Kraków)

It was Saturday, 15 August 1942. The *Aktion* was raging throughout the city. For a week I had been hiding with my mother in a shop next to the building where we lived, while my father and brother remained in the flat. We did not sense that anything was wrong. My father had had his *Meldekarte* [registration card] stamped, which in those days was the best thing that could happen, since this document was supposed to protect him for the duration of the *Aktion*; for the same reason he kept my brother with him. It was six o'clock in the afternoon when the shopkeeper's son came to us in our hiding-place and told us that they were pulling people in even if their cards were stamped. As soon as we heard this we passed the information on to father, so that he should hide at all costs. But father had faith in his document, and would not hide. That was his downfall. Half an hour later the *Schupo* [security police] came; without further ado they tore up father's *Meldekarte* and took him and my brother away with them. To this day we do not even know which direction they were taken in. All trace of them was lost. In the meantime someone had told them about our hiding-place, as a few minutes later the police began to demand the key to the door. When, after they had knocked and kicked the door for some time and the caretaker, who knew about us, would not give them the key, the Gestapo broke the door down. To get into the shop you had to pass along a short corridor. At the moment that one of the officers tried the handle of the door, we panicked and set off to hide in the next room; I accidentally kicked a basin, which made a loud noise. Now we were convinced that we were doomed. You can imagine our surprise when, a moment later, we heard one of the *Schupo* saying that they could leave, as there was nobody there. We were saved. And it was only then that I realised what a

18

terrible tragedy had been played out in the course of that one hour. I was alive, but my father and little brother were gone. I wanted to cry but I could not. I felt as if I had turned to stone.

There was a great deal more that I lived through during the four years of the German occupation, but that *Aktion* I shall never forget. I remember clearly how, during the November *Aktion*, I ran from the ghetto under fire from the Ukrainian policemen. I shall never forget the daily march through the gate, to the sound of music, and at the same time, of rifle-fire and of the falling of bodies. I can still picture 5 and 6 January 1943: the ghetto ablaze. And finally, 1 June 1943, the liquidation of the ghetto, and the murder of women, children and the elderly in the Janowska camp.

I can see all this and live through it anew, but all those dates are dominated by 15 August 1942, the deaths of my father and my brother. I do not know if anyone who has not experienced the hell of the *Aktions* can understand me; but I, who many times experienced them personally, and who was directly affected by the loss of those dearest to me, today – for the deaths of my father and brother and for the torment of six million of my brothers and sisters – a hundred times over, I accuse the German nation.

(Archive of the VHJC in Kraków, statement no. 292)

---

6. PESLA WALTER

Born 25 December 1934 in Ostrowiec Kielecki; daughter of Izrael and Perla

(*Statement taken by Dr Laura Eichhornowa, Kraków*)

On Saturday, 7 October 1942, my brother came home in the evening and began to cry, because a friend of his who was a policeman had told him that the next day they were going to transport the Jews out. My brother could have become a policeman too, but he had a good heart and did not want to push the Jews around. There had already been a commotion amongst the Jews during the previous week; they did not even bake the *cholent* [a dish served on Saturdays], because no one had a thought for it. My brother and my uncle made a shelter of boards in the yard. The yard belonged to my cousin's grandfather. The shelter was big, but very low. I could stand up in it, but my mother had to sit down. The whole family got into it, and four other people, so there were 44 people inside in all. The shelter was built underground by the fence; only a little bit of it poked out above ground-level, and through that tiny opening we could see what was happening outside.

We took some food with us, but only enough for one day, so on the second day there was nothing to eat. My brother hid at the house of his friend, the policeman, and arranged with us that when he gave a good hard kick, it would be a signal for us to let him in. My brother was very good and saved a lot of people, but he was not able to save our sisters. From our shelter, I saw people walking, all being marched along together; children were crying, and their mothers begged the Germans to shoot them, the mothers, rather than their children. Whenever a mother clutched her child tightly to her breast, one of the Germans would tear the child from her and kill it, and leave the mother; they did this to everyone, out of malice.

Then a carriage came by full of younger and older children. A big dog belonging to Peter, a German SS officer, was running after them, and the children kept crying and shouting. The Germans chased after people, beat them with their rifle-butts, and pushed around the young and old and the bigger children. One mother shouted 'Leave my child alone', and a German killed the child right in front of her.

On the third day my brother told my sisters that they could come out, because they had work cards. He said that nothing would happen to them, that people at the places where they worked were safe, and that other people were even paying large sums of money to get a job at those places. My sisters did as he said and left the shelter, and the Germans lined up all the young people who were going to work. No one expected anything to go wrong. But when they began to pick out the older and weaker ones, my sisters tried to join those who were to stay, but they did not manage to and they were sent to their deaths. And the next day my brother came home and did not tell mother anything about it. When mother asked 'Where are my children?', my brother said that they were at work.

But I knew what had happened because my brother had told me.

(Archive of the VJHC in Kraków, statement no. 455)

7. FRYDA KOCH

Born 12 September 1932 in Drohobycz
(Statement taken by Iza Lauer, Kraków)

We lived in Borysław. When the Germans came, the Ukrainians began rounding up Jews for forced labour. To begin with, people came back from this work, but after one street-raid, instead of sending people to work they took them to the police station on Pańska Street and killed them there. Afterwards my father removed the bodies on a wheelbarrow, because someone had to bury them. My brother and I hid in the attic under a pile of rags. The Ukrainians looked all round the attic and beat the rags with great iron-covered sticks; they found us, and one of them said: 'Cholovik i zhinka, budet horoshe myaso' ['A man and a woman, there'll be some good meat'], but then they saw that we were children and they let us go, for at that time they left children alone. From the blows I received, under the rags my back was covered in bruises.

For some time things were quiet. Then the Ukrainians and the German commandant went from flat to flat taking people

21

according to a list they had; on that occasion they took invalids and the sick.

There was terrible hunger. People were all swollen. You could not even find pigweed or other sorts of grass. Hundreds of people were dying. I did not go hungry at this time because my father was a confectioner and he had a job, and even helped other people.

The third *Aktion* took place in the spring and lasted a week. People said that children would be taken. I hid in the cellar and my brother on the roof, behind the chimney stack. Opposite us there lived Schwarz, who was always well-informed because he had friends in the *Ordnungsdienst* [Jewish police]; his children were playing on the verandah, so we knew that they were probably going to leave children alone. The next day we went to our uncle's. Uncle worked in a chemist's, and there were ten people hiding in the storeroom. It was very stuffy with all those medicines, but aunt found out that there was going to be a search at the chemist's so we all left. At night we hid in the lavatory. There was one old Jewish lady in there who lay all night without moving, and we thought she had died. In the morning uncle put us in the attic over the chemist's shop. I was not allowed to stand at the window, but uncle could see people being taken to the station, and we knew that they were going to their deaths in Bełżec; some people said it was by electric chair, others that there were electrified plates; I do not know exactly what it was, but I know for sure that they were going to their deaths. In the town everyone was being arrested. They paid young Polish boys to show them where the Jews' hiding-places were. We spent three days in the attic; we had had a bag of bread and potatoes, but it had been left behind in the lavatory. After three days, when things got quieter, my brother went down and brought it up; we ate the potatoes, even though by then they were rotten.

Father was caught, but he managed to escape. We went back home. Many of our friends had gone. Father knew that something had to be done; he set up a big rubbish skip in the yard, and dug a hide-out underneath it. Around the yard he put up a tall fence.

Two months later there was another *Aktion*.

Mother would not hide under the skip, so we went to our uncle's; by this time he had a shelter under the floorboards. There were 13 people inside. The Germans came to the chemist's and tried the floor, but they decided that there was nothing there. In the shelter you could either lie or sit hunched up. The food had been put in beforehand. We spent four days in there. My cousin was caught. He tore a strip from his shirt, made an armband and wrote *Ordnungsdienst* on it, and so they let him free at the station. Then several people did the same thing and the Germans ordered armbands to be stamped. When the *Aktion* was over, at night we went home. I looked around the room and could not believe that this was my home. It was clean, everything was in its place. And I had already got used to living in the shelter, where stones kept falling on us and it was so cramped.

Once again things were quiet for a few weeks. Father ran the confectioner's; our cakes were famous and were said to be the best. But what of it? Other people had less but were luckier. There was one Polish confectioner who victimised us, and kept having us fined; he tried to take our ice-cream machine, and father had to bribe him to leave it for us, but in the end he took it anyway. It was through him that, later, they took father and another Jewish confectioner, Linhard. That informer is in prison now.

Every day I used to go a long way out of the town to meet the peasant women on their way in and buy milk from them. One day, as I was on my way back, a Polish woman stopped me and told me not to go into the city because they were pulling people in. I thought it was just a round-up for forced labour. Then I met some of my girlfriends who were running away from the town. We did not want to stay together, so we split up and I went over the '*Schmelz*' (a square that was covered with bits of iron, tramline rails and other types of rubbish) and went to hide at a Jewish lady's who was an acquaintance of ours. Then the grown-ups went to hide in the attic and we went up there too. When the Germans came sniffing around, we hid in a hiding-place that could not be seen from outside. You went in through a trap door in the attic. The Germans came up to the attic but they did not find the hiding-place. I was terribly afraid, as I did not know what was happening at home; perhaps they did not know that there was an *Aktion* and they had all been arrested. On the fourth day there was a break in the *Aktion* and my father came to see how the lady's children were, as she worked for us and had been hiding in our house. I cannot describe his joy when he saw me. They were all convinced that I had already been taken to the Colosseum cinema, where the people who had been arrested were assembled. Father had taken a risk; he had been to the *OD*, where he had paid money to have food brought to me and had promised 5,000 złotys if I were released. Father and I went home, or rather to the hiding-place under the rubbish skip. At that time working Jews were given armbands with an 'A' stamped on them, and people wearing these were not pulled in. That *Aktion* lasted a whole month.

This happened in the autumn of 1942. Every Sunday there was a break. We went back up to our flat and made pancakes for the whole week ahead. The *Aktion* was also usually called off in the evening. My father paid one man who had an armband, and the man came and knocked on the fence when the *Aktion* was over. Then father went out and made us something to eat. But we stayed inside. There were five of us there: father, mother, grandmother, my brother and me. It was very cramped, there was nowhere to put your legs. We all lay on top of one another. This lasted for a whole month. Father had an ulcer on his gum which was very painful, and he kept taking medicine.

The people in the cinema were starved for the entire month. They did have soup sent by the Jewish canteen, but it was only a drop in the ocean.

After this *Aktion* people began to talk about the extermination of the Jews. Father built a hiding-place in the yard. My uncle and my cousin built it with him, and the women and children lent a hand. It was a pit the size of a room; there was a drain through which water could be poured into the yard, and there was a supply of air through a crate that was built into the hiding-place. He was also going to put in a gas pipe and to stock the hiding-place with food.

However, that Polish confectioner had a German commission visit us, and as father admitted that he had bought goods for baking on the black market, he was fined. When the Germans came back again we thought that it was an *Aktion*, and we all ran away. Then they went out into the yard, where the digging was still going on; they took all the things that we had stored in the hiding-place, and of course found out about the hiding-place itself. Our whole plan had come to nothing. The men of the *Ordnungsdienst* said later that the Germans had admired the hiding-place and had said that they would never have discovered it.

All the same, father partitioned off part of the hide-out and made it secure, but no one would help him and they did not believe it could still be of any use.

Now it was only an 'R' sign [*Rüstung* – munitions work] that could protect the Jews. Father managed to obtain such an armband. On the first day of the sixth *Aktion* he was arrested but released because he had the letter R. The next day he came to see how things were with us; when he got home the Germans were there. There was a lot of flour in our flat; father tried to buy his way out, and gave one of the Germans 1,500 złotys, but the German ordered him to take the flour to the police station. We learnt all this from a Jewish policeman, because father never came back. The German had said that this Jew was a black marketeer and had tried to bribe him; he ripped father's 'R' sign off and ordered him to be taken to the Colosseum. There they held people for one day, and the next day they took them down near the abattoir and shot them. But father was not taken to the abattoir. He was killed in the cinema, and everyone said that the confectioner who had informed on us had had a hand in it. We were in the shelter and had no idea of what had happened. It was a few days before mother told me. My uncle, the chemist, had given mother three doses of poison, in case things got bad. Mother wanted us to take the poison right away, but we would not agree and told mother that she had no right to do that to us, as father might still be alive.

The *Aktions* continued, and people stayed in hiding.

My mother heard about a hide-out in Dereżyce near Drohobycz. This was a walled soup cauldron which could hold ten people. Mother paid the watchman, and we were going to spend the rest of the war there. One Jew brought us food, but only one week later Jews were banned from walking round the town, so he could not bring us anything and we had to leave. We were in a terrible state there: there was no water, the air condensed and formed drops on us which were saturated with diesel fuel. We cooked on a primus stove; there was no question of washing, and for our needs there was a bucket which was emptied at night.

We returned to our part of town. After a while there was a round-up. We tried to escape into the woods, but on the way we were attacked by some Polish boys who threw stones at us and stopped us from getting away. Mother gave them some money and they left us alone. We set off back home. On the way a Polish lady stopped us and told us not to go into the town as there was gunfire there. We hid under a small bridge. It was springtime, but it was awfully cold. It was a beautiful spring day; in the distance we could see children playing. How we felt then! We thought about taking the poison. I said to mother that when we got home I wanted to have a drink of hot tea, and then everything could end. Then, from our hiding-place we saw that Jews were out on the streets. We went up and it turned out that the Germans had shot a spy, and that there had not been any *Aktion* against the Jews. I had some hot tea, and although my mother and brother wanted to commit suicide, I no longer agreed; I wanted to live, I wanted to live so much. Everything was so beautiful all around. Now

I can describe what I experienced, but I cannot express what I felt. Mother began to try to get me a place at one Polish lady's. My brother could not and would not live in a hide-out. He could not manage without water. We found a place at the house of one Polish lady. I spent six months there. Up till Whitsun I lived in the flat, and then in the attic. On one occasion the neighbours saw me looking out of the window, and I had to hide in the living room behind the wardrobe. Later I moved back to the attic, but I did not lie on the bed any more, as it was very hot near the roof and it was cooler to lie lower, on the floor.

Mother paid 1,500 złotys for me to stay there. They only fed me twice a day and I was very hungry between meals. I could tell the mealtimes from where the sun fell on the roof. Sometimes I was able to go down to wash; when it was very hot they let me stay in the living room behind the wardrobe.

At the end of May the landlady brought the news that the district had been cordoned off. I was very worried. I sensed that my mother and brother would be arrested. I did not want to believe this, but it came true. Uncle wrote to me pretending to be my mother, and he continued to pay for me. I packed my things, I wanted to go to mother; I wanted to kill myself. In time I learnt the truth.

The people I was staying with found out that several Poles had been shot for harbouring Jews, and they were afraid to keep me any longer. At this time in Borysław there were various *Aktions*, which I do not know much about. The remaining Jews, about 1,500 in number, were held in some barracks, in several buildings. My uncle was there, and my landlady took me to him. A few days later I moved to a garage where women and children were living. It was easier for me to hide there. To begin with uncle brought me food, but then he stopped as he could see that I was managing by myself. I peeled potatoes and went to do housework and scrub floors. In the winter they buried stores of potatoes, and every other day I got a bucketful of potatoes, which I sold to buy flour and barley.

From Mrs Flachs I would get double helpings at supper and breakfast. Mrs Flachs was the manageress of the barracks' canteen; she was very good to children and helped out the poorer people. She managed to get some shoes for me. I always had enough bread, but I could not eat it; I would sell it and make myself some soup or buy some black pudding. The Jews who went out to the town would bring back foodstuffs and sell them.

In the barracks there were two German officers who kept order. They were not so bad. But then two more came, one of whom was called Münzinger, and they were terrible. There was also the Jewish militia, about 20 men, and they caused us a lot of trouble. I remember Maks Steinberg, who once hit me on the head with his truncheon. And the worst of all was Walek Eisenstein, who used to reveal the locations of hideouts. I shall come back to him.

The Jews began building hiding-places in the woods. They dug pits, stocked them with food, installed stoves and connected up a water supply. They did this work at night.

One day Hildebrand, the head of the Gestapo from Jasło, arrived. A general assembly was called; Hildebrand gave a speech in which he said that everyone was to be transferred to Jasło, that children and all belongings could be taken, and that everything would be all right there.

People began escaping. Mrs Flachs arranged with the people that each hide-out would take in one child, and she gave each one 3 kilograms of food (flour and fat); as well as this she arranged a hide-out for the orphans, with one lady guardian. I was supposed to go into a bunker with one family, but then I saw that they were reluctant to take me; I complained to Eisenstein so he would order them to take me, but he did not help me. The Jews even ran away from the militia, and in the barracks there were only 15 people left. For a few days we were alone; I cooked for one man and ate with him. When the date of the transfer passed and everything was quiet, the Jews began to return to the barracks. When quite a lot of them had arrived back, one day the Germans cordoned

28

off the barracks. A lady woke me and warned me; I got dressed, picked up the bundle that I had ready and went to leave the garage; suddenly a German came in. I took fright; I threw down my things and subsequently forgot about them. I could see people going to the men's barracks. I went there too. They broke the lock on the potato store and 20 people hid inside. On the way I managed to grab two rolls. We spent the whole day there. But in the evening I did not know where to go. At night everyone gathered in the yard; there were others who had nowhere to go either. We left by the rear of the barracks and went into the woods. It was night-time, and it was raining; we were muddy and cold, and we were tormented by the thought of how it would all end. Would they catch us? We wandered around the wood right through the night; in the morning we spotted smoke rising. It was a hide-out, camouflaged with leaves. They opened the trap door. Even though we spoke Yiddish, they were afraid of us and when we went in they held axes. There were three people already there, and 11 of us joined them. There was not much room.

In the Abbey Wood there were many hide-outs, one next to another. They formed a special commission there, led by Mundek Schwarz of Borysław. There was an order to take in all the Jews, and the members of the commission inspected all the hide-outs and assigned people accordingly.

I stayed in the hide-out we had come to first, as father's cousin was there. Things were fine for me there. There was enough room inside, for many of the 'financiers' had returned to the barracks. From here they were taken to Płaszów. That was the first transport from our barracks.

The commission used to send people to the barracks to find out what plans the Germans had regarding the woods. Eisenstein was paid to leave them alone. In the meantime, a fair number of Jews had returned to the barracks.

Our hide-out was discovered on one occasion by some Polish boys. We ran away into the woods, but they did not give us away. They were boys who previously had worked with our people. Another time a Jew was caught in the barracks; he was beaten up by the Ukrainian militia and told them the location of three of the hide-outs. The commission learnt of this and warned us; we ran away to the neighbouring wood and hid in a fallen pine tree, the branches of which formed a hiding-place.

The next day the commission sent us in threes to other hide-outs. Also a new hide-out was built for those who had lost their own. In our old hide-out they dug out my barley and took it to the new one. In the new one there were 20 people. After a week there we had to leave, since the owners of the hide-out wanted to take in some financiers so as to have enough to live on. In the night some of the Jews would leave the wood and buy supplies of food. In the evenings potato soup would be brought to the hide-outs, where there were pipes for cooking. In the meantime a new hiding-place was built; it was walled with cobblestones, and a lavatory was installed. We moved in there; there were about 12 of us in there, all poor people who did not have their own hide-out. We all went hungry. The commission sent us barley, but it was not enough.

People complained about the commission. There were many who were starving, while the members of the commission used to buy cakes for themselves. People wanted to go and buy things for themselves, but the commission would not allow it, to avoid the hide-outs being given away. Previously the commission had collected money to pay Eisenstein. On one occasion, one of the Jews wanted to go and see his wife, who was German, so some people from the commission escorted him there. They spotted some Ukrainian militiamen outside the wood; the men from the commission hid, but the Jew was startled and revealed himself. He was arrested, and gave away all the hide-outs.

We did not know what to do now, or where we should run to. At the crack of dawn the next morning people dispersed into the woods, but they did not manage to hide; there was a round-up and we were all caught. I stayed in the bunker under some rags and would not go out. It was only when the Jews who had been caught came back for their belongings and told me that the Germans were going to burn the bunkers, and when I saw the canisters of paraffin they had ready, that I went out and joined the others.

The Germans formed us into a column and led us to the Abbey Path. Here they separated the people from the different hide-outs, and beat the men from Borysław severely to force them to reveal the whereabouts of other hide-outs. They did not beat the men from Drohobycz as they knew that they were financiers who did not know where the bunkers were. They beat people about the head and on the backside with knouts, and shouted 'Zeigen, zeigen!', then they led us back to the barracks. I liked the way things looked now in the barracks; the children playing outside were clean and washed. That was only a first impression after the woods. When you looked more closely at the children, they were in tatters and looked rather poor.

Mensinger walked about on a hilltop with a pair of binoculars, watching to see if there was anything moving in the woods. Once they caught a Jew who pulled a gun, but Mensinger beat him to it and shot him in the leg. He was then taken to the barracks, and he and another Jew were shot.

On one occasion everyone was summoned to a muster and they shot two people, I do not know why. The German officers warned us that if any of the inhabitants of the barracks should go into the woods and be found, they would be shot. To emphasise this they shot three Jews.

I was living with a girl I knew and liked very much, and for some time things were quiet. There were only musters. At one of them it was announced that there was going to be a transport. By this time the barracks were being guarded by the *Lagerwache*, and it was not so easy to escape. And then Hildebrand arrived; the barracks were cordoned off, a muster was called and the very next day the transport set off. A few people managed to hide in the barracks. I heard they were issuing supplies of food for the journey; I went to the kitchen with another man, and the cook hid us in the potato store where I had hidden at the beginning, though I had forgotten about it. The next day things were quiet again. I do not know how many people were put on the transport. An acquaintance of father's took care of me. In the meantime the front was drawing closer. The Soviets were already outside Lwów. We were afraid that there would be another transport. People kept watch at night. One night my guardian woke me up. The barracks had been cordoned off. At that time we had a hiding-place in the bathhouse. I slept in the disinfection room; there were a lot of people there. From there you could get into the bathhouse through a small window. In the bathhouse there was a huge stove that one of the Jews had built in such a way that it could be used as a hiding-place. We got into the stove, and in our haste we forgot to turn the gas off; there was boiling water overhead, it was awfully hot, we were soaking and there was no air. We left the trap door open, but people began to suffocate.

One child became delirious; one of the men was gasping for breath. Then the Jew who had built the stove came; he guessed that people must be in the stove, and he turned off the gas and put the cold water on. Despite this the man inside, whose name was Nowak, suffocated. The boy, Nowak's son, who was eight, was delirious and shouted 'Don't hit me, leave me alone!' and would not let even his own mother touch him. Mrs Nowak and her daughter were also suffocating. She left the hiding-place, took the boy with her and said that if she was not given water she would give the hiding-place away. One of the men went to get some water and was caught. Then they caught the woman and I heard her shouting 'Go in there, go in there, my husband had suffocated!' Another man could not stand it and ran away in his underwear. When they caught him, he returned, with one of the Germans, for his clothes, and it was a real miracle that the Germans did not look inside the stove. To begin with there were ten people in the stove, then some left and others came in; in the end six of us survived. In the afternoon things were quieter, we were able to go outside for a few minutes to get some fresh air.

Gypsies attacked the barracks to rob them. That time our people were taken to Auschwitz. There is a girl with me here who escaped from that transport. Her name is Elżbieta Abraham. At night we left the stove; we were now fearfully cold. We left the barracks at the rear, through a lavatory, and made our way through the bushes to the mine. Four people went to hide at the flat of some Aryans they knew, and one elderly lady and I were ordered to go to Patacze, where we would be able to join people at the 'Heiz' who had come in from the woods. As we were passing by one of the mines the Germans stopped us. The lady remained, but I ran away. She told me later that one of the Germans had gone to get a dog and had chased after me, but I escaped across the backyards and he could not find me. She begged the German to let her go and he did. So you can beg Germans to do things? Aha! She must have had some money with her.

I ran without knowing where; I was going to knock on someone's door, but I was afraid. I lay down to sleep in some bushes.

At dawn I set off again; I knew where I was now. I went to the Polish lady's where I had stayed before. But they said that they were rounding up people for the *Baudienst* colony; I did not want to stay there and I went to some Poles I knew in the town. They took me in.

Two weeks later the Soviets arrived.

(Archive of the VJHC in Kraków, statement no. 516)

8. MENDEL ROSENKRANZ

Born 28 October 1928 in Horodenka, near Stanisławów; son of Leon and Gita Ladenheim

(Statement taken by M. Hochberg-Mariańska, Kraków)

In 1939, when the war broke out, there was a great commotion in Horodenka, for many Polish soldiers and civilians began to flee the country – Horodenka is situated only six kilometres from the Rumanian border. Saul Gloger, who was a barber in Horodenka, was called to the Orthodox church, and there he gave Minister Beck and Marshal Śmigły a shave and a haircut. Then, when he left the church and began telling people about it, the Polish police arrested him for panic-mongering. He was in prison for two days; they released him after the great bombing.

On the day of Yom Kippur the Soviets entered Horodenka. Just at that time I started school, in the seventh class. The school was changed from having seven classes to ten. My father had given up running the shop because heavy taxes had been imposed; co-operatives were formed everywhere. It was possible to do business privately, and we did very well out of it.

War with Germany broke out on 22 June 1941, and within two or three weeks the Hungarian army had arrived. In Horodenka there were street battles, with the Hungarian patrols attacking the retreating Soviet forces. The Ukrainians assisted the Hungarians, instructing them in how to encircle the enemy.

For the first five months there were no Germans at all in Horodenka. The Hungarians behaved perfectly well towards the Jews; the only thing they did was to round up people for forced labour. In the course of those five months only one Jew lost his life; he was rather crazy, and had put up resistance and tried to strike a Hungarian soldier. He was beaten up so severely while he was in custody that he died. The worst-behaved were the Ukrainians. There was a Ukrainian

34

nationalist military party in Horodenka called the Sich which planned to organise a pogrom of Jews. We found out about this and Dr Schneider, the town doctor, went to the Ukrainian general to ask him to intervene. The Hungarians searched the premises of the organisation, confiscated their arms and arrested one of the leaders, Baskulo.

After those five months the Hungarians moved east and the Germans arrived. At once a German administration was set up headed by *Obersturmbannführer* Doppler, who wore a Gestapo uniform, as *Kreishauptmann* [regional commander], and *Kreislandwirth* König, who was also in the Gestapo. The German military police arrived – a German *Sonderdienst* and the criminal police comprised of Poles, mostly from Silesia. The Germans came in November 1941, and the first *Aktion* against the Jews took place as early as 4 December. At that time there was not yet a separate district for Jews; they were merely banned from living on the main street. These regulations were introduced by the Germans the moment they arrived. Under the Hungarians we had worn yellow armbands; the Germans introduced white ones with the star of David on them. At this time there were 6,000 Jews in Horodenka, 5,000 of them from the town itself and 1,000 who had been resettled from Hungary.

The *Aktion* began on the morning of 4 December. No one had expected it. The police cordoned off streets and began dragging people from their homes and assembling them in the synagogue. Father hid us in the attic, my two sisters and me, and went to see what was happening. They arrested him, and we never saw him again. On that occasion they took 2,600 people, men, women and children; the first transports were driven by road to the woods at Semakowce, and on the Friday morning the rest were taken there on foot. There a single huge pit had been dug. The Jews were shot and thrown into the pit; children were simply thrown in alive. But the pit was not filled in on Thursday but on Friday, and at night ten children and a few women, who had only been injured, had climbed out of the pit, where they had been lying under corpses. They told people how it had been there. A board was placed over the pit, and five people stood on it at a time. They took all their clothes off, and then they were shot. Among these had been the doctor from Horodenka, Dr Schneider. He had not been undressed completely: they let him keep his shirt on. But he said: 'You have so little, take my shirt too. It's a good, new shirt.' And he took his shirt off himself and put it with his other things. One of the women who had survived was pregnant, and two weeks later she gave birth in hospital. Here, she let on somehow about the pit in the woods. The Gestapo came to the hospital, took her and the baby, and shot them in Kołomyja. They also took the other survivors. Only one woman is still alive; she is living in Stanisławów and is called Dora Glatzerowa. In the course of the first *Aktion* they shot the entire *Judenrat*, including the *Obmann*, lawyer Hessel. Later they set up a new *Judenrat*.

The second *Aktion* took place on 13 April 1942. In the meantime, they had established a ghetto and imprisoned all the Jews from the whole of the Horodenka region. The ghetto was not walled off, but was guarded by the Jewish police. After father died, we made a living by selling things. My elder sister and I went to work on the road, carrying stones. A clerk from the *Arbeitsamt* in Kołomyja, who had been bribed, tipped us off that there was going to be another *Aktion*, and everyone hid in bunkers. We also had a bunker; it was in the yard; you lifted up a stone and went inside. That time the Germans took 75 people and shot them at the *Judenrat*. Afterwards, we buried the bodies in the Jewish cemetery. At this time the ghetto was more strictly administered and was guarded more closely; malnutrition and typhus appeared. Many people died of typhus. I do not remember how many Jews there were in Horodenka at this time. We went to work under escort by the Jewish militia. Our militia were not so bad. We knew that in Tłuste the *Ordnungsdienst* behaved appallingly, but we had no one like that. They were not particularly helpful, but they did not interfere either.

In July or August 1942, I do not remember exactly, a registration of all Jews was announced. Posters were stuck up on buildings to say that on Monday morning everyone should report to the market square, and that the registration would take place there. In the *Judenrat* they said that 750 Jews would be allowed to stay in Horodenka, and they would be given an 'A' [*Arbeit* – work] sign to show that they were in work, while the rest would be sent to Kołomyja. Everyone was afraid of this resettlement, and the rich paid up to 100 dollars in the *Judenrat* to be included on the list of those staying. On Monday morning people went to the market square, but not everyone, for some of them were suspicious and hid in the bunkers. I also hid with my mother and my sisters. *Kreishauptmann* Doppler began the registration, and suddenly cars carrying Gestapo officers drove up, and the Gestapo opened fire on the crowd. Everyone was rounded up and held in the big building that was known as the 'mansion'. The *Aktion* lasted from Monday to Friday – the Gestapo searched houses, attics and cellars and in the bunkers. We remained in our bunker. We stayed there till Saturday; we hardly had anything to eat, just a little bread. Everyone from the 'mansion' was transported out to Bełżec; they released only 50 skilled workmen and also a few of those who collected refuse (*Altstoffwaren*). Some people were sent to the Janowska camp in Lwów. We knew that in Bełżec people were killed by electrocution.

On Saturday morning, when everything was quiet, we left the bunker. There were others who had gone into hiding like us. We were given jobs in the Jewish warehouses. Everything was being gathered in one place. There were separate warehouses for saleable goods, for furniture, for crockery. That lasted for another two weeks. After those two weeks they began rounding people up and transferring them to the ghetto in Kołomyja. It was at this time that they took my mother and little sister; I never saw them again. At night my elder sister and I packed our things into bundles and ran away to Tłuste. We crossed the Dniestr at a ford. From the people who escaped with us to Tłuste I learned that all those skilled workmen who had been given an 'A' sign in Horodenka had also been taken and shot in Tłuste. Horodenka was *Judenfrei*.

On Thursday we arrived in Tłuste. There were no ghettos or *Aktions* there. The *Judenrat* had only had to provide a contingent of elderly people to be killed – 200 people. People there even refused to believe everything we told them, though Tłuste was only 35 kilometres from Horodenka. But on Saturday there began to be talk of an *Aktion*, and people began to panic. The *Aktion* started on Monday. Everyone was rounded up, and those who tried to escape were shot. We were all led to the station and loaded into railway wagons. A few young, healthy men were selected and put in a separate carriage, and were given bread and water for the journey – it was said that they were to be taken to the Janowska camp in Lwów. The rest were probably being sent to their deaths in Bełżec. We travelled the whole day, and towards evening we broke a window in the train and jumped out, first me then my sister. We walked back across the fields to Tłuste; it took us three days and nights. We slept outdoors. My sister went into villages to buy bread and to ask the way, while I waited in the fields. In Tłuste there were still quite a lot of Jews, and it stayed like that until spring 1943.

In the meantime there were several *Aktions*. On one occasion my sister was caught and taken with some others to Czortków, but after they had been starved for a week they were released; all that happened was that they were given some sort of injection. Afterwards everyone went down with typhus, and others caught it from them; many people died then. It was said that those people had been injected with typhus and released so that everyone else would become infected.

In the spring, I do not remember which month, the ghetto was closed down completely. Some of the people were transferred to the ghetto in Czortków, and the rest to the camp at Karolówka. My sister and I ended up in the camp. This was a farm where 50 Jews worked. There were no police, and no one guarded us. The farm was administered by a Pole,

Ziółkowski. He was not so bad, though when he got drunk he would beat people. You could get by there. I went out to work for some farmers, so I got better food and brought back bread for my sister. It was like this till 23 November 1943. On that day, in the morning, six Ukrainian militiamen and one German arrived; they rounded up a group of people in the yard in front of the stables and shot them. They shot my sister, and I ran away. A few of us were left; we hid in the fields, and the next day we went back to the farm. The bodies of all those who had been shot were lying in a sort of hole made after a tree had been uprooted, where we used to tip rubbish. We often used to say that we might end up in that hole ourselves. They were all lying there, and we covered them with earth. I saw my sister, who had been shot dead.

A few of us remained on the farm till 1 January 1944. By then the front was drawing closer. The administrator was afraid to keep us any longer, and ordered us to go wherever we wanted. So we split up, and I went to Lisowiec, where there was a similar farm. But here I realised that I would not be able to stay, so I went back to Karolówka. This time we were allowed to stay; things were not so strict, and the evacuation was beginning. The Ukrainian nationalists began to be active. They were murdering Jews in all the camps. At this point we split up and went into hiding. That same evening, this was towards the end of February, I came to a Basilian monastery, two kilometres from Karolówka. I went into the stables and spent the night there. In the morning the housekeeper came in; she asked no questions, and I did not say anything either. She brought me some bread and milk. I took a rake and began tidying up the courtyard. A priest came; he looked at me and also said nothing. They brought me food at midday and in the evening. And this went on from day to day. I stayed there for more than a month; then the Soviets arrived. I was afraid to stay there any longer, for the Banderists, the Ukrainian nationalists, were everywhere, so I went to Jagielnica, where the Red Army had already moved in. They took me on a truck and I travelled to Horodenka, thinking that maybe someone would come back, or that perhaps I would collect my things. But I did not manage to. I was advised to go to Czerniowce, as you could earn money there. I spent a few months there trading and I made some money, but then I went back to Horodenka. Twice the militia stopped me and took everything I had. I went to Stanisławów, and the rabbi was organising a transport to Kraków. People told me I should go, and that I would be able to learn a trade. I should like to become an electrical engineer.

(Archive of the VJHC in Kraków, statement no. 1)

Chapter Two
THE CAMPS

1. W.J. SACHS

(Written account sent in – no further details provided)

In the first few days of August 1944, in the face of the approaching Soviet forces, there began the evacuation of KL Kraków-Płaszów. It was at this time that they evacuated the majority of the women, including my mother, who I gave water to right at the end, as she was sitting in the kitchen with 135 other women waiting for the transport. The next day over 5,000 men, including myself, were also evacuated. We sat for three days and three nights, our legs splayed, lying on top of each other so to speak, in fearful heat, without water. When we arrived in Mauthausen a great number of corpses were lifted out of the carriages. It was then that I understood the kind of thirst that can drive a man to drink his own urine. We arrived debilitated by thirst; for three more days we were kept in the sun with one litre of cabbage water and a hunk of bread.

Then, for three days we carried rocks, and were beaten and shot at, in the most terrible quarry in Germany – it was notorious throughout occupied Europe for the 186 steps which you had to climb at least seven times a day. And if that was not enough, an SS officer and a *Capo* stood over us, the rocks were heavy, the sun burned our shaved heads mercilessly, and the gravel cut our bare feet. I went down with gastroenteritis, as we fell upon some cold water that had been stagnant so long it was green, and we drank it, ignoring the fact that we were being beaten on the back of the neck or pushed to the ground. I also saw the terrifying agony experienced by those dying of a twisted bowel. These wretches pleaded for death; the SS officer would laugh and say to them: 'Using a bullet on you would be a waste of 18 pfennigs'; a few minutes later he would be shooting healthy people.

After three days of this labour we were transferred to KL Gusen II, seven kilometres from Mauthausen. There we worked hard, 12 hours a day. We got up at half-past three in the morning and we were often on our feet till ten at night; all day long we were beaten and tortured, soaked to the skin and frozen, eternally hungry. And the lice were the last straw. This lasted till half-way through November when, as a result of a kick, I developed an ulcer on my leg. I ate no bread; I lived on a litre of soup a day alone, so as to be able to arrange sick-leave in return for the bread I had saved. After a few days I was so dreadfully hungry that I ate my portion of bread and the next day I had to go to work. I was dragged back to work; the beating I received could only be described by the sticks that were broken on me. And so I went hungry again, eating no bread, and I stayed in the block. I needed just a few more days to get well again when, at six o'clock in the morning of 1 December, Schreiber, the block orderly, came and said that the next day I would have to go back to work. For me that was a sentence of death by beating. At eight o'clock my friends from the night-shift arrived and said: 'You're lucky. They're sending the sick and the weak from the sick-room to the gas chambers; you'd have gone yourself.' I was the only volunteer.

I think that 1 December 1944 was the most terrible day of my life. Dressed only in my thin cotton *Häftling* clothes, with no underwear, shoes or hat, lashed by the wind, I struggled through the snow and mud from eight in the morning till one at night. My leg swelled up like a balloon, I had a fever, and my toes were frozen. We were then taken to the block, where we stayed for several days without dressings or medicine. It was only then that our medical cards were sent. I was in bed for two months.

Half-way through January 1945, the first period of starvation began in the camp; for 22 days we were not given a single piece of bread, just a litre of watery turnip soup without any flour, fat or salt, for the salt was used to put down on the roads in front of the kitchen. At this time there had begun the evacuation of the camps in the east (Auschwitz, Gross-Rosen, Sachsenhausen and so on). The sick-room filled up. There were now four of us to a bed. It was then that a 'death block' for Jews was set up, into which they crammed as many Jews as came. The record was 1,470, though also that day 75 deaths were recorded. The Aryan personnel refused to work in such conditions, so a Jewish staff was chosen, and I began work as a nurse. Naturally, I was not supposed to treat the sick but to keep order, distribute food and carry out the bodies of those who died. The Jews lay five or six to a bed. The strong stifled the weak. They came to us not to be treated but to die. It was only thanks to a friend who brought me food, and to the doctors I knew, who found me a job at the right moment, that I survived everything. Otherwise I would have been burned in the crematorium long ago. The days and weeks passed in this way until the second period of starvation set in at the beginning of April; this time people ate excrement and there were two cases of cannibalism. We starved until the Americans came, on 5 May.

Some 2,000 of our comrades were gassed and burned a week before liberation. I do not know by what miracle I survived it all. As I write now, I remember a children's game. A small child picks up a handful of sand and says: 'I had this many children.' He throws the sand in the air. Some of it falls on the ground. 'That many died,' cries the child; he catches the rest: 'and this many lived.'

In this way, for five years we were thrown in the air and caught or dropped.

(Archive of the VJHC in Kraków, statement no. 114)

---

2. GIZA LANDAU

Born 5 May 1932 in Tarnów; daughter of Józef and Erna Beller

(Statement taken by M. Hochberg-Mariańska, Kraków)

Mother tried to persuade me that we should cross to the Aryan side, but I did not want to. I had a feeling that we would get caught; I preferred to go with everyone else, wherever we had to. One day they loaded us into a lorry and drove us to the camp at Płaszów outside Kraków. That was in October 1943. The reception we received at the camp was terrifying. I do not know why everyone was so set against people from Tarnów. There was a Jewish commandant called Chilowicz and his wife, Finkelstein, and others too. They hurled abuse at us; at musters it was forever 'Drop!' and 'Stand!' – in mud and water. To begin with mother and I worked transporting earth in wheelbarrows for the road. Then we worked in the *Gröss-Schneiderei* [the main tailors' workshop], sewing uniforms. On our way to work we used to pass a sort of mound where people were shot and burned on pyres. There were executions the whole time, and people who had been caught with Aryan papers were brought in from the city; there were many children among them.

On 14 May 1944 there was a muster for the whole camp. They began to read a list of all the children. Everyone realised at once what this meant – after all, children were superfluous, like the old and the sick, and they had to be shot. When my name was read out my mother did not want to let me go, but she could not conceal me and they were searching for people according to their number. So I stepped forward and mother went with me. Gestapo officer Müller was standing there; he pushed mother back, saying 'Not you, you're still able to work'. My mother was beside herself but, as always, she made up her mind to save me. I was standing at the other end of a line of children, and mother had to run down the whole line to get to me. But two Jewish policemen were standing there, the worst two in the camp, Kerner and Marcel Goldberg. I do not know how it happened that they let mother through; one pretended he had not seen anything, while the other said: 'It'll be too late in a moment.' Then my mother rushed up to me, grabbed me by the belt of my overcoat and dragged me back to her place in the line. In this way she saved me yet again.

On that transport they took all the children, the sick and the elderly. A few children hid in the latrines; one fell under the lorry, and when it drove away the child stayed behind and was saved. Some of the mothers went to die with their children, but not all were permitted to. One mother went to her death because she thought her child was on the transport, but it turned out that the child had stayed behind. That was a terrible day in the camp. The loudspeakers played to drown out the crying of mothers; the entire camp shook from the wailing. The mothers had to turn their backs in order not to watch the children being driven out. The next day Chilowicz's wife attended the muster, checking to see if any children had survived; this made her furious. Mother dressed me in knee-length boots and did my hair so that I looked more grown-up; then she placed me among the shorter women so I did not look like a child. In this way I stayed in the camp and worked as a seamstress. Whenever possible I avoided showing myself to the Germans.

In July we managed once again to get out of a transport; this time it was at the station, because there were too few carriages. It was then that they shot Chilowicz, his wife and some others, and laid the bodies by the latrines. There was a muster at one o'clock in the afternoon and everyone had to file past, look at them and read a notice saying that they had been shot because they had arms and had intended to escape. Goeth, the German commandant of the camp, would ride in on horseback; then there were always casualties. People shook with fear whenever they saw him; he was a handsome man, but a criminal.

On 21 October 1944, nothing could be done any more and we were put on a transport to Auschwitz. We travelled in closed wagons; it was crowded and stuffy. Everyone was already bidding each other farewell, for we knew that we were destined for the ovens and the gas chambers. Even though so much was talked about this, no one imagined exactly how it would be. In the evening we arrived at the station in Auschwitz and at once we were marched to Birkenau. In the distance the sky was red, as if from a great fire. I could not believe that people were being burned there; I had seen a great deal by then, but such a thing was difficult to believe. Out of the chimneys there came not smoke but fire. People asked the *Posten* (guards) what was burning like that; they answered that bread was being baked day and night, but we knew that that was not true.

We spent the night in a big hall. It was so terrifying that I cannot describe it. Some people were crying, others praying, yet others cursing, and some sitting in complete indifference – nothing mattered to them any more. Mother held me tight and begged me not to be afraid, and said that God was sure to help us and that we would manage to survive, just as we always had before. But I just pretended not to be afraid, because I did not want mother to worry; in reality I was petrified, and my whole body shook. They gave us nothing to eat, but I was not hungry. Besides, what would be the point of eating so much, since we were going to our deaths. Then the selection began, and that was the worst of all. We had to take all our clothes off; in the doorway stood Dr Mengele, and to one side he sent those who could live, and to the other those who would die. Then mother began begging one of the guards, a Czech woman, not to give me away, and I hid under a whole pile of clothing in the corner of the hall. There were other girls hiding there too, including some older girls. I lay there for more than two hours. I could feel someone standing on my stomach, and I had to use all my strength not to cry out. They searched to see if anyone was hiding there but they did not find me. I was half suffocated when my mother pulled me out. But I was alive, and I was with mother again.

Then we were washed and had our heads shaved, and we were tattooed with numbers. I received no. A26098. People said that it was good to have a number, but even so the children were constantly subject to selections and were sent to the ovens. Mother concealed me all the time, even from the block orderly. At the musters she always placed me so that I did not stand out. In fact, all mother thought about was how to hide me and how to save me. The whole time, day and night, you had to live in fear and uncertainty. Finally, we were transferred to Auschwitz and at last we were able to breathe a little more easily. To begin with, I worked with mother on the wheelbarrows, and then Commandant Hesler ordered me to stand by the gate and open it when someone from the authorities wanted to come through. I was fine there. Every day we got a quarter of a kilogram of bread per person and a quarter-litre of soup, sometimes even a half-litre. But the most important thing was not the food but the fact that here there were no ovens or gas chambers.

It was like this till 5 January 1945, when the evacuation of the camp began. We were lined up, given a small loaf of bread and a lump of margarine for the journey, and marched off hurriedly. The Russians must have been very close by then, as the Germans were in a great hurry. We were not allowed to stop even for a moment, day or night. If someone bent over to straighten their shoe or to have a rest, or if someone grew weak and could not keep up, they were shot on the spot. We marched down side-roads, through woods, in the snow. All along the way there were corpses, some of them even in a sitting position. I tried not to look but it was impossible to avoid them. After two days we were put into open wagons. There was no food or water whatsoever; there was no more bread, and we ate snow. No one believed any longer that they would survive.

We arrived at Ravensbrück, which was a women's camp. Here 30 people slept in one bunk, without a blanket. There was sickness, famine and squalor. Every day people were dying like flies. From there we were transferred to Neustadt. We were kept for two and a half days in open wagons. The dead were thrown out onto the snow and lay where they fell. No one resembled a human being any more. I could hardly see, and my mother also looked like a corpse. We were marched to some stables; we lay on the straw, and there was no water to wash with and nothing to cover ourselves with. I really wanted just to die, but mother begged me to hold out. They gave out coffee and a piece of bread to everyone, but you had to fight to get to the cauldron. I do not know how mother still had the strength to get food for me. There was one

Lagerälteste who hated Jews; she stole all our soup and beat us like a thug. At that time the women were dying terribly, there was an outbreak of typhus and *Durchfall* (diarrhoea). We stayed like this till 2 May; there were fewer and fewer of us every day. Then they organised a *Blocksperre*, and boarded up the doors and windows; we were inside, and everyone said that they would blow us up or burn us alive. But they did not have time, for the Americans arrived and liberated us. To begin with I could not believe that the danger was really over. But they began to give us food, lots of chocolate, and then I finally knew that the war was over.

We travelled home, partly on foot and partly by various means of transport. Then mother went to Sącz and to Gdynia to try and get our factory back and to look for father, for someone said that he was still alive. At the moment I am living in Zakopane in a children's home, and I am also going to school. I would like to forget about the camps, but I cannot because the other children also went through a great deal and they are constantly talking about it.

(Archive of the VJHC in Kraków, statement no. 1071)

3. MARCEL GRÜNER

Born 28 September 1934 in Kraków; son of Hersz and Sydonia Sternberg

(*Statement taken by M. Hochberg-Mariańska, Kraków*)

What I remember is this: when we arrived in the ghetto, father joined the *OD* (*Ordnungsdienst*), that is, the Jewish police, because my uncle, his brother, got him onto the list. Father had a uniform and a cap and knee-length boots, and he used to go on duty. Various people came to him to ask him to use his influence with the Germans or with the Jewish administration, and whenever he could he helped them. Sometimes I went out to the city with him, as he had a permanent pass. Once, when a friend of his was arrested by the criminal police on Szlak Street, we took food to him. You paid the Ukrainian at the gate and you could hand over a package. The Germans who used to come to the ghetto were called Kunde, Heinrich and von Maluczki, who was in the Gestapo.

In the main ghetto we lived at 29 Limanowskiy Street; it was an *OD* building. After the resettlement, when the ghetto was divided into ghetto A and ghetto B, we were moved to 29 Józefińska Street. In ghetto A lived the Jews who were in work, and in ghetto B all the others, who were the first to be put on the transports.

When the Jews were being transferred from the ghetto to the camp, all the *OD* men were kept behind to carry out the liquidation, but father did not want to be part of it and we went to the camp. In the ghetto the liquidation was carried out by the remaining *Zivilabteilung* of the *OD*, the secret police. They included Spiro and Pacanower; I do not remember the others.

In the camp at Płaszów father found me a place in the brush factory, because it was said that children who did not have a job would be shot. In the factory we made shoe-brushes and clothes brushes, polishing brushes and bottle brushes. There was a set quota: you had to make 50 brushes a day. When I could not manage it on my own, one of the grown-ups helped me.

Father was on duty at the gate with a German or a Ukrainian, and then later he joined the *Aussenkommando* and went out onto Wielicka Street demolishing houses, where the *Wachskaserne* later stood.

On one occasion there was a huge muster in the camp; I do not remember the date. Everyone had to take their clothes off, put them under their arm and walk across the assembly ground, and the *Lagerarzt* [camp doctor], Blanke, just stood there watching. Whenever he did not like the look of someone he sent them to a table where their name was written down and they were given a red card. Then later those people were sent out on the first transport. Each block received a list; the people's names were on it and they had to go. All the children, even those who had a job, were supposed to go to the *Kinderheim*. Everyone was afraid of that because they put children from the *Kinderheim* on the transports. The children were lined up on one side and the camp administrator, *OD* officer Chilowicz, came and picked out the children of the *OD* and various acquaintances of his. But Commandant Goeth came up and shouted at him that he was picking out too many children, and he began to make the selection himself. He called out Romek Ferber, because his brother was *Lagerschreiber*, Wilek Schnitzer, whose father was head of the Madritsch company, Zbyszek Gross, as his father was a doctor in the camp, Genek Güntner, for his father was a *kapo* in the central warehouses, and two girls, Marysia Finkelstein, the adopted daughter of the *Lagerälteste*, and Ewa Ratz, whose mother was a servant to a German, the Führer of the *Schutzhaftlager*. The other children, including myself, were to be taken to the *Kinderheim*. We stood on the yard in the open air, fenced in with barbed-wire and guarded by German women soldiers. Father went to the commandant to ask for me to be allowed to stay. To begin with Goeth got angry and threatened to have my father shot, but then he let him come and take me away. Of 400 children 15 were saved. We were in the guardhouse and, as the children were being led to the transport, another 15 escaped and joined us. The 30 of us stayed in the guardhouse for two weeks. We could not go out into the camp because the other people, whose children had been taken away from them, could not bear to look at us, and wept day and night.

In 1944, I think it was in the summer, father and I were put on a transport to Gross-Rosen. There were 700 people on that transport. Not all of them stayed in Gross-Rosen – the majority went on to the hard-labour camp at Brünlitz in the Sudeten mountains. Everyone wanted to go there because it was a pottery factory, the Emalienwerke based in Zabłocie, and everyone tried to get into the factory. The factory was run by a German, Schindler, and people said that he was good and helped Jews. Father was not able to get onto that transport and so we stayed in Gross-Rosen. My mother had not travelled with us but had stayed in Płaszów.

We spent a month at Gross-Rosen. It was not so bad there for us. I used to drive to the baker's for bread and received an extra quarter-loaf. We got quite different, civilian clothes there. There were no children's clothes and I was given a jacket that hung off me and huge boots with foot cloths.

After that month, one day we were put into a train carriage and that evening we arrived in Auschwitz. At first we were sent to Auschwitz I; we spent the night there and the next day we went on foot to Birkenau. By that time they had stopped burning people and some of the crematoria had been demolished, but we did not know this for certain, and we thought we were going to the gas chambers. It was only when the tattooist came and began to tattoo numbers on us that we finally believed that we were not going to die.

We were in D camp; I was in block 29 and father in block 9, but we were able to go and see each other and talk together. For the first few days father had an extremely hard job lifting iron posts and rails and aircraft parts. After a few days his legs were all swollen and he looked terrible. He tried to change and managed to get work as a shoemaker, making things out of leather. That was easier for him.

I kept thinking about my mother, where she was and whether I would ever see her again. They told us that various transports were coming in, including some from Płaszów. Whenever I saw women through the barbed-wire fence, I ran to see if I could spot mother. One day I saw a *kommando* of women carrying some bunk beds along the street on the other side of the fence. I went up to the fence to look, but mother was not among them. Then suddenly one of the women started to shout: 'Marcel! Marcel!' I ran up; I recognised the voice, but I could not recognise mother at all; she was barefoot and in rags. She could not stop, she had to go with the other women, but I ran along the fence and we were able to talk like that. The women returned several times for more beds, and each time I ran along with them for as long as I could and talked with my mother. Mother kept crying. I comforted her, saying: 'Don't cry, Mummy, everything's bound to turn out all right.' Then I ran to the shoemakers' and told father that I had seen mother. He managed to get some shoes for her from the shoemakers, and he threw them over into her camp, which was next to ours. It was not easy to do this but he managed. The first time he tried, one of the shoes got stuck on the barbed-wire and it was only when the *Aussenkommandos* came back from work that a *kapo* took the shoe out.

The camp began to be closed down. I wanted to leave with father, but children were ordered to stand back, and only those over the age of 15 were taken. Father said goodbye to me and I was left on my own. As for my mother, I do not even know when she left. Then all the children were led out onto the road; we were supposed to be going to Auschwitz I, but there was a rumour that everyone would be shot on the way. I was not in the least afraid; nothing made any difference to me. I myself saw one boy, who had frostbite wounds on his legs and could not walk, begging one of the SS to shoot him; but the SS man refused. On the way, a taxi drove up carrying some Germans; they said something and then the SS left us, got on motorcycles and drove off. We walked to the camp on our own and there, two days later, the Soviets arrived. I returned to Kraków on foot and, part of the way, in a Soviet truck.

(Archive of the VJHC in Kraków, statement no. 8)

4. WITOLD JAKUBOWICZ

Born 24 December 1928 in Kraków

JAN JAKUBOWICZ

Born 15 February 1932 in Kraków
Sons of Leopold and Fryderyka Schlesinger
(*Statement taken by M. Hochberg-Mariańska, Kraków*)

In Bochnia, the majority of the Jews were working in the trade centre, called the Städtlische Werkstätte, which specialised in making clothes, and in the HKP (Heeres Kraftfahr Park). Most frequently people tried to get into the second, which was safer and where the conditions were relatively good. One of us, the younger one, attended the Jewish community centre day-room, and the older one worked in the HKP as a carpenter.

The first *Aktion* took place towards the end of September 1942. The transports were sent east to Bełżec; the elderly and the sick were taken from the hospital to Boczków outside Bochnia and were shot there. Of 5,000 people, officially 400 remained, of whom 300 were in the HKP and the rest were the *Judenrat*, the *Ordnungsdienst* and others who had attached themselves to them. During the first *Aktion* we had intended to hide in a bunker, but we did not organise it properly and only Witold, the elder one, went into hiding; the other people were already on the transport, in the barracks from which they were loading people into railway wagons. We waited on the square for two days, unable to escape; in the end it was our uncle who got us released through the foreman of the HKP. The very next month there was a second *Aktion* aimed at those without work. In the meantime quite a lot of people had come in: those who had been in hiding came out, and people had come in from Dębica and Brzesko. In the course of the following year the district was converted into a work camp;

the commandant was Oberscharführer Müller and his second-in-command was Gebell, a notorious murderer.

Towards the end of October 1943 there took place the final *Aktion*. In the morning 900 of the SS and 800 military police cordoned off the camp. The people from ghetto B, those without a job, were sent to Auschwitz; those in hiding or trying to escape, and those who put up resistance, and also many children and elderly people who had survived till now were rounded up and shot in an alleyway, and then burnt in Solna Góra in three wooden cottages. In all, about 300 people were shot, maybe even more. The people from ghetto A, those in work, were sent to the camp at Szebnie. We remained with our parents in a final group of 250 people. Of these, 100 remained behind, and we were sent in a group of 150 people on 27 October 1943 to the camp at Szebnie near Jasło. We spent eight days in Szebnie. On 4 November there was an *Aktion* there. There were 2,650 people, including our parents, sent to Auschwitz. When a muster was announced, everyone knew at once that there would be either a shooting or a transport. Since old people and children were shot in either case, father hid Janek in the upholstery workshop under a pile of pillows and quilts, and he spent a whole day and a night there. In the meantime our parents were put on the transport, and Witold got onto a list of 120 people to be sent to the camp at Pustków near Dębica. Fortunately the Jewish administrator of the camp put us down together on the list; he wrote that Witold was 18 and Janek 15, though in fact we were 15 and 11. Two days later, on 6 November, the trucks arrived and we were driven to the camp at Pustków. We were no longer with our parents, but fortunately we were together.

We spent more than eight months in Pustków – until 26 July 1944, to be precise. The camp in Pustków was divided by four rows of barbed-wire into two parts: a Jewish camp and a Polish camp. At that time there were more than 600 Jews, all men; twice, a transport of 100 was taken away, which meant that up until the time the camp was closed down completely there remained over 400 of us. At that time there were no mass shootings in the camp; all they did was to take people, both Poles and Jews, who had been in the bunker [the camp detention block] in the Polish camp, and hang them from telegraph poles and then burn them in the small crematorium on the hill behind the camp. From where we were two people were sent to the bunker, one of them, whose name was Rapp, for bringing in tobacco from outside the camp where he had been working building barracks. Rapp hanged himself in the bunker because he did not want to give away the people who had given him the goods. Both their bodies were burned. We could not see the crematorium because it was in the wood, but we saw the smoke when they were burning people.

For the first four months there was little food – each day 250 grams of bread, 10 grams of margarine and two portions of soup, which was just water with beetroot leaves and cabbage. After this time things got a little better; the food ration was doubled and the soup was a bit thicker, with buckwheat or potatoes. In Pustków we worked as carpenters. There were also other workshops there: brushmakers, an upholsterer's, tinsmiths, basketmakers, tailors, shoemakers, saddlers, varnishers, wickerwork, locksmiths, a photography section (*Bildstelle*) and car mechanics (*Autohof*). The Germans called the camp *Heidelager* or desert camp. The camp was run by the SS Truppenübungsplatz unit.

Sometimes we saw executions in the Polish camp. Once they hanged someone from a telegraph pole for trying to escape. They had to hang him three times: the first time the rope snapped, the second the hook broke off, and it was only at the third attempt that they actually managed to hang him. We also sometimes saw them beating people. We had no contact whatsoever with the Polish prisoners; any move towards the Polish camp could be punished by death.

In July 1944 we learnt that the front was drawing closer and that Soviet troops were outside Rzeszów. We got this news from our *capos*, who talked with the Germans, and also sometimes from the Polish *capos*. They began packing the machinery. In the final few days they set up a small plant to produce wood shavings, but actually it was operative only for one day and produced just enough material to pack the things. The Germans did not have time to dismantle the machinery in this plant as it had been concreted in.

On 26 July 1944 we were assembled into columns, given two small loaves of bread for the journey and loaded into five wagons at Pustków station. It was terribly hot and people were fainting from lack of air or water. We did not know where we were going. The SS men from the escort said that we were going to somewhere near Berlin; but after travelling for two days and nights we arrived at Auschwitz. At once we were driven onto the 'platform of death' near the gas chambers. The whole of our transport was to be sent to the gas. But Ruff, our *Lagerführer*, argued for us and had a letter from the SS Generalmajor that we were supposed to be sent to work. We knew that he was arguing not out of kindness of heart, but because he wanted to stay with us and not be sent to the front. We were also fortunate in that the gas chambers were working at full pitch; a transport of Hungarians had just been sent there and there was no room for us. We were directed onto the line to the Birkenau camp and there we were taken off the train. The whole transport went into a huge hall where we were ordered to undress and leave everything – we could take with us only our shoes, belt or braces and bread. We did not know what awaited us beyond the door. We had heard such a lot about the gas chambers, that you are supposedly going to the bathhouse, and we did not know whether this would be real showers or the gas. But it was the showers, and afterwards we had our heads shaved and we were issued civilian clothes with a red stripe down the side. Even as we were being shaved an order arrived to wait, as the matter had not been cleared up. We knew that it was our lives that were at stake, and that a death sentence might still be passed. Finally, we were sent to the quarantine block. Over the course of two days we were examined twice by the doctor; two people were rejected as being unfit for work. Then we went once more to the shower block, where we were issued striped prison uniforms and had numbers tattooed on. The same day, 29 July 1944, we were lined up on the muster ground and put in with a transport of Jews from the Lublin region. We do not remember exactly how many of us there were in all, but there must have been about 1,000 people. We were loaded into trucks, some were taken to Jawiszowice, and some, including the two of us, to Gliwice. In Gliwice there were no people yet, just concrete barracks surrounded by electrified fences. We both worked in Gliwice – the elder as a carpenter again, the younger as a messenger. We did not go hungry there – we were given half a kilogram of bread daily and two helpings of soup, and Janek, the younger one, got extra food from the SS kitchen which we both ate. This was Gliwice III camp – a factory producing bombs and mines. Jews, Poles, Hungarians, French and Slovaks worked there together. There were no special executions at that time, just beatings and what were called 'sports' as punishment; for example, for not making your bed properly (*Bettenbau*) the punishment was 'down and ups' or squat thrusts, or standing motionless and facing the wall for two hours. There were body searches every day, and you were not allowed to have with you a handkerchief or even a scrap of paper or a hunk of bread. Your pockets had to be empty; if they found anything at all you were beaten with a stick or a length of rubber. We stayed healthy the whole time; in fact we always made an effort not to fall ill, for that was dangerous. We knew that if someone was ill for more than three days and the *Lagerführer* found out, he would send him to Birkenau, where he would be completely 'cured' in the gas chamber. We used to wash ourselves down to the waist in cold water in the yard, right until the water in the pipes froze.

In Gliwice III the commandant was Hauptscharführer Spicker, and his deputies were Unterscharführer Moritz and Rottenführer Zahorodny, a Rumanian. The last one was the worst, he behaved like a madman – either he would give you anything, or he would get furious and beat you for the slightest reason. The block commandants were Germans, criminals who wore green triangles: Heini Keimling, Kurt Wolf and Willi Weiss. They were professional killers who gave the most frequent beatings. Keimling was lame and had a walking-stick which he used to walk with and to beat people with. He would strike you on the head with the walking-stick. Weiss hit you with an open hand in the face, Wolf hit you on the jaw with his fist.

In January we knew that the Soviet offensive had begun because specialists in bomb and mine manufacture came from Zieleniewski's factory in Kraków. One of them arrived, delivered a letter and returned at once. He told us that Soviet forces were outside Kraków. On 19 January all the SS's luggage was loaded onto handcarts; we were formed into columns and told that we were going to move further west, and that anyone attempting to escape would be shot. We set off, pushing the carts along the main road to Wrocław. We left at four in the morning, because the Germans did not want to cause panic in the town. With one break of an hour in the afternoon, we walked till 10 o'clock in the evening. We reached a town called Eidelsdorf or Edelsdorf – we do not remember exactly. There was a civilian camp there and we spent the night in one of the barracks. There were 600 of us from Gliwice III. The next day, 20 January, we moved on, and in the afternoon we crossed the Oder by a wooden bridge which only 50 people could cross at a time. Then an SS soldier drove up on a motorcycle; he talked to our commanding officer, and then turned to us and told us that the Soviets had been forced back 100 kilometres beyond Kraków, and we would circle round, cross back over the Oder and return to Gliwice. The same night we crossed the Oder again and came to the camp at Blechhammer. There we were to spend the whole of Sunday and then return on foot to Gliwice. However, at five in the morning everyone began to panic. They said that Soviet troops were only an hour's drive away; 100 people set off westward with the carts of the SS, the rest remained on the assembly ground. Various camps had been led there: Jaworzno, and Gliwice I, III and IV. There was terrible confusion, and no one knew what to do. The Germans closed the gate, and one of the SS told us to get away because they were going to blow up the whole camp. So then people broke the gate down and began running away. On the road we saw trucks full of corpses in striped camp uniforms – they were the people who had tried to run away on the march. Some people took fright at this sight and stayed in the camp, others set off westwards after the Germans. We escaped into the woods with a group of 40 people. The next day, Monday, the SS arrived, surrounded the camp, and from the watch-towers began firing rifles and throwing grenades. Those who managed to escape told us that it had been a terrible massacre, and that almost everyone had been killed.

On Tuesday morning we left the woods, all 40 of us. Nothing made any difference to us; we set off east, towards Gliwice. No one stopped us any more; the Germans were running away and paid no attention to us, and it was only near the camp in Gliwice that an SS officer stopped us. We told him that we were under orders to go to the camp and wait. He believed us, and in this way we found ourselves back in our own camp. There we were greeted by the *Werkschutze*, Silesians who had already taken off their uniforms and laid down arms. For two days we were under fire from the Soviet artillery, which was bombarding the town over the camp. But this did not frighten us. Though the walls shook and crumbled from the explosions, we lay calmly on our bunks. Finally, when the cannon fire died down a little, we ventured into the town. We met the first Soviet patrols. The soldiers ordered us to go to the Germans' flats and put on some new clothes. In the flats there were only women and children. We put some clothes on and set off. And since the road had not yet been cleared, we had first to return westwards. In this way, in two weeks of walking we reached Częstochowa; from there, partly by train, we travelled to Kraków. In Częstochowa our group split up, and on 4 February just the two of us reached Kraków. We calculated that since we had left Gliwice on 19 January we had travelled about 400 kilometres on foot.

61

In Kraków, we went straightaway to our old flat, and then to uncle's flat. But there was no one to be found anywhere.

(Archive of the VKHC in Kraków, statement no. 9)

Chapter Three
ON THE ARYAN SIDE

1. HENRYK MELLER

Born 1932 in Kraków
(Statement taken by Iza Lauer, Kraków)

We received a resettlement order, and I was sick. We went to my aunt's flat, as uncle made overcoats for the Gestapo and he and aunt were able to stay in Kraków. We stayed there for two weeks, until I got better, and then we moved to Bochnia – mother, my nine-year-old sister and me. In Bochnia lived my grandmother, two uncles and an aunt. Mother sold saccharin in the ghetto. In Kraków there was my aunt, my father's sister, who was married to an Aryan and lived as an Aryan. I used to travel to see her almost every day; she gave us bread to eat and to sell. I carried ten kilograms at a time. The trains were very crowded. My aunt said that if there should be an *Aktion* in the ghetto I should come to her. I travelled like this for almost two years. One day, I left for Kraków by train at six in the morning. A lady came to my aunt and said that there had been an *Aktion* in Bochnia, and that my mother and sister had been taken. My uncle was working in Kłaj, so he sent a car for the family. Mother was not at home; only my grandmother and aunt took the car. I had no reason to return to Bochnia. I spent perhaps a year at my aunt's.

In 1943 my aunt was taken by the Gestapo because they suspected that she was Jewish. At this time I was in the country. My aunt often sent me into the country, where I worked as a farm-hand and my aunt paid for me. When the payments stopped after she had been arrested, the people I was staying with threw me out. I came back to Kraków, and I did not know what to do. My aunt's sister-in-law, a Catholic, gave me some bread and 40 złotys. I found a haystack in Stara Olsza and spent a few nights there. Later I 'moved' to the railway station and slept there. Of the 40 złotys, I had 25 left. I bought 100 copies of the *Goniec Warszawski* newspaper and sold them for 50 groszy each. In this way I did business. After two months things got easier as I was making money, but I was badly infested with lice because I was sleeping under benches at the station. When the wrong guards were on duty – I knew all of them by then – I would go to Słomniki, where I would spend the night at the station there. Sometimes one of the *Bahnschutz* would come after me with a dog. Then I would go to Miechów for the night and sleep there. I got to know the lads at the station and I began selling cigarettes. Sometimes I was pulled in during a raid; a Gestapo car would come along but with boys like me they only searched us and then let us go. There was a major there who was in charge of the station and who we nicknamed 'Greyhair'; he used to beat people terribly with a knout and confiscate the goods we were selling. A couple of times I was caught by the *Bahnschutz*; they took my money and my goods, beat me up and threw me out, threatening that they would hand me over to the police. I went to the Stella cinema and spent the whole night outside it. I got awfully cold.

My aunt was released because she was the wife of an Aryan and had a grown-up Aryan child. I could not stay with her because the secret police were always hanging around to see if there were any of her Jewish relations there.

I found one old woman who put people up; she was very good to me even though she knew I was Jewish. I paid 20 złotys per night. First I went to the delousing station. Now I started to do well. I bought more and more cigarettes and made more and more money. There was one lad at the station who knew me and went round telling the other boys that I was Jewish. The boys were all right, but if someone wanted, for example, some Sport cigarettes and they did not have any, they would call over: 'Hey, Jew-boy, give us some Sports.' But this did not do any harm. It got to the point where I was earning five or six hundred złotys a day. I ate and dressed well, and I had a suitcase with various goods for sale. I did business in the morning; in the afternoon I went to the cinema, and in the evening there were a lot of people about so I did business again. I lived like this for a year. I must have been caught a hundred times by the *Bahnschutz*; they would beat me up and confiscate my goods, but that was nothing.

In the meantime they 'resettled' the old lady I was living with and she moved to her daughter's; there was no room for me there. I took my suitcase and left it with our former maid, and went selling things. I went to various railway stations to sleep.

One day I met Lusia, a Jewish woman, and her son. She had come to my aunt's; she was engaged in smuggling cigarettes. Aunt told her to take me to Warsaw; I went with her. I started selling things there but it did not go very well, so I went back to Kraków with Lusia.

Sometimes I would go and visit my aunt.

In the summer of 1944 the secret police caught me at the station. They caught three of us. They came there and beckoned to us, saying 'Give me some cigarettes'; and then they took us to the police station on Gertrudy Street. They asked what my name was and where I lived. I gave them a made-up name and address. They sent us to the lock-up on Skawińska Street. We were given nothing to eat there, and we were infested by lice. My 'Granny' brought me food. They could tell I was Jewish there, so I had to admit it.

Later they said that everything was in order, that they had checked the address, and they sent me to Bronowice. It was good there; in the mornings we went to work at the manor, and in the afternoons we played; on Sundays we were allowed to go home. After a week I ran away because I was afraid that I would be found out. The lads lent me some money; I bought some cigarettes and made 600 złotys in the course of the day. One of the secret police came looking for me; I knew him from Skawińska Street, so I moved away and went to the cinema. In the evening I got on a train and went to Warsaw, to Lusia. She knew people there in the party [the Bund], and they had a birth certificate made for me. Then I travelled to Radzymin, where I found work with a farmer in Mokre. I worked there right till the end. I tended the cows and in the winter I threshed the corn. No one knew who I was.

(Archive of the CJHC, statement no. 830)

2. JÓZEF LEICHTER

Born 4 February 1933 in Medynia Głogowska near Łańcut; son of Izrael and Bajla

(Statement taken by Dr Dawid Haupt, Przemyśl)

Things were getting worse and worse for us. We lived in constant fear because every so often the Germans descended on the village, beating and robbing us. They sent my eldest brother to do forced labour somewhere near Nowy Sącz. He was 16 then, and was made to work hard clearing the forest and breaking stones to build a new road. It was three months before he returned home.

In the village the local boys used to attack our house at night; they would break windows and, dressed as Germans, they would steal our things. They terrorised all the Jews in the village, and when the Germans came to the village they informed on us. The older people took no part in this and strongly disapproved of them (the younger ones).

The night before 1 August 1942, the village messenger informed the Jews that they should all leave as the next day the Germans were going to transport us out to the ghetto in Łańcut. Only a few people acted on this advice, while others either hid in the village or ran away into the woods. As far as time would allow, we gave all our belongings to the neighbours to look after. At night father would go back to the village to get supplies; after a few days he found out that the German police were searching the woods, and that any Jews they caught were being executed on the spot. Father also learnt that Izak N., a Jew who had been caught, had been beaten up and had revealed the location of one of the hideouts; the Germans had found several Jews there, dragged them out and shot them, then they shot Izak N. and his wife and child. Because of this, father decided that each of us should go his own way. My elder brother Dawid and I spent two more days in a different part of the woods, and then we went to another village, Krasne. There, we told people that we had been evacuated and that we were looking for work, which we found. When we had been there for three weeks an official came from the police and asked for our documents; when we were unable to give him any he said that he could see we were Jewish, and that he would take us to the police. Because of this, the very same day, we ran away from Krasne and set off walking towards the Rzeszów district. After a terribly difficult journey we arrived at the village of Nowy Borek. The moment we entered the first house we came to, the owner recognised at once that we were Jewish, and told us that a woman with a child (we understood that this was a Jewish woman) was looking for two boys. We guessed that this might be our mother, and without saying anything to that man we went out to look for her. We went from house to house until, finally, at around midday we met her in another man's house where she was working as a maid. Mother was so moved when she saw us that she could not say a word. We called her 'auntie'. We went out of the house into the garden and here we told her where we had been and what had been happening to us. Mother told us that she knew nothing about our father or our eldest brother.

Mother gave us something to eat and that night we slept in the same house as her. In the morning the owner told us that he was afraid to keep us as he had guessed that we were Jews; so my brother and I went to look for work, and when we could not find any, we asked for some bread. Most people could tell that we were Jewish and chased us away from their houses; but there were some who took pity on us, and even wept at our fate. Around midday we met our mother and little sister. The man had also thrown them out as he was afraid to keep Jews.

That day the four of us set off on our wandering. In the evening we came to the village of Kielnarów near Rzeszów, where mother and Dawid found work, and I had to hide out in the country, where my mother brought me food. In the evening the son of the farmer, Prędki, recognised my mother, whom he had seen before in our village. Despite this he was going to keep her on and try to get some documents for her, but his farm-hand, who could tell that my mother was Jewish, threatened to inform on them if she did not leave. My mother left that house and found work somewhere else in the same village, and I became a shepherd-boy for Prędki, after he had sacked the farm-hand. I worked for him for three months, after which he sent me away because the other farmers had frightened him by telling him that for harbouring a Jew he could be executed.

In the meantime mother was in our home village of Medynia, and here she learnt that our father and eldest brother were living in the woods outside Łańcut. There were 15 of them in all, including aunts and uncles. My father and brother had not seen each other for three months after they had split up in the woods for the first time. Each of them had wandered around the villages and worked as a hired hand; they never stayed anywhere for very long, though, as people suspected they were Jewish. After three months they both came back to the woods, where they met.

Mother visited them in the woods and spent just one day with them. She told them where she was living and how things were with us. The next day she returned to Kielnarów, where I had also found work with a farmer, Kazimierz Piecuch. After a month I had to leave as he was afraid to keep a Jew. From then, for two weeks I could not find any work and had to get by on what I could beg. At that time mother did not have a permanent job either and every day she went looking for work in a different place. The farmer from Kielnarów concealed my sister for several months, even though he knew she was Jewish.

Looking for work, I came to the village of Nowy Borek, where I began working for a farmer called Jan Trojanowski. I worked there for a year and a half. I tended three cows and helped with the housework. One day the farmer came home and said to me that an old friend of his from another village had told him that I was Jewish, and that people said so in the village where I had worked before. He demanded that I tell him where I was born, and he said that he would write to the village administrator there and get him to check whether my parents (at that time I gave my name as Jarosz) actually lived there, and whether I really was from there. My boss took me to the shop at the farmers' club, where I was given an exam on the subject of the Catholic faith. I passed the exam, since I knew my prayers off by heart – my previous boss Mr Prędki had taught them to me. He had given me a prayer book as a present, and I had learnt the prayers from it. Although I had only spent one year at school, I could read printed letters and so it was easy for me to learn Catholic prayers.

Despite all this, the head of the farmers' club wrote a letter to the administrator of the village of Kamień, as that was where I had told him I was from. Two weeks later a reply came back saying that no family by the name of Jarosz was known there. That evening the administrator summoned my boss. I went to bed and pretended to be asleep, but I stayed awake because I wanted to find out what the administrator had said and what he had decided to do with me. I had decided that if my boss came back and told his mother (he was not married) that he would turn me over to the police, I would put my clothes on and run away that night.

Late in the evening my boss came home and told his mother that I was Jewish, but that despite this he would keep me on, as I was hard-working and the administrator had advised him to keep me on. So I continued to work for Trojanowski. In the winter I cut the chaff, ground the corn in a hand-mill, tended the cattle in the stable, mucked out and so on. I also took milk to the dairy every day. Some of the village boys used to try to frighten me by telling me that they would hand me over to the police, that I was Jewish and that the police would take me away soon. Once I was seen by a farmer from the village where I had worked before, and when he found out that I was working for Trojanowski, he came to my boss and warned him not to keep me on because he was putting his life in danger. In spite of this my boss did not sack me, but from that time on he stopped sending me to the dairy with the milk so as not to remind people that I was there. My boss and his mother were good to me and they took pity on me. They did not want me to go wandering, and they tried to help me stay alive. They also said that I was loyal, that I worked well and that those who had been there before me either stole from them or would not work, or ran away at the busiest time for work on the farm.

I had heard nothing about my mother or elder brother for several months, and I knew even less about whether my father and oldest brother were still alive. I missed them all very much and sometimes I would cry and cry, when no one could see.

The village boys also used to upset me by saying that my mother (whom I called my auntie) had already been shot by the Germans, and that they would shoot me too. I did not believe them, but I was terrified that something had happened to her.

During the harvest of 1944 the Soviet army arrived. The previous day my boss went out to meet them to tell them about the location and size of the German forces. All the inhabitants of the village left their homes and hid in the fields, in the shelter of some rocks.

I went there too, taking my boss's cows with me. The next day my boss came back with the Soviets and took me and the cows home. The very same day my mother came and told me that my brother Dawid was still alive. She did not know anything about my father or my eldest brother so she set off to go to our home village, Medynia Głogowska, to find out what had happened to our family and to our other relatives who had gone into hiding with father in the woods. In the meantime I continued to work for Trojanowski. A month later my mother came back and I learnt from her that I no longer had a father or an eldest brother.

(Archive of the CJHC, statement no. 891)

3. PAWEL DUTMAN

(Written account)

I had relatives in Ciechanów. When the Germans occupied Poland, I began to travel to my relations to get food because it was impossible to earn any money in Warsaw. In 1940 the Germans made the ghetto. They took all the Jews from the Warsaw district and put them in the ghetto. It was terribly crowded in the ghetto, and people were starving. But there were still Jews living in Ciechanów, and as long as I kept going there my family did not go hungry.

In 1942 they began to transport the Jews out of Ciechanów. I went there one more time to help my relatives, but I was stopped at the border by the Gestapo and put with a group of Poles who had also been caught. The Gestapo commandant from Nowy Dwór was there, and he began questioning me about where I was from and whether I had any papers. I did not have any, so he said that I was a Jew and began hitting me because I would not admit it. I worked there for a month. We were given 100 grams of bread to eat, and half a litre of soup that was so thin you could drink it without a spoon. When the work was finished, all the Poles were transported out to Prussia, and I was left on my own; there were no Jews there as they had all been taken to Warsaw. There was a Polish boy working there and he advised me to escape, because they were going to shoot everyone. My heart was beating; what should I do? In a short while I would die. But I decided not to give in till the very last moment. In the morning, when the Gestapo drove in to have breakfast, I was at work, but not far from the building there was a tall embankment; I let myself down from the embankment and ran between the houses, where I waited for an hour. There was a wood nearby, and I ran away into the wood. When I had got 30 metres from the road, shots rang out behind me. But I managed to escape deep into the wood. I spent two days in the wood and then I went into a village because I was very hungry. I went to a farmer and asked him for some bread, for I had not eaten for two days. But I could not get into Warsaw as the roads were blocked off by the military police.

My parents must have thought that I was dead, and here I was wandering about. I wanted to cross into the Reich, because I had friends there. But to do that I had to cross the river Narew. Night fell and it was ten kilometres to the river. I set off at one o'clock and reached the village of Otrzewnica. I went to a farmer and asked for some bread, as I was completely exhausted and had no strength left; and then I carried on. Right through the night I walked across marshes and through water, and at dawn I reached the Narew. But there was no one to be seen as it was early yet. At seven o'clock I crossed to the other side. I had friends who lived not far away, and I went to them. When I arrived there I had nothing but the trousers I was wearing; they gave me some clothes to put on and found a farmer who was prepared to take me on, and I went to him. I was fine there, all I did was tend the cows; but I felt sadder and sadder. Up until July things were quiet there.

In July the Germans made a camp and rounded up the Jews who had escaped to the Reich from Warsaw. One night there was a round-up in Poniechówek, but the Gestapo did not know about me. In the afternoon all the Jews were taken to the fort; on the way the Poles stood and watched as the Jews were being brutally beaten. My farmer came back from the town and told me what was going on. He knew that I was Jewish. I was really worried because it was the same Gestapo officers who had caught me on the Narew. But people did not know that I was Jewish. In the third fort those barbarians murdered the Jews. I used to tend the cows not far from the fort. They were given 100 grams of bread a day, and not always even that; and they had to carry water in barrels from the river – two Jews would be harnessed to a cart and a German would sit in the cart and whip them. It was terrible there, for they had to pull the carts uphill. So many Jews died hauling that water! Five or six of them died every day, and thousands died in the fort. After three months they began transporting the

74

Jews out. They brought them in from the whole district and took them away. People went to see how many bodies had been left behind. But I was afraid to go in case they recognised me. Three days later I went to the fort and had my fill of looking at corpses. They dug graves six metres long and six broad, and arranged the bodies in layers. They estimated that 30,000 Jews had been executed or starved to death by the barbarians. A few days later I found out what had happened to those who had been taken away. They had been taken to Olszanica, to the woods, and had been given salted sausage. They began drinking lots of water, and many of them died straightaway; the rest were taken to the ghetto in Legionowo.

I stayed with the farmer till February. In February an order was given to bring all Jews to the commandant's office. I had to leave and to start moving from one farm to another; for the rest of the war I lived like that.

(Archive of the CJHC, statement no. 659)

4. ANZELM LANDESMAN

Born 1933 in Skałat

(Statement taken by I. Gliksztajn, Bytom)

There were seven children in our family. I got up one morning. *Aktion.* I ran away in one direction, my mother ran somewhere else, and my younger brother somewhere else again. As I was running the Germans fired at me and wounded me in the head. I fell down. They thought I was dead and they trampled all over me; I did not even gasp, I just lay there. When the Germans had driven away I got up and went to the hospital, where I had my head bandaged. When I got home my parents had gone. I stayed at a farmer's I knew. Later the Germans came again; they caught me, kept me in the synagogue and then put me on a truck to Tarnopol. From Tarnopol

75

everyone was sent to Bełżec. My sister tried to escape from the truck and was shot dead. The reason she failed was because she had tried to run away during the day; my brother and I ran away in the evening. A German shot at us, and wounded my brother in the leg and me in the face. Janek was wounded twice in the head and in the face. But we still managed to escape; we only moved at night. What should we do? We split up: my brother went one way and I went the other. I went into a village and went up to one cottage. There were just two Ukrainians living there; I told them that I was from Drohobycz, that people were starving there and that I wanted to work for them. They were pleased that I would tend their cows. I spoke Ukrainian well because at home I used to play with the neighbours' children. I could say prayers in Ukrainian and in Polish. I worked for them, and I forgot Yiddish; sometimes in the stable I would almost say something in Yiddish to the horse, but something stuck in my throat and would not let me.

The village administrator came and asked for the names of my father and mother. I said: 'Michał and Nastusia.' I also made up names for my grandfather and grandmother. Once, when I was grazing the cows, I heard a familiar voice singing. I ran to the road and looked; it was my brother. I raised my hand, crying and shouting. He stood up and climbed down from the cart; he was also crying. Then he drove on, and I never saw him again. I worked there till the winter of 1944. Later the Soviets came, and I thought that there were no Jews left any more; but I went to Skałat to see our house, and spotted my uncle walking down the street. He brought me to Gliwice.

(Archive of the CJHC, statement no. 905)

5. SZLAMA KUTNOWSKI

Born 1929 in Warsaw

(*Written account*)

Even the people we knew best started to shout '*Jude*' at us. An order was issued that all Jews over the age of 13 should wear armbands. Some Poles were deceitful; they registered as *Volksdeutschen* and stole the property of the Jews. At the end of 1941 the Germans made a ghetto in a holiday camp that had been for Jewish children from orphanages. This place was called Henryków.

We lived in a garage. There was a brick floor, and we made a ceiling of boards. While we still had reserves of food we lived off them, and when they ran out I started going to Marki to earn money. In the winter the snow fell into the place where we were living. The men had to work for the Germans, the women also did various jobs, and they began transporting the children out to Majdanek and Treblinka. Father was taken to a camp. In the camp people were beaten and not given anything to eat. On the road to Marki lived a forester who had a 19-year-old son, and that son used to beat up the Jews the whole time.

After some time I found out that in Pułtusk you could get cheap food, because it was in the Reich, but that if they caught you at the border they sent you to a punishment camp. Despite this, people used to go there and made money. I told my parents that I wanted to go. My parents advised me against it, but I took no notice; I left them crying and I set off. When I left, there was nothing to eat at home. I took with me our last few złotys. Jews were not allowed to travel by train, and I had to pretend to be a Pole. With God's help, I managed to get there. I crossed the border and bought a few things, which I took home. My parents were very pleased, but they were afraid for me to go again. But we had no other means of support, and I had to carry on smuggling.

Father fell ill in the camp and was released and allowed to

77

return to the ghetto. I travelled with Poles. Some of them behaved deceitfully towards me. Once, on the way, they took away the things I had, and they were going to hand me over to the Germans. I told them that I would stop travelling by train, so they let me go, and from then on I travelled alone, without any companions. One day, when I got back home as usual, I found no one there; the barracks had been set on fire and a lot of people had been killed. There was nothing for it; I had to go to see Zaleski. Zaleski was a man my parents knew, but he was two-faced; he would not let me spend the night there, and he told me to leave my goods with him. He had been good to us while he could use us, but now, at such a difficult moment, when I needed help, he behaved deceitfully. I went to him and asked him if I could stay the night. He refused. He told me that there was a cellar near the railway station, and that it would be warm there. 'You can leave your goods with me. Tomorrow you can take your things and go to the ghetto in Warsaw, that's where your parents were taken.' I did as he said. I spent the night in the cellar, but when I went to get my things, not only did he not give me them, he was even going to hand me over to the military police. I got frightened and begged him to let me go. When we went out onto the street and set off towards the military police head-quarters, I thought to myself that it makes no difference, either way I would die. I started to run away. He was fat and he could not catch me. I ran off towards the railway and hid far away from the station. When a train came I got on it and travelled to the Reich. Unfortunately, as I was crossing the border the border guards caught me and took me to the guardhouse. The guardhouse was in Lemany. I spent a day and a night there, and the next morning they took me for questioning. The commandant was a good man and heard me out. I told him that my parents had been taken to Germany; I said that all I had left was an aunt in Pułtusk and that I was going to see her. In the end they let me go, and I promised that I would not cross the border any more.

Then I went to the village of Zambiska, to a farmer that I did

78

not know. His name was Ciemierych. I had to work hard for him, but I had enough to eat; he was very good to me, and he did not know that I was Jewish. He sent me to confession and to communion. When he found out that I was Jewish, he continued to be good to me. Some Poles I knew came to that village. After a while, when they were caught at the border, they said they knew where there was a Jew, and that if they were set free they would hand him over. Those Poles lived near Ciemierych. Some of them were from the Durka family. Mrs Durka was very bad. She had a daughter who was often visited by a German military policeman called Wrona. It was him that they told I was Jewish. Wrona first came to see me on 20 October 1942, while I was chopping wood. He asked me where I was from and why I did not have any papers, and that was all. Ciemierych's people protested and told him to fire me. He said that it went against his conscience to throw me out into the freezing cold, without a roof over my head. Two weeks later Wrona came back with the commandant of the military police. They made a search of my farmer's place and they found some meat. They took Ciemierych and the meat to the police headquarters. The next day I found out that Ciemierych had been sent to prison for four years.

I was kept in a cellar with a Polish man who had been arrested for trying to escape from a camp in Germany. He worked all day. Twice a day he was taken for questioning, where he was beaten every time, and then he was sent back to the cellar for the night. I was taken for questioning three times a day, and was tortured each time. At night we told each other about everything. When we had to go for questioning we would both cry. On 20 January 1943 I was beaten terribly, and the next morning I was handed over to the Gestapo. They tied me to a cart and drove me to Pułtusk. It was evening before I arrived. In the evening they put me in a cell with Kowalczyk. He had been imprisoned for political reasons. In the night he tried to persuade me to escape with him. I was afraid, I did not want to escape and I did not dare to. The next morning I was taken to the commandant for questioning. They crushed my finger in the door so badly that I still have a scar today. They trampled on my stomach and asked if I was a Jew, but I did not confess. The third time I refused to confess, the commandant interrogated me. Then they passed sentence on me: the following morning at ten o'clock Kowalczyk and I were to be hanged.

In the night we filed through the bars and escaped. That night we slept in the village of Płacochów. When I reached Winnica I learned that my mother had written a letter to Zambiska; I could not write back because I did not have a permanent place of residence. In Winnica I stayed with Mr B. He was bad. He did not even treat me like a human being. I did not want anything from him for free, because I was engaged in smuggling and I had money. B. was someone Kowalczyk knew. I told Kowalczyk everything and said that I wanted to move somewhere else. He said that in a few days he would be going to Ciechanów, and that then I might be able to work in his brother's factory. I asked him if he could have some documents made for me. He said that he had a cousin who worked in the German civil service, and two weeks later he told me to go to the local authorities to pick up the identity cards. I took some photographs to the office, and Kowalczyk's cousin treated me well. Kowalczyk's brother in Ciechanów also treated me well. Things were fine in the factory, though I had to deal with all sorts of people; one of them was Fatba, the manager of the factory. He was terribly cunning, and was determined to get rid of me. He had a brother who was a *Volksdeutsch*; the brother took bribes, and when someone did not pay him he would threaten to have them sent to Germany. Kowalczyk knew everything I had been through in prison with his brother. He kept thinking up various excuses for me so I would not have to face a medical commission, because he was well aware of the danger I would be in. All the same, Fatba took a bribe from me.

Before I had been there very long the factory was taken over by the army as it had been a wine and vodka factory. When all the workers were taken to Germany, I got out of going. I was caught in a round-up in September 1943. Children of 12–15 were held in the church in the village of Lubiel. In Lubiel we were guarded by the military police and among them was Wrona, who was notorious throughout the district. I was terrified because I knew that if Wrona noticed me I would be dead. For two days I hid my face in that church, until lorries came and took us to the railway station. We travelled in goods wagons. On the way some people cried, others laughed, but no one was happy. No one faced the same danger that I did. We reached the town of Algerapp. There were 2,500 of us in all. In Algerapp we were taken to the square in front of the *Arbeitsamt*. Rich Germans would come to the square and buy people like cattle. We were chosen to be sent to an ammunition factory; there were 25 of us boys, and we were sent on to Hanover. I felt good in Hanover, better than in Poland. The Germans did not know who I was and when I walked down the street I did not have to look round to check whether someone was shouting '*Jude!*' at me. I had an identity card and the Germans were not aware of who I was.

My foreman was a very bad man. We had to get up at six in the morning and go to bed at eight in the evening. The food I got was awful, but I thanked God for it anyway. Every night the English and the Americans played us the music of bombs dropped from planes. There were air-raids every night, and in the morning the rubble was cleared. The raids made us happy; they made the Germans cry.

The Germans transferred us from Hanover because the factory was destroyed by bombs. We went to Hamburg. Before we got there, the factory there was bombed. There was nothing for us to do, so we were trained as messengers. Some time later I read in a newspaper that an uprising had been organised in the Warsaw ghetto, and that the ghetto was on fire. I read this with tears in my eyes. At night I kept dreaming about my mother and other people in my family. We got up every day at four in the morning; we slept in air-raid shelters. We were working for the army by then, and we struggled on in this way till Christmas 1943. In December we were transferred to Jadwisyn, to the park that had belonged to Prince Radziwiłł. There we were guarded by the Nazis.

Every morning at five o'clock we had to be on the square. From there we were taken down to the River Narew, where we dug trenches. It was terrible there. They beat us and hardly gave us any food, and we had to go on working. The earth was so hard that you could not push your spade in, and the Germans forced us to work the whole time. We young people had a good time when we were alone together. Things were like this till 10 July 1944. On that day the Germans transferred those of the boys who were left, because some of them had run away, and some had been killed. They took us to Wyszków and set us digging trenches again; we were given food from the kitchen. On 15 July the kitchen was hit by a shell and from then on everyone just ate whatever they could lay their hands on. It was like this till 18 August. On that day the offensive began and we were moved to the Narew. When the Russian army reached the Narew we were transferred to Płońsk and assigned to various companies as messengers. I was sent to Serock. I slept in bunkers, and there were times when I went three days on end without food. Bullets were whizzing overhead and I did not have a chance to cross to the Russian side. They began evacuating civilians from the area. Because of this I met people I knew, and strangers. One day I met a boy like myself, a Jew, who was with his sister. I had been sent to work in the stores, and I could take any clothing I wanted, because the stores had been broken open. I gave the boy two blankets, a sweater, some shoes and one set of underwear.

I struggled on like this till 16 January 1945. The final days were tough. On 14 January the offensive began; I was given an order to take a report to the battalion at Ćwiercie, but I stopped at a village off the road called Eyrzyki and from 14 to 16 January I stayed in hiding. At one o'clock in the afternoon the Soviet army moved in and I was liberated. Straightaway I went to a Jewish major who was in command of a tank unit. I told him everything, and he sent me to

Rembertów, to the RKU. From Rembertów I was sent to the Jewish Committee. At the Committee in the Praga district I met my friends, Ejchel and Bursztyn, and travelled to Lublin with them. In Lublin I am staying in an orphanage.

(Archive of the CJHC, statement no. 273)

6. REGINA RÜCK

Born 15 July 1935 in Jodłowa, near Brzostek; daughter of Pinkas and Čyla

(*Statement taken by Iza Lauer, Kraków*)

When the war broke out we were living in Jodłowa. Father had a shop selling artificial fertiliser, and he owned some woodland. Later we were resettled in Brzostek. We were allowed to take bedding and clothes but not furniture. Mother gave a lot of things to a Polish friend of ours to look after.

Father hired a cart and we drove to Brzostek. There we lived in the synagogue with all the other people who had been resettled. The poor people had stayed in Jodłowa; the Germans drove them into the woods there and shot them. We were told about this by mother's brother, who had managed to break away from the group and run away deeper into the woods. He escaped with his two sons and they dug a bunker. They slept there, but someone noticed and the police came. They shot uncle, but his sons got away.

Father was taken to the camp at Pustków.

Near us there lived some good Poles; they learnt that the Jews in Brzostek were to be shot and they tipped us off so that we could escape. Mother gave them all our things to look after; she put my sister on her back and took me by the hand, and we ran away to the woods. A few times people let us stay the night, and a few nights we slept in the woods.

Mother met a Jewish lady friend of hers in the woods; she

83

wanted to help my mother and said that mother should give her one child to look after, so my mother left my younger sister with her and went on with me.

In one village mother left me with a Polish man; she brought him plush bedsteads and tablecloths and various other things. I lived in the attic then, and I did not see the light of day for six months. That is why I wear glasses now. I was not allowed to walk about at all, in case anyone heard. They said I could walk so long as I was completely quiet, but there was straw there and it rustled. I only got up when I had to go 'to one side' – there was a pot for that – and apart from that I just sat and slept a lot, because it was dark. Three times a day the man's wife came and brought me something to eat; she talked to me in a whisper and she could not stay long because the man's mother was a bad woman, and she would have informed the Gestapo straightaway. When it got warmer the children came to see me too. I felt better then. The old woman went out to graze the goats and did not know where the children were. In the attic it was dark, for everything was blocked up with sheaves of corn; once the threshing began it started to get lighter.

Sometimes mother came to see me; she was very worried because she did not know where my sister was. My mother was working for some farmer and living there; later they would not keep her on, and she went from place to place and spent more time with me. She wanted to take me with her, because my eyes were hurting more and more.

The old woman began coming up to get food for the goats and they were afraid she would see me, and when I heard her coming I was also really frightened because it would have been disastrous both for me and for them, so I buried myself deeper under the straw.

Mother took me and found me a place with another farmer, and there I tended the cows. My mother found out that my sister was living at a priest's, that she played with him and loved him very much, and that the lady who had taken her was living there in the attic.

Mother did not tell the farmer anything about me, and they did not ask me and did not know that I was Jewish. Later they refused to keep me on. Mother took me with her, but now she had nothing, as she could not go back to Brzostek for our things.

Mother taught me to say that my name is Genia Król, that you 'write it' Genowefa, that I come from Kalisz, and that my mother is dead and my father has been sent to Germany.

She took me to a village and told me to go alone to one of the houses and ask for work. We said goodbye and she left. I went in and asked if they would take me on to tend the cows. They agreed. It was not good for me there because they were poor. There was not much to eat, my clothes got torn and in the summer I had to wear shoes as I was not used to going barefoot, but the shoes wore through during the summer and in the winter I had no shoes and I had to go barefoot in the snow because the people there had no money to buy me shoes. I still have frostbite now in my feet. In the winter I peeled potatoes, cooked them and drained them, and I looked after a little child and carried it around.

In the meantime the priest's housekeeper would not keep my sister any more. Mother left her with another farmer's wife, but the Gestapo used to come there. They kept the child in a package tied with a twist of straw.

Mother went to Lwów. The farmer drove the child out beyond the wood and left her in a field. There a local woman was reaping corn; she saw the child and took her to the village administration. Another woman took her, saying that she was hers. The little girl said that her name was Marysia Król and that she had a sister called Genia in the village of Hechły. That lady wanted me to be with my sister and came to look for me. I was delighted that my sister was there. The people I worked for did not want to let me go; they said they would give some corn and potatoes, that they would buy me some shoes and that I would be all right. But I wanted to go to my sister. We lived next to each other; we often visited each other and we were happy there.

Then mother came and took us to Kraków and put us in a boarding-house.

(Archive of the CJHC in Kraków, statement no. 489)

---

7. HENRYK PIECHOTKA

Born 1932 in Włocławek

(Written account)

We lived in Otwock near Warsaw; the Germans were going to move us out. Father found out from a policeman that they were going to take us away in the morning. We ran away in the night. We crossed the river Świder. Fear drove us on. My mother was not with us – she was in Lublin. We came to Pruszków. After some time we found mother. She arranged places for us with different farmers. There were three of us brothers. I was nine when I was separated from my parents and my brothers. At the beginning it was terrible. I had to work to earn my keep. I did not think I would last out.

Once I ran away from the farmer. But I had no choice, I had to go back. My parents explained that in that way I would survive. Mother often came to see me. I tended the cows, worked in the fields and so on. I spent a year with that one farmer. People began to be suspicious, as I was careless and went bathing with the other boys. I ran away and, without my mother knowing, I wandered to a place a few villages away. There I explained that I had lost my parents – that the Germans had killed my brother and father, and that I had lost my mother and my other brother during our escape. At that time I was too stupid to understand what it meant to be an orphan. I got up for work at dawn and went to bed late in the evening. I slept in the cowshed, and I had lice the whole time. I spent two months digging potatoes. I worked hard but I was satisfied, for I wanted to live through the war, because I was

86

sure that my mother and younger brother were alive, and that I would see them again. In that village there were often round-ups. Those times were hard to bear. I was terrified of the military police. When they came, I used to take a pitchfork and start mucking out. Somehow things always went well. I often saw Jews who had nowhere to go. I went to church and to confession, just to keep going somehow. For three years now mother had had no news of me. Now, after the liberation, I know how it would have been if my father and little brother had survived. I met my mother and my other brother in Żyrardów.

(Archive of the CJHC, statement no. 369/2)

8. TAMARA CYGLER

Born 14 March 1935 in Będzin; daughter of Samuel and Rachela Erlich

(*Written account*)

One day (we were already in the ghetto by then) – it was 22 June 1942 – at six in the morning I heard my mother's voice waking me up. She told me to get dressed quickly because the Gestapo were outside.

I got dressed as quickly as I could, my hands trembling, and ran out to the hide-out our neighbours had hurriedly got ready (one of them was the president of the Jewish community, the other commandant of the Jewish militia). Suddenly I heard the fierce shouts of the Gestapo: '*Alles raus!*' We were going to stay where we were, but the shouts grew louder. We decided to go out. The murderers, seeing people come out, rushed at us. Surrounded by soldiers, we were led out onto the street, where small groups of Jews were being formed under the eye of the Gestapo. The president of the community and his wife did not walk with everyone else, they went along the pavement with the Gestapo. So my mother went up to them and asked them to take me with them as their own daughter. The president's wife agreed, and they took me with them. We were led to an assembly point where there were already many Jews. We waited there for a very long time and I could not find my parents in the terrible crowd. After a few hours the president's wife was sent to another part of the square, where I finally found my parents.

After a short rest we began to do gymnastics. It was a hot day, and the Germans had thought up one more torture. The gymnastics consisted of standing up and squatting down. Suddenly I heard shots, one, two, three. Those who refused to do the exercises paid for it with their lives. At last they began to segregate us; my parents and I were designated to be evacuated. We were put in a big queue near the barracks. Pushing and beating us, they led us up and down like cattle, making us suffer in any way they could. It was hot and close, and many children died of suffocation. At last they packed us into wagons which were to take us to our place of execution. We decided to jump out of the train at the first opportunity. Near Nowy Będzin we jumped out. First father jumped, then later I jumped with mother, holding her hand. Mother recognised straightaway that we were near Mała Środułka, where there were still Jews living. As we were going down the street we met Mr Szeftl. He took us to his flat and bandaged our wounds. The next day we went back to Będzin, where father was already waiting for us. Six weeks passed quietly; ten days before the next transport mother handed me over to my dear guardian, Genowefa Pająk.

One day, as usual I was at my friend Halinka Herszfinkiel's house, when suddenly my father came and told me to come home as there was something very important. A lady was sitting there who had a very nice, young face. Mother was asking the lady if she could take me in for the rest of the war. People thought that the war would last five or six months at the most. The lady agreed and took me in. After dinner I went to her flat. There were three children there – Sonia, Waldek and Manun. I felt happy there and I did not want to go home. After I had been at Mrs Pająk's for five days I went to visit my parents. Mother and father said goodbye to me. Father was crying, but mother was very calm. In the evening I went back to Mrs Pająk's, where I ate supper and went to bed. In the night the Germans cordoned off the ghetto and began transporting everyone out. After that I never saw my dear mother and father, that was the last time. I shall never see them ever again.

Once the secret police caught two Jewish girls who were staying with my adopted mother, so she asked me to go and stay with some of my friends for one night. I had lots of friends in Będzin, but when I went to Mr Szulc's (my mother's friend's husband) he told me very politely to go and ask someone else, because he had no room. I suggested that I could sleep in the yard, where there were lots of barrels (there was a brewery there), and I asked him to let me spend the night in one of the barrels. He answered that he had already told me once to go elsewhere. He told the caretaker of the building to take me to Dr Bren, my mother's friend, who had promised her that he would help me if I was ever in trouble.

It was a dark night, people were being taken away. Trains loaded with human freight were flying like birds towards their destination. To the ovens and gas chambers, where a place of execution had been prepared for them. The trains flew one after the other, as if they were chasing each other, as if they were racing.

As I went down the streets I stared in horror at the trains; I imagined how, inside them, living people were suffocating, my parents among them, and as I watched that terrible sight I imagined the groans of the children and the heart-rending cry of 'Mummy!' coming for the last time from the mouth of a suffocating child. The last time! Suddenly I had an idea that saved me: I would go to the Nowy Rynek and spend the night in the bushes there. That is exactly what I did.

In the town things were quiet for the moment; there was not as much going on as there had been in the night. At six in the morning I went back to my dear guardian, Genowefa Pająk. I went up to the attic, as everyone was still asleep. My dear 'mother' was not asleep, though; she was watching over everyone. The next day she took me to Dąbrowa Górnicza to her friend Helka Gil, whose husband was German. I spent two and a half months there. 'Mama Genia' (Mrs Pająk) had to give her all the things that she had got from my real mother from the ghetto. Mama Genia paid for my stay there. Two months later I went back to Mama Genia; I was in rags and had nothing. After several weeks of constant worry I moved to the country near Częstochowa, to Wreczyca. I tended the cows there and I was starving hungry, I even ate from the dog's bowl I was so hungry, but I did not say anything to Mama Genia, because I did not want to worry her. In the country I looked after two cows, a heifer and a calf. Everything was terrible there, I thought that my time there would never come to an end. After two months I moved to Wojkowice-Komorne, to Mama Genia's brother-in-law. I was fine there for a short period, while Mrs P. was ill with cancer and was in hospital. Then Mr P. was good to me, though of course it cost a lot of money for me to stay there. I spent seven or eight months there; it was there that I fell ill with typhus. Mama Genia brought me back to Będzin (she had an X-ray taken on the way) with a temperature of 39 degrees: I was ill for a long time, over two months. Finally I got better again. A month after my sickness someone knocked on the door. Mrs Pająk was not in, she had had to go into the country. They started kicking the door and shouting that it was the Gestapo. We opened the door. There were very many of them. They had surrounded the whole building, because they thought that there were partisans and Jews there. They went into the kitchen, where there was a goat, and asked if there were any partisans there, and we answered: 'Go and look.' They searched the place, but all they found was the goat. They searched the main room. They found a German raincoat there, but later Mrs Pająk proved that it belonged to a German that she cooked for. They also found some overalls, 1,500 marks and part of a motorcycle, so they thought that Mr Pająk was in the resistance and handcuffed him. They were going to shoot him on the spot, but first there had to be a hearing. He proved that he was innocent and two weeks later they released him. He had been tortured terribly. That was the day before the Russians arrived.

(Archive of the CJHC, statement no. 525)

9. LEON MAJBLUM

Born 14 December 1930 in Brzezany

(Statement taken by Dr Dawid Haupt, Przemyśl)

. . . At that time my father, my sister and I were hiding in a bunker in the ghetto. We were starving there. When the supplies of food that some of the other occupants had were shared out, there were often arguments and even fights. After 14 days of suffering we were discovered by a young Pole who had started working for the Germans. He terrorised us, forced us to give him money and then handed us over to the Gestapo.

When the Gestapo and the SS surrounded the building where our bunker was, we were in a hopeless situation. We knew that we were bound to die, and so my father told me to try to escape across the police cordon. I did what he said, and left the building; another Jewish boy joined me. The SS, seeing us escaping, fired a whole volley of shots at us; the other boy was killed, but I managed to get away unharmed. My father and my sister died that day.

I went to a Ukrainian lady I knew, who let me stay the night and then ordered me to leave in the morning. From there I went into the country and went to a forester's lodge asking for work. I was taken on as a shepherd-boy, but I could not stay there for more than three days because the boys who tended the cattle with me recognised that I was Jewish, and subsequently made sure by undressing me by force. I had to move on. In Józefówka, where I found work as a shepherd, I spent four months. When they also realised who I was, the farmer threw me out. I went to the Polish colony at Glinna. For some time I carried milk to the dairy co-operative, and when rumours started about me being a Jew, I ran away. Half an hour later, the Ukrainian militia came to where my boss lived to arrest me. The village boys obligingly ran after me, caught up with me outside the village and tried to persuade me to come back, not telling me that the police had come for me. However, I did not do what they said as I had a feeling that something bad would happen to me in that village.

This time I wandered to the village of Wylszanka near Jezierna, where I spent the whole winter working for one of the farmers. It was the end of April 1944. One day a boy came up to me in the fields and said that I was a Jew, and threatened to tell the police. Since I knew that the German–Soviet front was not far away, I took my beloved dog and set off towards the front. After living through hunger and all kinds of difficulties and dangers, I finally managed to cross the front. Once I was on the Soviet side, I was arrested on suspicion of being a spy.

I was kept in prison for four weeks. I was interrogated a countless number of times. I was so exhausted by what I had been through that I had no desire to live. In the interrogations I was listless, my ears rang and I could see spots in front of my eyes. On one occasion I was visited in prison by a Jewish Soviet major and we talked for quite a long time in Yiddish.

I told him the whole hellish story of my experiences and misfortunes. I obviously must have convinced him that I was not lying, and on 2 June 1944 I was released from prison and put into a children's hostel. From there a Jewish lady I knew brought me to Przemyśl, where up till now I have been living in the Jewish Children's Home.

(Archive of the CJHC, statement no. 672)

10. BRONISŁAWA GOLDFISCHER

Born 15 April 1930 in Lwów; daughter of Szulin and Sala
(Statement taken by Dr Dawid Haupt, Przemyśl)

In December 1942, it was obvious that sooner or later all the Jews in the ghetto would be eliminated. In the face of this my father, wanting to save at least me, found a place for me with a Polish family whom he paid 15,000 złotys. Mrs Stokłosowa and her children cared for me warmly and were good friends to me; they risked their own lives to save me from dying. The money they received from my parents, and more besides, they spent on my keep and my upbringing.

Up until April 1943 I saw my parents from time to time. At that time they were working in the bottle factory on Serbska Street. That was where we used to meet. On 1 April 1943 someone sent a *Kripo* agent to Mrs Stokłosowa's; he walked into the living room and asked at once where the Jewish girl was, the blonde one who played the piano. That was me. At that time I was sitting in the next room. Mrs Stokłosowa stayed calm and said that there was no Jewish girl in her flat, but that her daughter was blonde and played the piano; then she took him in and showed him her own daughter. She showed him her identity documents and the plain-clothes policeman allowed himself to be convinced.

After the agent left, Mrs Stokłosowa sent me to her sister, who did not know then that I was Jewish. I spent the night with her, then in the morning I went back to my parents. I waited in front of the bottle warehouse for the column of Jewish workers. When my parents saw me they turned white with fear. I told them what had happened in the course of the last day; I stayed with them in the factory, and at night I went into the ghetto with the column. I hid in the ghetto till 25 April 1943. As there was to be an *Aktion* the next day, I set off to work with my parents, and once I was outside the ghetto I slipped away from them unnoticed and went to Mrs Stokłosowa's.

Despite the danger they were in because of me – they risked their own lives by taking me in – they looked after me like one of their own children, and it was thanks to them that I survived.

I last heard from my parents on 14 May 1943, when they sent me a letter and a parcel. After that I heard nothing more from them.

While I was living at Mrs Stokłosowa's I left the house, went on errands and talked freely with people. In our flat one room was let to a German soldier whose girlfriend, a Polish girl, told him that I was Jewish. Mrs Stokłosowa paid him 3,000 złotys to stay quiet about it. He kept his word.

On one occasion Mrs Stokłosowa put on a wedding party for a former pupil of hers who invited lots of people to the wedding, including a Polish man she knew who later turned out to be an intelligence agent for the German police. During the wedding party I was serving at table and I happened to notice a swastika under the lapel of the man's jacket. I went white with fear, and he noticed and asked why I was so frightened. I answered that he reminded me of someone I never wanted to see again. Three weeks later he came back to Mrs Stokłosowa's when I was alone there. I pretended not to be bothered by him, and he said that I was very good at playing the part of an Aryan girl. Then he searched the wardrobe, and to his surprise he found a photograph of me in a special dress kneeling to take communion. My parents had had that photograph taken in the ghetto by a photographer they knew, before they sent me to Mrs Stokłosowa's.

This obviously misled the agent, because he asked me a few more questions about my papers and left, saying that he would be back at some point when my mother was at home. He never appeared again, however.

One day on Pełczyńska Street I met a Ukrainian policeman who had once blackmailed my mother and who knew me personally. He recognised me at once and asked what I was doing on the streets of Lwów. Since I could not think of an answer, he said he would only let me go if I gave him the diamond ring he had once seen my mother wearing. When I told him that my mother no longer had it, he did not believe me and ordered me to take him to her. I was upset and angry and snapped back my answer: 'I just wish you would go to where my mother is!' and I ran away.

A few days later I met a Polish girlfriend of mine who did not know that I was Jewish and who worked in a hospital. She told me that a Ukrainian policeman had been brought to the hospital with shrapnel wounds (at that time Lwów was under bombardment by Soviet planes) and, partly in a fever and partly consciously, he kept saying that on Pełczyńska Street there was a young Jewess in hiding; she was short and blonde, and was supposed to have brought him a diamond ring. Three days later the policeman died.

(Archive of the CJHC, statement no. 888/II)

11. MARLENA WOLISCH

Born 1936 in Lwów

(*Statement taken by Iza Lauer, Kraków*)

When the Germans came, we moved from the old market square to the ghetto. And when there was to be an *Aktion* in the ghetto, all of us – father, mother, my brother and sister and I – went to the Polish part of the city, very close to the ghetto. We had papers and none of us looked Jewish. One day they caught my brother. A lady told us about it. Father went to get him out. The Gestapo would not let him go. From that moment we never saw either of them again. My brother was 18; my father was a grammar school teacher.

In the building where we lived all the occupants were Jewish. Someone probably informed on us, because they searched the building; they took mother with them, but they refused to take me or my sister. We ran after them and asked them to take us, but they would not, so we ran behind the truck all the way to the Janowska camp. We could not see mother because there were so many people in the truck; but she threw us a note to say that Irka should look after me. Irka, my older sister, was 15. She sold some things very cheaply (like a sewing-machine for 200 złotys). She left the rest and we had to move out of our flat because our Polish neighbours kept bothering us. We spent the whole day wandering the streets, and we slept in the hallways of apartment buildings, on the stairs.

Irka had 3,000 złotys stolen on the tram. She had been stupid; she was only buying some cakes. Sometimes we went to Irka's girlfriend's; they let us in there, but they were afraid of the Ukrainians. No one was prepared to put us up for the night. We did not have any papers as they had been left in our flat. There was a priest that mother knew. Irka went to him; he had some documents made for us. He wanted to take Irka on as a maid, but she did not want to be tied down. One day we met our aunt, father's sister, and she told Irka to leave me with Aunt Marysia, a Ukrainian who was married to one of our uncles.

Aunt Marysia was often visited by her mother; she was not her natural mother but had looked after her since she was a child. She shouted at her, asking her why she harboured Jews – for Aunt Marysia's husband was also Jewish.

Uncle went to work in the ghetto and we were always worried when he came home late. At night the screams from the ghetto kept us awake.

Aunt was very sick, and I could not get any ice for her. She spat blood and parts of her lung. She baked cakes which she sold on the square; she would sell 200 cakes in an hour.

One day, when aunt and I were out, two Ukrainian militiamen and a Gestapo officer searched the flat. They broke the door down; they found uncle in the bathroom and took him away. They stole a lot of things, and ordered uncle to carry out suitcases and knapsacks full of things. They sealed the flat.

When aunt saw all this she went to a neighbour and cried her heart out. When I came back, my aunt heard me knocking and came out of the neighbour's flat; she told me everything and sent me to her mother to say that her brother, who served in the SS, should come at once. But he came too late; in the meantime the militiamen had taken my aunt away.

I had nowhere to live; Aunt Marysia's friend from the same building took care of me. The militiamen came to the building every day. I went to Aunt Marysia's mother, but she would not let me stay long at her flat. I wandered round the streets, and in the evening I went back to my aunt's neighbour. I was terrified because I often met policemen, and I was afraid that they would recognise me as they had my photograph. The lady who was looking after me wanted to put me in a home, but it was difficult because I had no papers.

At the same time in the ghetto they had started killing children again, impaling them on railings and breaking their skulls against the wall. I saw this myself.

The lady was frightened to keep me in her flat; at night I slept on a trunk in the corridor outside the door of Aunt Marysia's flat. It was terrible; the militia kept coming in.

The lady took me to the Polish Committee, but they would not accept me without any papers. After a long struggle they took me in. Two weeks later I was sent to a home at No. 80, Dworzańska Street.

Two of the nuns, the mother superior and one of the nursing sisters, guessed that I was Jewish. Despite this they let me stay till the Red Army came; then my aunt took me away, and now I'm staying with her.

(Archive of the VJHC in Kraków, statement no. 441)

97

12. IRENA SCHNITZER

Born 1938 in Kraków; daughter of Roman and Rozalia
(Statement taken by Iza Lauer, Kraków)

As soon as the Germans came, my mother sent me with a lady who lived near us to her cousin in Warsaw. The Germans transported my mother, father and sister out of Kraków. My aunt lived with my cousin at a Polish lady's, but she was afraid to keep me there, because she said that I 'look like that' and that they did not 'look like that' at all. A nun that we knew took me to a home. Things were bad for me there. The teacher recognised that I was Jewish and she told the other children. The children beat me and called me a Jewess. The teacher would not even listen when I told on them. Then my aunt came; I told her how bad it was for me there, and my aunt took me to Warsaw. I only spent one night at my aunt's as the next day another lady took me to Bełżec. I called her 'auntie'.

At the beginning it was fine in Bełżec, but then the Ukrainians started going round the countryside and killing people. People hid in the woods and in various hide-outs. At the station there was a huge tub (an iron cauldron) and written on it, in German, was 'undress for bathing'. The Germans filled the tub with gas and all the Jews inside died. The boys who were on duty told us about it. They also saw the smoke in the night from where they were burning the Jews.

I was all right at that lady's and I was not afraid at all because even though the neighbours knew that I was Jewish they did not tell anyone. To begin with my uncle paid the lady, but even when the city was bombed and he did not send any more money, she still continued to look after me. Later she took me to a home in Lublin. But before long she took me away again, as they did not give you much to eat in the home; and she brought me to Kraków.

(Archive of the VJHC in Kraków, statement no. 469)

13. HALINA SCHÜTZ

Born 10 July 1928 in Lwów; daughter of Izydor and Klara Klapper

(Statement taken by M. Hochberg-Mariańska, Kraków)

When the war started we were living in Lwów and we stayed there till the time the ghetto was organised. I do not have anything special to say about that period. My parents knew a Pole who arranged 'Aryan' papers for us. In the summer of 1942 we moved to Kraków – my parents, my grandmother and I. We had birth certificates and some other papers, and I had a school certificate. I was called Halina Klof. We did not live together in Kraków – I lived with mother, father lived in a different place and grandmother somewhere else again. One day our neighbour, whom we got on well with, got drunk and started calling us names because of some wood that had supposedly gone missing from his cellar. That was the first time we heard someone say to us 'Jews!'. The next day the neighbour had sobered up and apologised to us; but before long a woman informer came to us and she was given 500 złotys not to give us away. But we had to move to another flat and we no longer lived together.

On 1 August 1943 my parents went to a christening given by some Poles they knew, and I went to see my grandmother on Boże Ciało Street. It was one o'clock in the afternoon. When I got to my grandmother's flat, a stranger opened the door and asked me who I had come to see. I realised at once that something bad had happened, and I told him that I had come to visit my friend, because in the same flat there lived some girls of my own age – they confirmed this. But the secret policemen – there were two of them – took me into another room and began questioning me; they did not believe that I was a Catholic and that I did not know my grandmother. I had a St Teresa medallion round my neck. They asked if I knew that Jews were not allowed to wear these. I pretended not to know what they meant, but it did not do any good, and

99

they took grandmother and me to the military police station on Podbrzezie Street, and left us there at the mercy of the Germans. From there we were driven to the Gestapo headquarters on Pomorska Street. They wrote down only our names and dates of birth – false ones, of course, because neither of us admitted to being Jewish. We were taken to the Montelupich prison, and two days later from there to the women's prison on Helclów Street.

We spent two weeks in the prison. Grandmother confessed right away that she was Jewish, but she did not reveal that I was her granddaughter; she maintained stubbornly that she did not know me. I was interrogated three times and each time I was beaten so badly that in the end I could not stand it and I had to confess. But it was not just because of the beating. I might have withstood being beaten more, but I had no documents with me. And, of course, I could not give my parents' address at any price, for I knew that that would be the end of them. They already had officially issued *Kennkarte* and were registered as residents. It could have saved me, but it would have been the end of them. Three times I gave false addresses. Of course, they checked and none of them proved to be my real address. So they beat me even more. In the end it was so hopeless that I confessed.

In our cell, apart from us, there were 45 Jewish women, 15 Polish women, all prostitutes, and a few gypsy women. We ate quite well thanks to the RGO [Central Welfare Council] who sent us soup and food parcels. After two weeks 25 people, including 14 women from our cell and 11 men from the Montelupich prison, were driven to Jerozolimska Street, to be sent on to the camp at Płaszów. Grandmother and I were among them. As soon as we arrived we were surrounded by Ukrainians carrying machine guns; Commandant Goeth came, John and another Gestapo officer whose name I do not remember, and the segregation began. The Commandant read out a list: nine of the men from Montelupich and one young girl called Paula Adolf were sentenced to death as political prisoners. Along with them three older women were sentenced to death; one of them was my grandmother. The rest were allowed to live. We were guarded so closely that I could not even see my grandmother for one last time.

I spent eight months in the Płaszów camp; I worked in the furriery section. The work was not too hard; the worst thing were the musters, standing on the assembly ground for three hours at a time; and also getting up at four in the morning and other such difficulties.

I myself saw them hang a young 16-year-old boy just because at work he had been singing a Russian folk song, 'Chubchik'. They hanged him three times because the rope snapped on the first two attempts, and we had been ordered to gather on the assembly ground and had to watch. In the camp there was a man called Chilowicz, the commandant of the Jewish police, and his wife, who mistreated the women, calling them the worst names and taking revenge for the slightest thing. I also witnessed the shooting of ten people for attempting to escape, in September 1943. Among them was a woman with a small son of seven. The little boy was very frightened of dying. He held on to his mother and asked: 'Mummy, does death hurt very much?' She cried and said, 'No, only for a moment'; and then they were shot. A German with a pistol shot first the child, then the mother.

In December 1943 I saw the elimination of a group of the *OD* brought in from the ghetto. On our way to work we used to pass the 'hill' where their bodies were afterwards burned on a pyre.

The first transport from Płaszów left in November 1943, and the second in March 1944; at that time I was sent to Skarżysko Kamienna. About 500 women went there. I worked in an ammunition factory, in Werk A. We made cartridges for small-calibre weapons; I put the holes in the shells. There was malnutrition and typhus there. Only money could buy help from the Poles who worked with us in the Werk. Those with typhus were mostly shot; for this reason the sick would stay off work on the sly, spend a few days in bed in the barracks

101

and go straight back to work, so as not to have to go to hospital. I also got over typhus in this way. In July 1944 the men and some of the women from Werk A were transferred to Częstochowa, and the rest of the women, including me, to Leipzig.

The journey lasted four days and four nights. In Leipzig everything we had with us was taken away from us: clothes, underwear, small stocks of food. We were given prison underwear and striped prison uniforms.

Once again we worked in a munitions factory, making grenade parts. The food was reasonable to begin with, then it got worse and worse and in the end malnutrition set in. On 14 April 1945 the evacuation started. In my group there were 150 women; we travelled on foot for 14 days, day and night, with only short rests, and in fact without a destination, for we were surrounded on all sides. We twice crossed the Elbe. After 14 days, out of 150 women there were 65 left – the rest had been shot dead by the SS. They shot people for stopping without permission, for trying to get food and, most of all, they shot anyone who could not keep up. The hunger was terrible. When we set off we had each been given one packet of margarine, a packet of conserves, two spoonfuls of jam, and two spoonfuls of sugar. In the course of 14 days of marching we were twice given soup. We were not given any bread, either at the beginning or on the way. After 14 days, in the night, after crossing the Elbe, the SS disappeared and left us. We went to the town of Oschatz where there was a camp, and there we decided to wait for the liberation. There they still had a civilian police, the so-called German gendarmerie. But the local people already started taking care of us, as the Red Army was only ten kilometres from the town and the Americans were even closer. Nearby there was a prisoner-of-war camp with English, French and American prisoners. They got to us by pretending to be from the Red Cross and brought us food, lots of tinned foods and chocolate. We were under surveillance for three days. Then the first Americans arrived by truck, and the next day the Russians came in. I was in

Germany from the beginning of April to 15 June. I got my
strength back a little, then I set off back to Poland.

(Archive of the VJHC in Kraków, statement no. 121)

14. JOSEK MANSDORF

Born 21 December 1931 in Tarnów

(Statement to the Historical Commission in Tarnów)

One day, when the Germans were already in Tarnów, a car
pulled up in front of the building where we lived on Widok
Street. Three SS officers got out and came into our flat, asking
who lived there. When father said that we were Jews, they
beat him up and ordered us all out of the flat and into the
yard. They took the best things from the flat and drove away.
Once, when they had already ordered people to wear armbands, I was walking along Lwowska Street carrying a few
boxes of sweets to sell in the shop. A German policeman
grabbed me by the armband and tried to take the sweets
away. Because I cried a lot, he took me to the community
authorities and there, after they had asked me about where I
had got the sweets from and where I was taking them, they let
me go home. After that I was afraid and I stopped taking
sweets to the shop. Apart from this, I do not remember anything in particular.

Four days before the first evacuation I heard the neighbours
tallking about it. My elder brother was living in Wola Lubacka
near Jasło. My parents sent me by train to tell my brother to
come to Tarnów. There were various problems and we could
not go back to Tarnów straightaway, so we sent a Polish man
to Tarnów to find out what was going on there. He brought us
a card telling us not to go there. They were evacuating people.
The man went there again to find things out and came back
with the news that our mother, brother and little six-year-old

sister had been put on a transport. Our older, 19-year-old sister, who had been ill at the time, had been shot dead as she lay in bed. My brother had been there when they said to her: 'We've no use for good-looking Jewesses'; they laughed, and then shot her. My brother was taken to the market square; he stood there all day, then in the evening his documents were stamped and he was allowed to go home. I was told that my brother had gone to look for me, and that father had escaped into the country during the evacuation.

I went back to Tarnów. Two days later both my brothers arrived; father did not come back to Tarnów again. He stayed in the country. Later, one brother was sent by the *Arbeitsamt* to the aircraft factory at Mielec as a metal-worker. My other brother was shot dead by a Gestapo officer called Romelman. He was 20 years old. I was left on my own. I had one other sister, but I did not know what had happened to her during the evacuation because just at that time she had had to travel to Kraków. I registered at the *Arbeitsamt*; I was given a work card and told to report there twice a week.

When the ghetto was made, a tinsmith called Weiser moved into our flat with his family of six. I asked him to go to the *Arbeitsamt* and to try to find a job for me where he worked. We went to Müller, the director, and asked about this. He refused; I was too young. Weiser told me to go to work without a referral from the *Arbeitsamt*. For three months I worked like that. He told me to take my armband off and to buy butter, eggs and lard outside the ghetto, and to bring it into the ghetto in the evening. When the workers were returning to the ghetto in the evening, I put my armband back on and went in with them. That went on for three months. I still reported twice a week in person to the *Arbeitsamt*. Once I was sent to work for a week at the 'Mieszczanka'. During this time Weiser found another boy to do the job. Then, unexpectedly my sister came back to the ghetto. She had been in Kraków the whole time; she did not have a residence permit anywhere. We lived like this till the second evacuation.

With the Weisers, we made a hiding-place underneath the

living room. The entrance was from the hallway. One part was open, and the other part was where we hid. During the second evacuation the Gestapo broke open the boards in the first part of the hide-out, where a lot of wood had been stacked. They moved a few planks aside, but they could not see any people as it was dark inside. We could see one of them, though, when he poked in his head and his hand, carrying a revolver. Then he took his hand out and said to another officer that there was a lot of wood there, but that apart from that there was no one there. Right through the second evacuation the patrols kept coming, but they did not come into the hiding-place. Two days after it was over we went out. The flat had been ransacked. We had nothing to live on. I wondered what we should do. I borrowed 500 złotys from a man I knew and went to the Polish part of town; I bought some cigarettes there and in the evening I sold them in the ghetto. Until the third evacuation I sold cigarettes. Once I was noticed by a secret agent from the Polish police while I was standing with my cigarettes. I ran off, scattering the cigarettes behind me. He shot at me three times, but I ran away into the next building where there was a passageway into another street. Later I went back home, very frightened and with no cigarettes. I stopped selling cigarettes.

I was 12 years old. I went to the fence around the ghetto. There I got to know some Poles, who began to bring me butter and eggs. I bought linen and cloth in the ghetto and traded with them. Things were like this till the third evacuation. We hid again in the same hide-out, but there was no evacuation. We waited there for a whole week. On Sunday I lit the stove and put on some coffee; my sister was going to do the laundry and wash the floor. A moment later our neighbour ran in and said that the evacuation had begun, and that they were three houses away. My sister got up quickly, and we barely managed to hide. I had only just finished tidying the wood in the hide-out when they came into the flat. We did not take anything to eat with us. We spent five days in the hiding-place and ate nothing in that time. After five days had passed we came out. The Weisers had been taken away as they had not managed to hide. I went out onto the street but I could not see anyone. I went back into the flat, took some bread and butter and went back into the hide-out. We stayed there for several more days, then we went back up to the flat.

My sister wanted me to go to the Polish district without my armband and to go to Jasło to find out whether father was alive. After I had left the ghetto, I met someone from there that I knew. I found out from him that father was still alive. I went back to the ghetto and told my sister everything. She told me to go back to persuade someone I knew that we would pay them well to take us to see our father. I did not meet anyone and I went back. People said that we should leave our street. My sister went to the Polish district, but she did not come back, as there was a sentry at the ghetto wall. For two days I thought about how to get out of the ghetto, and I decided that when the workers were going out to work, I would dress in torn clothes like someone from the country and I would leave with them. I got dressed and put my arm in a sling, as if there were something wrong with it, to make it easier to take my armband off. As we got to the factory, there were Poles standing on the pavement, and there were German and Polish policemen. I slipped off my armband and held it in my fist. I took one step out of line, then I turned to face the group and asked aloud if anyone had anything to sell. The Jews went into the factory, and I walked away with a package in my hand. The Poles ran up and asked me if I had bought anything. I said that I had not. I went to Jasło the back way through the villages. I got to Jasło and went to see a Polish man I knew to ask about my sister and my father. They said they did not know about anyone; they put me up for the night. In the morning I went to Wola Lubacka. I went to see a farmer there; I looked through the window – and saw my sister coming. I went out to meet her and we set off together. We did not know where we were going. Night fell. I told my sister that I would go to Tarnów, that I would buy various small items like needles, threads and combs, and that I would go and try to sell them to the Poles. She agreed; we decided she would wait for me in the woods. I went and bought everything and went back to her.

It took four days. I walked without stopping or resting, day and night. When I got back, I told her that I would go to the Poles and if I found a good person I would admit who I was and ask them to take me in, saying I would pay well. I did not find anyone like that. One man asked if I did not know of a serving girl. I said that I knew of one girl who had been evacuated, and who was working for some people who did not pay her anything. Her clothes were torn and she had no money to buy new ones. She wanted to find work as a maid to be able to buy things. He told me that if I brought her to him I would get 100 złotys. I went for my sister and we went back to the farmer's. She was right for the job, and she stayed. I carried on towards Jasło. I found one very good farmer; I admitted to him that I was Jewish. He said he would keep me on. I stayed with him for a month. I told him about my sister and that she had various valuables, and asked him if he would not take her on. This was not true, but I wanted to go to Tarnów to buy some things and that was why I said it. He agreed, because he was smart and he wanted to get something for himself. I told my sister about everything and she said I had done well to find such a farmer because she could not stay where she was any more as they had realised that she was Jewish.

I reached Tarnów by the evening; I climbed the fence into the ghetto and spent all my money on goods. Friends helped us by giving us things for free. The same night I left the ghetto and went back to my sister, and we went off together to that farmer's. I hid a few things in the barn, left a few, and gave the rest to the farmer, saying that every week or two I would bring him something. Two weeks passed and I said I would go and fetch him something. In the evening I went to the barn and took some of the things. In the morning I went back to him and gave them to him. Every fortnight I gave him something, and in this way we stayed in hiding for a year. Then I

107

had nothing left except for 50 złotys. I borrowed 250 złotys from the farmer; I said that I would go to Tarnów, that he should keep my sister on till I got back, and that I would bring him lots of things. In Tarnów I bought a pack of cigarette papers, and took them round the villages selling them loose; I made twice as much as I had paid. I bought butter and eggs and took them back to the ghetto. I sold them in the ghetto and made 500 złotys. With that money I bought linen, and went to one of the villages and sold it. I bought butter and lard, and again took them back into the ghetto across the fence at night. I sold that and bought more linen for 1,800 złotys, and went back into the country. I sold that and again bought some food. I repeated this eight times. In two months I had 5,000 złotys. A quilt cover then cost 100–120 złotys. I went to see my sister to check how things were. My sister said that she wanted to leave, as people had found out. Without telling the farmer, I went to another village. I found a place for my sister with another farmer; I continued to trade, and I paid for her. I sold lard but not in the ghetto any more but in a clothing factory where Jews worked. There I sold food and bought various things.

In the meantime I had found a place at a farmer's where my cousin, who was a tailor, was in hiding. I went to see my cousin and asked him, since he sewed clothes for the farmer, if I could not stay there, even for just a month. But he refused. I met another Jew; we went into the woods and built a hide-out. In the daytime I went into the town, and at night I went back to the woods. It was already autumn. We survived like that for three months. I was thinking about how to arrange some documents for myself so that I could go and work in a village where I was not known. There was one 15-year-old boy I knew. I went to see him. I asked him what his name was, when he was born and what the members of his family were called. He told me everything. The next day I went to the priest, gave the name of the boy and asked for a copy of my birth certificate as I wanted to get myself a *Kennkarte*. He gave me a copy. I paid five złotys. The next day I went to the community administration in Ryglice and gave them the birth certificate. They told me to give them a photograph and they issued me with a *Kennkarte*. When I got back I heard about a farmer who was looking for a boy to work for him. I applied and he took me on. He asked for my papers and I showed him. He took me to the village administrator and registered me as his farmhand. I worked for him for a whole year, tending the cows. I got up early and tidied the place. The farmer was pleased with me. One day my father came to see me unexpectedly in the barn where I was asleep. I had not had any news of him, but people had told him about me. We talked all night. At three in the morning I told him to leave so that the farmer would not see him. He went, but as he was leaving the farmer noticed him and recognised him. He guessed who I was but he did not say anything to me. Then the whole village found out. But the farmer did not fire me and no one gave me away.

In July, when the Germans were retreating, the Gestapo came to the monastery in the village. They were billeted there. One evening one of the officers was passing by and noticed a figure in the distance; because the person did not stop when they were called, the officer fired at them three times. That someone got away; because it was dark, the officer did not notice that it was a girl. He came into our house and asked about a 12-year-old boy. I was in the attic then and I heard everything. I made a hole in the wall and hid. I fell asleep and slept till morning. In the morning I went downstairs. I was told to eat up and leave, as the Gestapo officer was looking for me. I went to see my sister. There were also soldiers billeted there, and she was working in an army kitchen. They needed a boy to carry water to the kitchen. I worked for two weeks in that German kitchen. Then the Germans left. I went back to the farmer I had been working for. There they knew by then that it had not been me [who had been shot at], and they told me to stay, though I did not want to because I was afraid. I went back to tending the cows. On Sundays I grazed the cows and went to church. I was there till September 1944. Then they began evacuating Poles from the village of Czarna, and they started coming to our village. Whoever had room put them up. There was no room in our house as there were a lot of people living there, so the farmer did not take anyone in. The people who had been evacuated found out that he was keeping a Jew, and they began coming and saying that there were so many people without a roof over their heads and he was keeping a Jew instead of someone else. He argued with them, saying that it was not true; he did not take anyone in and he kept me on.

In the autumn we had to go digging ditches. The boys from the village told one of the Germans that I could speak German. He happened to be looking for someone who could, so he called me and asked me where I had learnt German. I told him that I had learnt it from a dictionary while I was grazing the cows. He took me on as a translator. I stayed with him the whole time and things were fine for me. Someone told him that I was Jewish. One boy warned me not to go there any more as the supervisor knew that I was Jewish. I thanked him and I stopped going. My farmer asked me why I was not going, and I told him that they did not need a translator any more. I continued to work on the farm. I put on some different clothes so that I would not be recognised, as they were looking for me. One day one of the people who were looking for me came and asked about such a boy. The farmer said that there had been a boy like that but that he was not there any more.

I had begun to be afraid by then and I asked the farmer to keep me in hiding for a while. I gave him an overcoat in return for this. I told him to take on one of the boys who had been evacuated, one who was more or less like me, so that if anyone asked he would have someone to show. He took in an evacuated family, and he kept me in hiding and no one knew what had happened to me. People asked about me, but he said he did not know where I had gone. I lived in the cellar. The cellar was divided by a board. On one side there were potatoes, and on the other I lived. I stayed there till the

Russians came. Then the farmer told me to come out. I left the hide-out and I set off back to Tarnów.

15. ZYGMUNT WEINREB

Born 26 November 1935 in Kraków; son of Bernard and Bronisława Bornstein
(Statement taken by M. Hochberg-Mariańska, Kraków)

When the war broke out, father escaped to Baranów and mother and I stayed at home. There were bombings and we often sat in a bomb shelter. On 25 September father came back and on the night of 8–9 November 1939 he left for Lwów. Until the outbreak of war between Germany and Russia father wrote from Lwów and Krasne, then there was no more news.

On 13 February 1941 we moved to Niepołomice. Mother and I stayed there right until the end of October, then mother sent me to my aunt's in the ghetto for the winter, as the flat in Niepołomice was cold and damp. At that time everything was quiet in the ghetto. I returned to my mother in Niepołomice.

In August 1942 there was an evacuation of people from Niepołomice to Wieliczka, but mother knew by then what that meant, that from there you were sent further, so she decided we would both go to the ghetto in Kraków. Mother sold a ring and bought a Polish *Kennkarte*. Then she went to Maków Podhalański to look for a flat, and I was going to travel on to join her. I stayed in the ghetto till October and I was taken out just before an *Aktion* by my cousin, who knew the commandant of the Polish police. We went to the brickyard at Łagiewniki; I was to stay with Puchała, the watchman. My cousin had a pass and wore an armband, and I followed a few steps behind him. I stayed for a few days at the watchman's, and then my mother came for me. I was called Zygmunt

111

Zarucki, and my mother was Bronisława Zarucka. We went to Maków and registered there, and we were issued ration cards. We were always scared as there was a man there who knew us from Kraków, but nothing happened to us. Mother had to go to Kraków often to sell things, and that was what we lived on.

In May 1944 mother went one Wednesday evening and was going to come back on the Thursday or the Friday. She said that if she managed to sell what she had this time, then for a while we would be all right. She left, and she never came back. When she had not appeared by Sunday, I knew that something was wrong. And the whole village started saying 'That woman from Mirocha has not come back'. Mirocha was the person we were staying with. I was still thinking that the trains must have been crowded and that she had not been able to get on. But a few days later Puchała came to see me and told me that Mama had been at his flat and had gone into town, and that she had not come back. He gathered a few things and we went to the brickyard. I had to hide so that I would not be seen by Mila, a clerk from the yard who used to inform on Jews. I spent the whole day out in the fields, or in a shack when it was raining, and I did not go back to Puchała's till night-time. My cousin was also in hiding there; he was living in a cubby-hole. Round about 20 June Puchała went to Maków to fetch the rest of our things; but in the meantime they had found out everything there about us being Jewish, and they handed him over to the police. The police station in Maków phoned the brickyard, and Mrs Puchała found out. She came to my cousin and me and told us we should run away at once, as the police were coming back with her husband. We walked out into the country and wandered uphill and down. Then my cousin said that we should split up as otherwise someone would notice us, and he told me to sleep in the fields and to go the next day to Brodzińskiego Street. He also showed me the road from Borek Fałęcki to Zakrzówek. There was corn growing high there. I had a quarter-loaf of white bread with me; I ate it, fastened my winter cap under my chin, wrapped myself in my jacket and went to sleep just as I was. But the next day my cousin was not on Brodzińskiego Street, and I never saw him again; I expect they caught him. I wandered around the streets of Podgórze; then I saw a relative of our landlady from Maków as he was getting out of a horse-drawn cab. I ran away from him, but on the next street corner I bumped into him again. Everywhere I went I saw him; I do not know whether there were other people who looked like him, or whether I just imagined it. I was very hungry and tired.

I spent one more night in Zakrzówek, but in the morning I was half-dead. I met a tram driver and he advised me to go to the nursery on Polna Street in Dębniki. There they told me that they only took in younger children, and they told me to go to the Albertine Brothers on Krakowska Street. I went there, though I could barely walk. In the office I said that my name was Czesław Bojdak, because that was the name I had had at the brickyard; I said I had run away from my stepfather and that I had nowhere to stay. The lady clerk would not believe me and asked, 'Are you prepared to go to the police with me?' It was all the same to me and I went with her to the police station on Wolnica Square. There the policeman, I think it was the commanding officer, took me into a separate room and said: 'Tell the truth.' But I repeated that my name was Czesław Bojdak and that I was from Czyżowka Street – I remembered a street called that from when I had been wandering around with my cousin. 'Very well,' said the policeman, 'I'm going to call Police Station No. 4 there and I'll find out if you're telling the truth.' But he did not call, he just told the clerk: 'Everything's in order, you can take him in'. The next day there was something in the newspaper about a boy called Bronisław from Parkowa Street who had gone missing. I did not know anything about it, until suddenly the supervisor called me: 'Come here, Bronuś, admit it, you're Bronuś from Parkowa Street.' I thought she had gone mad, but she would not believe me and she took me to Parkowa Street; then I finally got angry and shouted that my name was Czesław Bojdak, and I told her to leave me alone.

I stayed at the Albertine Brothers and Mrs Thiel, the teacher, guessed that I was Jewish, and the Brother Superior did too, and they helped me a lot. They did not say anything to me, but the Brother told me to bathe in bathing trunks like the older boys, and the teacher got angry whenever anyone called me a Jew and secretly taught me things so that no one would be able to tell I was Jewish. But then everyone began whispering about me, so the teacher took me home with her and put me in a school where the headmaster, Mr Chrzan, knew that I was Jewish and helped me a lot. While I was at the Brothers I had one adventure: we went bathing at the Roman baths and while I was in the water the elastic in my trunks snapped and they fell off. When I started looking for them I almost drowned, but I knew that without them I could not leave the pool. After that I was terrified of bathing.

When the Russians arrived the Brother Superior read in the newspaper that there was a Jewish Committee, and he told me to go to Długa Street to find out if my father had registered there. And my teacher transferred me to another school as Zygmunt Weinreb and she had to put me into a home as people had begun to bother her because she was keeping a Jew. But I go and visit her and she always calls me 'Czesio', because she got used to calling me that.

(Archive of the VJHC in Kraków, statement no. 5)

Chapter Four
IN HIDING

1. ERYK HOLDER

Born 1937 in Stanisławów
(Statement taken by Dr Dawid Haupt, Przemyśl)

My father was an engineer at the power station in
Stanisławów. Before the war my parents lived in their own
house on Wysockiego Street in Stanisławów. My father
worked and things were fine at home. When the Germans
came my parents had to leave the house and we moved in with
my grandfather and grandmother. Then things got worse but
we did not go hungry, and father was still working at the
power station and also trading. Mother was a cleaner at the
railway generating station. I remember how one day the police
took us from the flat and led us to the Jewish cemetery. When
we got there there were hundreds of Jews, and more and more
of them kept arriving. There were men, women and children.
At one place in the cemetery there was a huge grave. The
people who were standing nearest the grave had to undress
and walk up to it, and one of the Germans shot them from
behind. I saw that with my own eyes. The children were not
shot but were thrown into the grave alive. At the cemetery my
mother somehow got lost in the crowd and ended up at the
front, close to where they were shooting people. So Mama was
just about to get undressed to be killed, but since it was
already late in the evening everyone who had not been shot
was ordered to go home. We finally met up with Mama at the
cemetery in the evening and we went home with grandmother
(I do not remember whether grandfather was also there).

When the ghetto was formed in Stanisławów we moved to
Śnieżna Street. Mama was taken while she was at work and
put on a transport. On the way she jumped out of the train
and broke her leg. Then she was taken to a work-camp, and
soon after she was put on another transport. I never saw her
again. Not long after that they shot my grandmother; I do not
remember now whether it was then that they shot grandfather, or whether it had been earlier at the cemetery.

117

When they shot grandmother we had to leave Śnieżna Street and we moved in with a lady in the ghetto. My father went on working at the railway and brought food home, and the lady cooked for us and did our laundry.

This did not last long. They began transporting Jews out of the ghetto again. It was at that time that my father took me with him one day as he left the ghetto on his way to work. He told me to walk a few steps behind him. When we were near the railway a man came up to me, took me by the hand and led me to my 'aunt'. I knew this man was Mr Łopatyński, because my father had told me at home that he would hide me. In the evening my father came to see my 'aunt', who was Mr Łopatyński's sister, and spent a few days with me. Father gave Mr Łopatyński all our things and our money and grandfather's, and showed him the place where he had buried some gold.

While I was at this aunt's, Mr Łopatyński built a hiding-place in his garden, and when he had finished it he took me to his house and hid me there. He had made a wooden cot there. There was also a big opening with a grate in the hide-out, but there was no glass in it. I was not allowed to go near the opening, as children played in the garden and they would have noticed me. I knew that no one should know I was in the hide-out. Mr Łopatyński's children did not know about me either. I spent the summer and the winter there, and the next summer, until the Soviets drove the Germans out. It was not bad in the hide-out. Mr Łopatyński or his wife brought me food a few times a day. I ate the same things as they did. Sometimes they gave me a bath, but only when their children were not at home. In the winter I lay under the quilt all day. I do not remember whether I was cold. I was only ill once – I caught a chill.

I never went up to the opening in the hide-out, though I could hear the children playing in the garden; and I always remembered that no one should see me. I was not afraid to be alone in the hide-out, and I never cried. But I missed my mother and father very much.

After the first few days, my father moved from aunt's flat to some barracks where Jews were living. For some time he continued to work on the railway. One day Mr Łopatyński came home from work and said that the Germans had shot my father. They had been rounding up Jews from work to take to the cemetery; my father started to run away, and a German spotted him and shot him dead. When the Soviet army drove the Germans out of Stanisławów, Mr Łopatyński took me from the hide-out to his flat, and a week later handed me over to the Hellmans, a Jewish family who had survived. When the Hellmans left Stanisławów they took me with them and put me into a Jewish nursery in Przemyśl. I am all right here, because there are other children here with me. I am now in the first year at school.

I had no brothers and sisters. While I was at Mr Łopatyński's sister's I played with her son Ryś. Ryś loved me and never did me any harm.

My aunt taught me to say my prayers, 'Our Father' and 'Hail Mary'. I knew that I was a Jewish boy and that because of that the Germans wanted to kill me.

(Archive of the CJHC, statement no. 889/II)

---

2. KRYSTYNA AND RÓŻA GOLD

Aged 14 and seven; no other details recorded
(Statement taken by I. Glicksztajn, Bytom)

... When father and mother were arrested on a train and sent to Germany, we were left alone at the mercy of the farmer. We paid him a lot and each day he gave us 200 grams of bread and six baked potatoes. The farmer and his wife and daughter knew that we were Jewish, but his son-in-law did not know, as he was in the NDP [the right-wing National Democratic Party, some of whose members were known to hold anti-semitic views] and he might have given us away. There were three openings in our bunker; on fine days there was a bit of light, but when the weather was cloudy it was completely dark. We lay there day and night. In the spring, when the snow melted, the water poured in and everything got wet, and in the winter it was freezing cold. We stayed there for six months, a year, a year and a half. The farmer's wife kept complaining about having to hide us; we gave her everything and we had nothing left. If someone had said 'give us tuppence or we'll kill you', we would not have had that amount of money.

We were so hungry that neither of us could walk any longer. In the end the farmer's wife would not even bring us water. Then my brother went out one night, drank some water from a puddle and died. We buried him at night in the woods.

One day uncle left the bunker and never came back. We stayed hidden there for 18 months, till the Russians came. We could not walk at all – even now our legs are still weak; and Róża is sad the whole time, she often cries and will not play with other children.

(Archive of the CJHC, statement no. 903)

3. MARIA KOPEL

Born 1932 in Krasnobrody

(Written account)

In our family there were six children. I was in the middle. In Krasnobrody the Germans were rounding up Jews, so my father, mother and aunt took the children into the country and hid at a farmer's. My youngest sister was three then; she had curly blonde hair and did not look Jewish. My mother gave one of the countrywomen 500 złotys and she took my sister in. One day my father, mother, aunt and brother bought some bread and went to give it to my sister. Later the village people told us that they [German soldiers] had ordered my mother to take her clothes off, but she refused because either way it meant death, so they killed her with her clothes on. Father was strong; they tied his hands behind his back and were going to shoot him in the head, but he kicked one of the Germans in the stomach and the German fell over and was knocked out. Then father grabbed a rifle and ran off towards the farm people; but they tied him up and killed him.

When the countrywoman found out that my parents were dead, it was raining, and she took my sister and threw her in the pond. But the seamstress was passing and she heard a child crying; she pulled her out and took her to Krasnobrody, and I do not know what happened to her after that. Some people said that she had been killed, others that a countess had taken her away. But the countess ran away when the Russians came, for she had collaborated with the Germans. The rest of us children stayed with the farmer, but in the winter he threw my five-year-old brother out, and he froze to death. The village people also killed my aunt; there were just four of us left. One day my elder sister told me to go to Krasnobrody to see if there were any Jews left there, as I looked the least Jewish and I would not attract anyone's attention.

I went, but I had only just crossed the bridge when I heard shouting and screaming. I stood and saw from a distance that the police had come and were taking my brothers and sisters away. I did not turn back any more but walked on, without knowing where I was going. I went through some woods, then there was some kind of open ground and some Jews from Krasnobrody were hiding there. I went to them and met my only remaining brother, who had escaped from the cart. We cried terribly – there were only two of us left now.

At five in the morning the police surrounded the open ground and the local people took us away. My brother cried, and he kept begging the village administrator's son to let me go. So the administrator's son left me behind the wall of a house, and took all the others away. I kept crying, and I wandered around the village, which was called Chudów. Then the administrator's son took me in and I worked as a servant for them. After some time, the Banderists came and killed the administrator's son. Because everyone knew that I was Jewish, I left and went to work for another farmer. He was very bad to me. He had a horse that bit; when I had to take water to the horse I was afraid to get close to it, as the horse used to knock the water over and then the farmer would beat me. I served there till the Russians came, then I went to Zamość and the Jews took me to the orphanage in Lublin. Now I am staying in Chorzów; I have not got a friend in the world.

(Archive of the CHJC)

---

4. FRYDERYK SZTAJKELLER

Born 1939 in Bielsko

(*Statement taken by Hilda Barberówna, Bielsko*)

… I lived behind the wardrobe; I did not get any supper and in the morning they also forgot to bring me anything to eat. When someone came close I stayed still; I never even went out into the sunlight. I never washed, I never had any toys. I stayed quiet and covered myself with the quilt, which was full of lice. I thought I would be there for ever. They said they would go to Częstochowa and leave me. I was going to cry but I thought, when they go I will come out from behind the wardrobe. Then the man of the house died. I cried terribly – who would cut my hair if I got lice? When I walked around the living room I was sad but I did not cry. There was a balcony there and they could have opened the balcony doors to let me see the sun, but they did not; they only opened the doors when I was a long way from the balcony. Later I lived under a table behind a curtain; they only gave me soup, though they had a main course as well. There were two girls there, Różka and Wieśka; they took food away from me, saying that I had had enough. Everyone there called me *Yevrey* [Jew, in Russian], only one of the girls called me Frycek. I was very pale; even one of the young children told me I was pale. The Germans sometimes came, but I was not afraid, because if they had said I was Jewish the Germans would have killed them too. Once one of the Germans shot a sort of golden ball into the floor; it made my ears ring. I stayed there for two years, and never went outside. Once they told me that if a German found out they would throw me into the water. I missed my father. Later on Uncle Rotman came and brought me *kasha* with milk. The Polish lady said it would be very good for me because I was pale. Then uncle took me to Katowice, and from there a young lady brought me to Chorzów.

(Archive of the CJHC, statement no. 906)

5. EUGENIA WELNER

Born 19 February 1934 in Kraków; daughter of Maurycy and Róża Weinstock

(*Statement taken by Professor Chaimówna, Będzin*)

On 31 July 1943, the day before the final general evacuation, my parents sent me to the village of Łazy in the Zawiercie district. I was left with a labourer called Winkler who worked at the brickworks in Łazy. My parents knew Winkler. A few weeks earlier they had arranged for him to take me in. He agreed. Father gave him various things, some money, rings, clothes and quilts.

Mr Winkler's wife came to fetch me. Mama told me that I should go with the lady, because if I did not, they would burn mother and father and me. I said goodbye to mother and father; I did not cry; I took some sweets, some cakes, my pyjamas, soap, a towel, some toothpaste and my toothbrush. I did not take any clothes because the lady was going to come the next day for my suitcase.

I left Nowy Będzin at 7.30 in the evening and arrived in Łazy at 9 o'clock. The journey went well. At the station in Łazy we were met by Mr Winkler and Mrs Winkler's mother. The lady's mother took me to Wysoka, a village three kilometres from Łazy. When I got to her house I met her husband and her daughter. I started to miss my parents and began to cry. They gave me supper and I went to bed. I slept with the daughter, whose name was Lucka. In bed I cried secretly. When I got up in the morning, it was Sunday, and I said my prayers from a book because I had not yet learnt them by heart. Later I ate my breakfast and we went outside onto the grass. For breakfast I had dry bread with cucumber and bitter white coffee. They had the same. Then I went to the Winklers' in Łazy. There I had to work. I darned socks and mended shirts. Then I washed the dishes, peeled potatoes, washed the floor and lit the stove. I ate the same food as them. Sometimes there would be bread with butter, for dinner potato soup, and for supper more bread and sweet black coffee. It was like that the whole time, until the lady had a baby. Then I had to wash the nappies, rock the baby and play with it. Winkler was a drunkard; he drank vodka, and when he got drunk he beat his wife and me, because he did not like me. He was always making me get back to work. It was like that the whole time. I looked after the baby for nine months. I never left the house; I even went to the lavatory in the house and the lady carried it out. None of the neighbours knew me, no one knew about me, because when someone came to the house I hid behind the wardrobe. The door was always locked. Twice some Germans came for vodka in the night. Mr Winkler opened the door to them; I was asleep in bed. One of the military policemen asked who the little girl was. My hair was dyed blonde. The man said I was his sister's child. I pretended to be asleep, but

I heard everything. The policeman tried to wake me up. I stretched in my sleep and settled down again. The other policeman would not let him wake me up. They did not get any vodka because Mr Winkler had buried it in the cellar. They went away. The next time they came late one afternoon in the winter. The man saw them through the window and sent me into the lavatory. I stayed in there for an hour. When they went away the lady came for me. I called them aunt and uncle.

One day when I was cleaning I broke a bottle of vodka. Uncle chased me and hit me in the face with a belt-buckle; but I hid in the lavatory and locked myself in. He stood in front of the door and said that if I did not open it he would break it down. But he did not do that. He stood there for two hours, until in the end aunt came and told me to give her my gold ring; she said she would pawn it and buy some more vodka. I agreed and gave her the ring. It was only then that uncle went away from the door.

When the Russians came and opened schools, my aunt sent me to school. Things were better for me under the Russians. Uncle told the Russians that I was Jewish. Now the neighbours thought that I was a convert. In May my father came for me; I cried for joy.

(Archive of the CJHC, statement no. 1238)

6. ŁAZARZ KRAKOWSKI

Born 23 March 1935 in Katowice; son of Chil and Necha Blumstein

(*Statement taken by Professor Chaimówna, Będzin*)

... When my mother was sent away to do forced labour, the next day my father handed me over to Włada. I was happy to go there – I was used to Włada as she had brought me up.

After I left the ghetto, on 23 June 1943, until 10 November 1944, I stayed in the flat the whole time, mostly under the bed. When there were no visitors there I would walk around the room, but quietly so that no one would hear. During the day there was no one at home as they went out to work. Mr Liwer stayed hidden at home. He was an elderly man. We read newspapers and books together, mostly religious ones because there were not any others there. I had enough to eat; father had left some money so there was enough for me. I did not work, except that from time to time I peeled the potatoes and stoked the stove. The days were terrible, sitting the whole time without moving in that stuffy room; the worst time was when I fell ill and needed a doctor. We went to Sosnowiec to see the doctor; I was terrified, and prayed that no one would recognise me. At the doctor's I pretended to be the lady's son. The doctor said that I had worms, and wrote a prescription for me. Two weeks later we had another trip like that to the doctor's; that time too everything went smoothly. On 10 November 1944 I went to live with the uncle of a lady I knew in the village of Bonowice. The uprising in Warsaw had just finished and they could take me in as a child whose parents had died in the uprising. There I came back to life. I was free. I could go wherever I wanted, and I simply gulped in the air. One day a lady came to uncle's who suspected that I was Jewish. She fired off lots of questions at me, which I was able to answer because, as I said, I knew my religion well; so she decided that I was not Jewish. Here I was liberated by the Russians. I stayed in the country till 1 May 1945. I went to school; I was popular there, and I was very happy.

(Archive of the CJHC, statement no. 629)

7. IZAK KLAJMAN

*Born 10 June 1934 in Będzin; son of Bencjon and Chana
Süsskind*

(Statement taken by Professor Chaimówna, Będzin)

We were living in the ghetto in Będzin. There, together with
our neighbours we built a bunker in the cellar. On 1 August
1943, when we heard that the Germans had surrounded the
ghetto, we went down to the bunker, our family and all the
neighbours – there were about 50 of us in all. The bunker was
about five metres long and three metres high. We stayed
inside from 12 o'clock at night till 12 noon. The whole time
Germans kept passing by. In the bunker there was a little
one-year-old baby. The baby began to cry and some Germans
heard it as they were passing. They began shouting: *'Juden
heraus!'* Because the entrance to the bunker was covered with
stones, we could not climb out quickly. The Germans opened
fire and killed one Jewish man. The men moved the stones
aside and we began climbing out. The last out was my grandmother, and one of the Gestapo beat her terribly with a rubber
truncheon. We stood against the wall; the Germans ordered
us to stand facing the wall. My 14-year-old sister began
begging one of the Germans, who was wearing a helmet, to let
her go; but he was going to shoot her for that. Then they
ordered us to line up and asked how many of us there were.
We answered that there had been 50 of us, but since one
person had been shot, there were now only 49. They ordered
us to go to the assembly point. On the way they drove us on
and beat us with their truncheons. They had also driven the
Jews out of other bunkers, and a large column was formed.
They led us towards the station. Near the barracks they
ordered us to halt. My sister took off the sign she had on
saying *Jude* and moved away from the crowd, and she and a
friend of hers went up to one of the Gestapo, saying that she
was a Christian and that she had only been in the ghetto by
chance. She asked him to let her go. The officer believed her

and let her go free. In this way my sister got away. When my mother saw this, she turned to me and told me to escape too. Just then the guards were being changed, and I squeezed between the soldiers in helmets. I was spotted by one of the SA [*Sturm Abteilung*] in a yellow uniform, and he struck at me with his bayonet. He meant to kill me, but I jumped aside and he only scratched me. I got away and ran into the nearby blocks of flats. A friend of my father's lived there. I knocked on the door of his flat, but unfortunately no one was in. But I waited till the man came back. He took me in straightaway, dressed my wound and left me in the flat. I went to sleep, and the man went into town to get me some clothes (I was dressed only in a pair of bathing trunks, as in the bunker it had been very hot and stuffy). In the evening my sister came too. She was terribly upset, she seemed half-mad. She kept on asking me where mother was. I answered that mother had been put on a transport. She did not sleep the whole night and kept waking me up. In the morning we had breakfast and my father's friend told me to go to the Małobądż meadows. He gave me a big scout shirt that belonged to his 18-year-old son, some food, and coffee in a flask. He told me to wait for him there till he came. I went there and sat on a small hilltop. In the afternoon my sister joined me, and drank my coffee. I was dreadfully thirsty as well because the weather was hot, so I went to a sort of dirty spring or puddle where there were frogs and insects, took some dirty water in the flask and drank it. My sister said nothing, but five minutes later she left. I waited until the evening, and at six o'clock the man came. I asked him to give me something to drink. He bought me a bottle of beer and I drank it. He took me to another pond, washed me all over with soap, gave me some bread and meat paste, pushed me into a stook of corn and covered it with loose straw; I spent the whole night there. In the morning, as soon as the sun came up, I woke up and got out of the corn. I walked around the meadow because I did not want to stay in one place. At about nine o'clock the man's daughter came and brought me some food and a blanket. She gave me a hug and told me to watch out. I wandered round like that the whole day, and at night I crawled back into the stook of corn and fell asleep. In the night the Germans came and searched in the corn, but they did not find me.

I dozed like this the whole night; I was terrified. In the morning, in the distance I saw a policeman with a dog. I realised that the dog would sniff me out, so I jumped into the river and went underwater, because I knew that the dog would not be able to smell me in the water. When the policeman went away I got out of the water. It was hard to stay in the water for so long. Another day passed. I did not eat anything that day; I could not eat because I was so afraid and nervous. At night I hid again in the stook of corn. In the morning the man came; he brought me more food and promised that he would take me away from there as soon as things got quieter. He told me to wash in the river so I would be clean. When he left I went down to the river. As soon as I reached the bank, some boys came; they somehow recognised me as a Jew and, to make sure, three of the bullies attacked me. They pulled my trousers down and started shouting 'Jew, Jew, Jew!' at the top of their voices. Then they grabbed hold of me, twisted my arms behind my back and started discussing what they would do with me: drown me, or hand me over to the German police. I took advantage of a moment when one of them let go a little; I kicked him and ran away. I ran along the Małobądż road as far as the Czeladź bridge. There I hid from them among the ruined houses. I waited for a couple of hours in one of the houses and went back to the meadow, because I had to wait for my father's friend there. When I got there a Christian lady saw me and called me over. When she heard who I was, it turned out that she knew my father, so she went to the parents of the boys who had been bullying me and told them about it. The boys got a hiding and from then on they left me alone. Also, that lady took me home and I stayed there for one night. At that lady's I got to know Leszek, a Polish boy. He was very clever, he knew everything about me, and we became friends. We played together near the house. At night they made me sleep in the summer-house. It was very cold there, and I got badly bitten by mosquitoes; I did not have my blanket or my jacket, as the boys had thrown them into the water. I had just a shirt to wear day and night. The next two nights I slept in the corn, and then my guardian came and took me home. I spent one day there. He gave me some underwear, clothes and shoes, and took me to his cousin's in the country, in Pustków near Kłobuck.

We went by train. He arranged with his cousin that he would pay her 50 marks a week. He paid for one week in advance and I stayed there. He did not tell her anything about me being Jewish, but told her that I was the son of a famous professor that the Germans had sent to Dachau, that my mother had died before the war, and that I did not have anywhere to live. She was a country woman, and so she did not even suspect that he was not telling her the truth. I stayed with that woman in the country for nine months. I did everything. I got up at five in the morning, took the cows out to pasture and grazed them, mucked out, and did everything on the farm that needed to be done, just like a real farm-hand. They called me Jaś there. They gave me the same food as they ate. But there were lots of lice, bed-bugs and fleas there that kept on biting me. I was covered in lice, even though every Saturday afternoon the woman washed my only shirt so that it would be clean for Sunday. Later, after a few weeks, my guardian brought me some shirts from Będzin, so I had more clothes. That was how my time passed in the country. After the nine months my guardian took me to his daughter, who lived in the country at a manor house. She was happy to take me in. I worked there as a shepherd again. I had to get up very early there and feel the chickens to see how many eggs there would be that day. They gave me very little to eat and I was often hungry. But the lady deloused me and often gave me a bath, and I was clean. I spent four months there. After four months the lady moved to her parents in Będzin, and I went with her. At their home I worked on the farm; I took the place of a serving-girl. I lit the stove, washed the pots, swept the floor and did everything. They fed me quite well. I stayed there until the Russians came. The whole time I never left the flat, and none of the neighbours saw me. Whenever one of their friends came I hid straightaway under the bed or behind the rocking-chair. I was so happy that I cried when on the first day of the liberation my cousin came to check whether by any chance there was someone from the family there. I heard my cousin's voice in the other room, and I ran out and flung my arms around him.

(Archive of the CJHC, statement no. 1224)

8. RENA KANT

Born 6 January 1932 in Brzana near Stróże; daughter of Izrael and Gizela Zahler

(*Statement taken by Iza Lauer, Kraków*)

In Jedlicze registration took place in the summer of 1942; but it was not really a registration but an evacuation. They looked through everyone's *Arbeitskarten*; skilled craftsmen were allowed to stay with their families, and labourers on their own. The Ukrainians surrounded the town and all the Jews were driven out onto the market square. Those without work were kept on the square. Trucks drove up; people were loaded on and sent off to Krosno and from there were put on a transport, I do not know where to.

That day I woke up early. My mother was not there, only my nine-year-old sister and my four-year-old brother. A Jewish militiaman ordered us to go to the market square, but to take only ten kilograms of things. So I picked up my brother and told my sister to follow me, and I said that we would go and hide. I knew that they took people away and murdered them, and I did not want to go to the market square. But my sister was afraid to move and did not follow

131

me. My brother and I went across the garden. I was afraid to go any further because there were lots of Ukrainians everywhere, and we hid in the lavatory. I do not know if someone gave us away, but before long a Ukrainian came and ordered us out; he asked what I was doing and where I was from. I told him that I had been to see my aunt and that I was on my way home; I said I lived nearby. I did not want to say that I was Jewish so he would not take me into the town. I went with him, supposedly to our house; I was carrying my brother because he had had rickets and he could not walk or speak. On the way the Ukrainian told me to admit that I was Jewish. I told him to carry on walking, and that he would see where I lived. He had a word with another Ukrainian, then he waved his hand and let me go. The whole day I wandered in the fields and the countryside. Some farm people gave us something to eat. I thought I might meet my mother, because she often went into the country, but she was not there, and I never saw her again.

After two days I met my grandmother and my aunt. They told me where they were going and told me to go into the town to get some food. I went to some Jews I knew who had stayed in Jedlicze. The evacuation was over. They were called Fries; he was the president of the *Judenrat*, and came from Katowice. His wife would not let me into the flat; she told me to wait outside till she brought me out some food. But I did not want to wait outside a closed door, and I went away with my brother. I asked some farmers and they let us come in, gave us something to eat and put us up for the night, even though they knew we were Jewish. I found my aunt at a forester's. She had not been able to continue with grandmother. Grandmother had turned herself over to the police. I was to go on with my aunt. My aunt said that I would not be able to carry my brother any more. I really was very tired by then. I had been carrying him all day. My brother was heavy, and I was completely exhausted. These days I would probably be able to carry him for longer. I left him in front of a house in the village. He cried as I walked away. I thought that maybe

132

someone would take him in. Fries told me that he was shot in Krosno. He was shot by Becker of the Gestapo. Sometimes I feel guilty about leaving him, but I really could not have carried him any longer.

I went with my aunt to the village of Zajice near Jasło. We lived there for a week at a Pole's we knew. Then there was a round-up in Jasło; we could not stay there any longer and we set off back towards Jedlicze. On the way a Polish lady friend of my mother's handed me a letter from my mother in Bobowa. We decided to go and see her. I got on the train in Jedlicze, and my aunt was going to get on at the next station. I never saw her again. Some Polish people I knew told me that my aunt had been afraid to travel by train and had set off for Bobowa on foot. I got there, but my mother was not at the address I had. There had already been an evacuation. I got on the train and went back to Jedlicze. There my uncle and my cousin were working in a factory. I had to hide in the attic because everyone went to work and no one was allowed to stay at home. There was another family hiding with me in the attic. Then uncle sent me to stay with a man. I was there for a month, but the neighbours began saying that I was a Jew, and the man sent me to his cousin's. There I lived in the attic for four months. Then the people were supposed to be resettled. But that was just what the Germans said; in fact, they put everyone on a transport. When my cousin found out about the move they were planning, he took me back to the Polish man's for a few days. But afterwards, when there was no one left in the town, the Polish people let me stay on. That man does not want me to give his name because he does not want people to know that he harboured a Jew. They were an elderly couple. I stayed with them for three years. To be safe, I did not leave the house. When a visitor came I hid under the bed; when someone noticed me, they said I had come from the country to bring eggs. I helped them a bit with the housework, and the people shared their food with me.

I only had two dresses, so the lady altered some of her old dresses for me.

When the Soviets came, I went into the country, because I did not want to hide any more.

In the country, some farmers took me on as a cowherd. I did not tell them that I was Jewish; I was still afraid. I tended the cows for four months, but it was cold and I caught a chill, so I went back to the elderly couple. When people asked who I was, we lied. It was only in the summer that I heard there was a Jewish Committee and a children's home in Kraków. I went to the Committee in Krosno and from there they brought me to Kraków.

(Archive of the VJHC in Kraków, statement no. 612)

9. TEMA KAPŁAN

Born 1928 in Knyszyn

(Statement taken by M. Turek, Białystok)

In 1942 a black cloud drew over us. The town was cordoned off by the German murderers. We went to the station to see what was going on. The station yard was full of people. They told us that the German government commissar had sent them home from work, saying that the Jews had a holiday today. We realised at once what this meant, and started running away. They fired at us, but with God's help we got away. The farmers would not let us in. We spent nine days in the woods, and we heard that there were still some Jews in Białystok and Jasinówka. We sent a farmer there to find out for us. In the meantime two boys came and tried to take us to the town. 'Why should you get frozen here; come to the town or they'll shoot you.' We gave them some money and went straight to Jasinówka. We stayed there till 25 October.

On 1 November the town was surrounded and they fired at us with heavy machine guns. The bullets flew over our heads, but with God's help they did not hit us. We went to a farmer we knew who lived on the road. He said he could only take one person in. My uncle stayed there, and I went on with my mother and father to look for somewhere else. We came to a holiday camp, where we stayed for two days. Then we found out that the farmer had given uncle away, and that uncle had been shot. Before his death uncle had asked to be buried in the Jewish cemetery. The farmers we were staying with heard about uncle's death and asked us to leave. We moved on. The farmer's wife gave us some bread for the journey to bring us luck on our way, and wished us good luck so that we should not fall into the hands of the murderers. We went to another farmer, and he took us in. He kept asking us what would happen if the Germans were to stay in Poland. We explained that that was impossible. But the wound in our hearts was very great. The farmer built a hide-out for us. The pigs walked about on top of it, and the entrance was under the horses' stables. We lived like that for 13 months, in the cold and filth; but we were happy not to be told to leave. But the police found us out and burned the hide-out down. We had to run away in broad daylight. German murderers and Poles were standing all around, and we had to hide in the corn. Shell-cases were falling around us. I envied all those people who had hide-outs. And I said to my mother and father: 'Have I sinned so badly?' Before evening we came out of the corn. The farmers surrounded us at once as if we had been gypsies, and began questioning us about where we had been hiding. We said that we had been in the woods. One of the farmers said that if he had known who had been harbouring Jews, he would have killed that person straightaway. Then they told the Germans that there were Jews hiding in the holiday camps. But the Germans had no time to search for us. We stayed there for three days without water or food. On the fourth day the farmer came and took us home. He built us a shelter under the floor. Two days later the 'Katyusha' [Soviet M-13 rocket launcher] began to play and we went down and hid in the farmer's cellar. The cellar was built of concrete. There were three other Jews with us who had been in hiding

135

at our farmer's brother's. The Germans came unexpectedly to the village, but fortunately they did not come into the cellar. A few hours later someone came into the cellar and said: 'What are you staying down here for? The Red Army's come!'

(Archive of the CJHC, statement no. 985/II)

10. ESTERA SZAJN

Born 27 January 1933 in Turka on the Stryj
(Statement taken by Hilda Barberówna, Bielsko)

For almost a year I lived in the ghetto with my parents. That was in Sambor. There began the *Aktions*, which I remember very well. Early one Saturday morning in the summer of 1942 my mother heard voices and shouted: 'The Germans are coming!' Straightaway I hid under the bed near the window. Mama hid under the other bed, our friend hid in the wardrobe, and father got dressed. The Ukrainians first burst into our neighbour's living room, demanding that they show their *Arbeitskarten*. Then they smashed our door in, came into the main room, and went up to my father and beat him. They shouted, 'Where is everyone?' They took father away. Then one of them bent over the bed and spotted Mama. One of them beat her with his rifle butt; I saw blood and jumped out at him. I tried to grab his arm, but he pushed me away. The Ukrainian took my mother away. When she came back she told us exactly how things had been. She had got away onto the balcony, and from there she had seen lots of Jews who had been caught. They gave the Ukrainians money, gold and dollars. The murderers took their valuables, but put them on the transport anyway.

From the balcony mother called to me: 'Estusia, quickly, hide under the bed.' I wanted to hide under the quilt and I argued with her. There were more shouts; mother got onto the

136

next balcony and was going to jump down into the yard. Suddenly a little boy called: 'A Jew! A Jew! A Jew!' Mother ran up to the attic and hid in the corner.

In the same attic was our neighbour with her three-year-old child. At one point the child began to cry and the Ukrainians found the woman. My mother witnessed the scene. The neighbour bought herself off with 2,000 Reichsmarks and a silver watch. All this time I was alone in our living room. Suddenly the Ukrainians came in. They looked in the bed, but by good luck they did not find me. I heard them opening the wardrobe. They found our friend. They demanded gold, and since she did not have any they took her away to put her on the transport. I was still under the quilt; I was so hot that I stuck my head out. After the *Aktion* was over they came back into our living room. I did not have time to hide myself and I just lay there without moving. The Ukrainians took my dresses from the wardrobe. Then one of them noticed me and said, 'There's someone there'; and the other one said, 'Shoot her!' I ran up to him and begged him, 'Please, sir, do not kill me, what good will it do you? You've already killed my Mummy and Daddy, and what did you get from that?' The Ukrainian shouted at me: 'What? I killed your parents?' When I saw his expression, I said, 'I'll give you everything, even the dollars that my father buried.' I only calmed down when he said: 'Go on, go back to bed; I expect you know that the train with the transport has already left.' I could not bear to lie down any more and I followed him into the next room. There he was putting on civilian clothes over his uniform. I startled him when I came in, and he was going to shoot me, but I ran away and locked our flat. I decided to go to our Polish neighbour's, but she would not let me in. Then I went to Olesia Kot, a Ukrainian woman. She took me to Bromer, a Jewish shoemaker. That was near the *Judenrat*. Father found out that I was at Bromer's and took me home; there we met mother. Then mother decided to leave me with Mr and Mrs Kumernicki. She paid them to look after me. One of the *Volksdeutsch* was supposed to take me there. On the way he left me with some friends of his and told them to kill me. But a Ukrainian took pity on me and took me to the Kumernickis' home. There were ten children there: Michasio, Petro, Marynia, Genia, Stefan, Petrunia, Toncia, Władzia, Gencio and Jasio. I was all right there. There was not much food. I had a sense of obligation; I washed the pots and helped as much as I could. I always had to hide. In the day I stayed in the guest room. At night I slept with the children on a single board bed, or on my own by the stove. I stayed there for two years. I heard about the closing-down of the ghetto and I thought about Mama.

One day in 1943 Gencio went to the neighbours. Those neighbours were bad people. They gave him something nice to eat and Gencio told them everything he knew about me. The lady, who was *Volksdeutsch*, came straightaway and laughed about the Kumernickis harbouring a Jewish girl. In the evening the police came. I hid on top of the stove, and shook with fear. They did not find me and they went away. I went to Mrs Kumernicka and asked her to carry on hiding me, maybe in the bed, but she was afraid to take the risk. In the evening I had to go to the woods. It was the summer of 1943. Gencio built me a hide-out with branches and I stayed on my own in the woods. Sometimes Marynia or Gencio brought me food. I did not leave the woods. When I felt hungry I picked berries and ate them. For two nights running it poured with rain and I got soaked to the skin. Gencio came and took me home. On the way I picked some mushrooms for Mrs Kumernicka. Through the winter, in the daytime I stayed in the hay in the stables, and at night I slept in the house. When the Soviet army arrived, Bromer the shoemaker came and took me away. He had also survived as an 'Aryan'. I stayed with him for a whole year, and then he put me in the children's home in Bielsko.

(Archive of the CJHC, statement no. 534)

11. MIRKA BRAM

Born 1936 in Kalisz

(Excerpts from statement taken by M. Hochberg-Mariańska, Kraków)

... Three days later the Germans came to Adampol and shot all the Jews who lived there and threw them into the well. They searched everywhere, in stables and barns. The farmer's wife I knew hid me on top of the stove and covered me with wood. But when the Germans left, she would not keep me any longer because she was afraid that someone would give her away. She took me to the village of Wyryki. There she took me to the village administrator; she told him that she had found me on the road and asked him to find a place for me somewhere as a farm-hand. The officer asked me where I was from, and I answered as Mrs Szusterowa had taught me: 'I do not have a mother or a father, and I walked here from Warsaw.' But the officer did not want to have anything to do with me and put me on a cart with a farmer who was going to Włodawa, and told him to take me to the town elders there for them to do something with me. But when we got to Włodawa it was already dark and the elders' office was closed, so the man set me down in the street and told me to go wherever I wanted. And I had no reason to stay in Włodawa, because everyone there knew me, so I ran away from there and set off back to Adampol. On the way I met some boys and they asked me where I was going. I told them that I was going to Wyryki, and they all started shouting 'Jew', and they ordered me to say my prayers. I knelt down in the road and I started to say 'Our Father', because I knew that, but I could not remember how to cross myself. And they shouted 'Jew, Jew...' and they took my coat. In the coat I had the prayer book that Mrs Szusterowa had given me in Adampol. I ran away and the next day I got back to Adampol.

Mrs Szusterowa told me I should go and see the priest in Włodawa, and that he would certainly help me. We went to

Włodawa across the gardens and fields so that no one would see us. She left me by the church and forbade me to go back to her house, because she was very much afraid. I went to the church and went looking for the priest, but I could not find him anywhere. So I asked a little boy: 'Where's the mister priest?', and when he started shouting, 'Jew, Jew!', I ran away again. But I saw the priest by the little house behind the church and I went up to him. I said: 'Good morning, Mr Priest. I'm an orphan, please can you help me?'

The priest smiled and said: 'Go and see Mrs Orzechowska, the doctor's wife, and tell her that I sent you.' And he gave me Mrs Orzechowska's address, even though I knew where she lived, but I did not say anything because I was pretending not to be from Włodawa. But Mrs Orzechowska and her husband recognised me straightaway and told me not to be afraid. I burst into tears and told them everything. Then Mrs Orzechowska sent me into the country to a priest she knew who knew that I was Jewish. The priest taught me how to talk so that no one would know I was Jewish, how you must not say 'Mr Priest' but 'father', and many other things. I stayed there for several days.

One night Mrs Orzechowska and her husband came and took me to the Red Cross at Chelmno and told me that now I was called Marysia Malinowska, that I was eight, I came from Modlin, I was born in Prużany, my father was a major, my mother had died and my father had been taken prisoner by the Germans. Mrs Orzechowska testified that she knew me and asked them to take care of me. From there I was taken by a rich lady; she had a second husband who was the son of a German and who wanted to be a *Volksdeutsch*. I was going to have to stand before a commission, and Mrs Preudowa asked me if by any chance I was Jewish, because if I was I could not go to the commission, since they would take some blood from my ear and they would be able to tell at once. But I did not tell her the truth, though I really did not want to go there. There were several Germans on the commission and they asked me about various things, about my life before the war, what my

---

mother had been ill with, and what I used to eat; and they looked me in the eye and told me to look at them too. I looked them straight in the eye and pretended not to be in the least afraid. And then they ordered me to walk to and fro across the room, because you can also tell a Jew from his walk. But somehow they could not tell, because they said that I could be a German.

(Archive of the VJHC in Kraków, statement no. 3)

12. BERL LIEBLEIN

Born 18 January 1930 in Skole; son of Markus and Lea
(Statement taken by Dr Dawid Haupt, Przemyśl)

... At night my cousin and I returned to the flat that the *Ordners* [Jewish police] had taken us from in the morning. As we were talking Yiddish to each other, my Uncle Aron Wilf came out of his hiding-place and concealed us up in the loft. For the next 24 hours we stayed there without eating anything; then we all escaped with uncle's family to the village of Korostów. There my uncle went to see a poacher he knew. The man's name was Michał Swystun. He hid us in his house for about six months, putting himself in great danger both from the Germans and the Banderists. The Banderists behaved particularly cruelly towards the Jews. One bandit in particular, Suslyniec, was notorious throughout the district for the atrocities he had committed; he had many murders on his conscience. He once lured 12 Jews to his hide-out, promising that he would conceal them, and then he and his gang murdered all of them. Another time he got hold of two young Jewish girls; he hung them head down from a branch, and lit fires under them; in this way they burned to death.

Swystun was most afraid of Suslyniec's gang, for if they had found us they would have murdered him and his family.

141

When more and more people in the village began saying that Swystun was harbouring Jews, he took us to the woods on Krasne mountain, near Paraska mountain. He built us a bunker there for six people, 50 centimetres high and three metres long. He brought blankets and a quilt for us from home. The entrance was hidden by a big block of wood that had been there for a long time, and by branches. The bunker turned out to be too small, and two weeks later Swystun helped uncle to build another bunker which was three metres long, one metre high at the entrance and 1.80 metres high further along. Swystun continued to look after us; he brought food part of the way up the mountain at night, and we carried it to our hide-out further up. Swystun was our guardian angel; without him we would certainly have died.

One day, as a result of long, heavy rains, our bunker collapsed and water got in; we sat inside, soaked to the skin, and the blankets and quilt were wet through. Fortunately, Swystun came at night and helped us yet again. He went to the village and fetched a saw and some other tools. He came with his brother-in-law and together they mended the bunker, propped it up where it was needed, chopped some wood and built a huge bonfire at which we dried our clothes and bedding. Swystun did not hesitate to steal a primus stove from his neighbour, and he brought it to our bunker, so that from then on we cooked on the stove and in winter we were warm. We had water nearby, and we washed frequently. Uncle kept us supplied with meat – as the need arose, he went hunting for wild goats and deer.

During the move from the first bunker to the second one, my uncle's nephew, Majer Wilf, broke his leg. And again Swystun helped; he set the leg himself in a wooden splint, and he and my brother-in-law carried him from where the accident had taken place to the new bunker.

In the summer of 1944 hard times began for us. The Germans sent Swystun to work at the front fortifying their positions. For two weeks we lived only off our reserves, cutting our rations more and more.

For two months we lived near the front. On one side of Paraska mountain was the Russian front line, and on the other the German line. At that time the Banderists had stopped their attacks and had run away in various directions. Despite this, we could not cross to the Soviet army, as we would have had to go across the mountain, and then the Germans would have spotted us from their trenches. On top of this, all the roads were mined.

In October 1944 the Soviet forces advanced and took Skole. Then we went back to Skole. The town was almost all burnt down, and the houses in ruins. The Soviet soldiers, especially the Jewish ones, received us warmly, and shared what food they had with us.

After we had been in Skole for a few days the Banderists attacked the town by night; a fight began in which a Jewish boy, Goldfischer, from Skole, was killed, after he had survived the Nazis.

The Banderists searched the house we were living in, but they did not find us because we had managed to get out and hide in the ruins of the house next door. We heard the Banderists asking each other if they had seen Wilf – my uncle. Someone had obviously hired them to murder him. Uncle suspected that it was Topolnicki, the Ukrainian teacher, who had a lot of things belonging to uncle and to other Jews, and wanted to get rid of inconvenient witnesses.

I left Skole and went to Lwów, where I was put into an orphanage, and from there I went to Przemyśl. I am living at the Jewish Children's Home in Przemyśl; I am going to school and I am learning Hebrew.

(Archive of the CJHC, statement no. 880/II)

13. MOJŻESZ KIN

Born 1931 in Narajów, near Brzeżany; son of Selig and Estera
(Statement taken by Dr Dawid Haupt, Przemyśl)

... In June 1943 I lost my mother. The *Aktion* had finished. My
parents, thinking that things were quiet now in the ghetto,
came out of their hiding-place and ran into some Ukrainian
militiamen who were searching the hide-outs where the Jews
had been hiding. My father realised instantly what was going
on and he ran into the lavatory to hide; he stayed there till the
policemen had gone away. They took my mother then, and
we never saw her again. We stayed in hiding for another week
in the cellar, then one night we got away to the Narajów
woods 16 kilometres away. Nine of us went together: four
from our family and uncle's family, in which there were five
people. In the woods we lived in the open in some thick
bushes. We had only our coats to cover ourselves with. Every
few days a group of us would go to Narajów to get food. We
lived like this till the autumn of 1943. Then we built an underground bunker with walls and a ceiling made of planks. We
put in some boards to sleep on. A good friend of my father's, a
Pole called Hajnusz who was the director of the glassworks,
put us in touch with another group of 16 Jews, so there were
now 25 of us. Hajnusz bought food for us and he and his son
drove up and left it in the woods, and at night we took everything to the bunker. Hajnusz brought us potatoes, flour and
kasha, and sometimes bread. We cooked in the bunker. The
most difficult thing to get was water; we had to go all the way
to a village outside the town called Huta, several kilometres
away from our hide-out. To save ourselves the journey, we
dug a ditch in the wood in which we collected rainwater, and
we used that to cook with.

One night five people from the bunker went into the
village for potatoes. On the way they were attacked by the
Banderists, and my uncle's son was wounded. The others
managed to get away. When uncle heard his son groaning

from the injury, he turned back intending to save him and help him get away, but the Banderists caught him; they killed his son, shot my uncle and then threw both the bodies into the water. Hajnusz told us about all this later.

During the winter the number of Jews in the woods rose to 65. On 16 March 1944 the Banderists attacked us. They had found out that a Polish man was supplying us with food, and had terrorised him into leading them to our hide-outs. When they came to our bunker they tried to trick us into coming out. They spoke to us in Russian, saying they needed mechanics and drivers. When we failed to come out they threatened that they would demolish the bunker and crush us to death inside. At this point everyone left the bunker; only two girl cousins of mine and I stayed inside. All those who went out of our bunker and out of the others on the Banderists' orders died. On that day the Banderists shot 51 people dead in the woods; only 14 survived. My father and both my brothers died then. From the bunker we heard the sound of the rifle shots. It was the Banderists, shooting those poor people who had hidden in the woods to escape death at the hands of the Nazi brutes. In the afternoon Hajnusz came to the woods, and when we recognised him by his voice, my two cousins and I left the shelter, and 11 more Jews who had survived came out of the other bunkers.

Hajnusz took us to where the massacre had taken place; there we saw a huge pile of bodies lying one on top of another on a demolished bunker in which people had previously been hiding. I could not see the bodies of my father or brothers as they were underneath a whole mass of other bodies, and there was no time to pull the other corpses off and bury them because there were still some Banderists about in the woods. Hajnusz told us that the Banderists had first killed the children, then the adults.

From that time all of us who had survived lived in one bunker. We agreed with Hajnusz that he would continue to bring us food up to the wood, but he never appeared again; later it became clear that the Banderists – these were young local Ukrainian nationalists – had burned all the farms of the Polish settlers, including Hajnusz's house, and as a result he had fled to Brzeżany.

We were deprived of Hajnusz's help, and we had nothing to live on. The nearest village of Polish settlers, Huta, had also been burned. At night we went there, took potatoes from the deserted clamps and cooked them in the bunker. In this way, living only on potatoes, we survived from March to July 1944, when we were liberated by the Soviet army. In the meantime the Banderists had sometimes returned to the wood searching for Jews, but we were on the alert and they did not find us.

I remember one more terrible story from my time in the woods. On 16 March 1944, after the murder of 51 Jews by the Banderists, when we left our bunker and went to where the massacre had taken place, we found there a young Jewish boy, Symcha N., from Narajów, who was lying seriously wounded on the pile of corpses. He told us that the Banderists had shot him and three other children; they had ordered them to lie on some potatoes and had killed them one by one. One of the Banderists had shot him twice in the head, and when he saw that he was still alive he shot him once again near the stomach. At that point Symcha had become unconscious, and when he came round, after the Banderists had left, he was alone on a heap of corpses.

We took Symcha to our bunker. There we could only feed him on potato pap and water. Despite that he slowly got better and in the end he recovered completely. He is an orphan, like me; he lost his parents and his brothers and sisters that same day in the woods. He is now living in Brzeżany.

(Archive of the CJHC, statement no. 879/II)

14. HERMAN AMSTERDAM

Born 26 October 1930 in Mielec

(Statement taken by Dr Dawid Haupt, Przemyśl)

... We decided to run away to the woods. It was on Yom Kippur, 1942. We did not take any bedding or food with us, and only about 3,000 złotys in cash. On Yom Kippur we fasted in the woods, and the next day we found a scrap of paper on the grass on which my aunt had written to tell us which part of the woods she was hiding in. We went there and joined our grandparents and aunts and uncles. There were ten of us. In that place we did not yet have shelters. We lived in the open air. The number of our friends in the woods rose day by day, and reached 50 people. We bought guns and ammunition from local farmers. We had rifles, revolvers, grenades and ammunition. The Jews bought food in the village at night, and my father even bought two sheep, which we slaughtered in the woods, so there was enough meat to go round.

We were not to live peacefully for long. A Polish forester told the German authorities that there were Jews hiding in the woods, and for the first time the police organised a surprise round-up and captured 30 of our comrades, who were savagely beaten and then shot.

In revenge for this tip-off, some of the village boys, professional criminals who sometimes hid in the woods and came to see us, shot the forester. The boys knew our hide-outs; they were on close terms with us and often brought us food and vodka. My aunt cooked and we ate with them. It was only in the autumn that they left us, and in the winter they stopped coming back.

For the winter the Jews built themselves bunkers and moved into them. We dug out our bunker at the top of a deep gully. On top it was covered with planks on which we packed clay, hidden by grass and branches. We had to walk three kilometres for water.

My father made us shoes from sheepskin and rags. At night

he would go with some others to the village to buy food, and when the money ran out he went stealing. For as long as it was possible, we stole potatoes, beetroot, cabbage and so on from the fields, and when that stopped father stole from the farms.

In the spring the village boys came back and built a separate hide-out for themselves. My aunt and uncle and some of the other Jews moved into their hide-out. One of them fell in love with my aunt and she became his wife. One night the boys came back drunk; they had an argument among themselves, and when they went to sleep one of them shot my aunt and her husband as they slept. After this the one who had fired the shots and his friends ran away from the woods. My father tried to take revenge for his sister; right after her death he chased after the culprit and even shot at him, but he did not hit him. Later, my father died by the hand of that bandit, who shot him when he was stealing food one night for the Jews; I shall come to this later.

In May 1943 there were again 60 people in the woods. More and more were joining us. They escaped from the ghetto or the camp and came to us in the woods. At that time my father built a new long tunnel underground which he had designed himself. It was a narrow tunnel with twisting corridors. The entrance was concealed with thin tree trunks, earth and pine needles. Father did this because he had heard that there was to be another round-up. These rumours proved to be true. A few days later, the German police cordoned off the woods in which we were hiding and organised a man-hunt. They passed near our bunker with their dogs; we heard their voices, but they did not find us. When the German army moved away, we moved our hide-out one kilometre away. Things were quieter now. My father and his friends started to go stealing again in the local villages, and one day they even brought a pig back. In July of the same year the Germans organised another round-up, but they did not find anybody. The day after the round-up there was an accident. One of my uncles was carrying a hand-grenade, and it went off and

148

blew him to pieces and wounded my father. We had some bandages in the woods, and these were used to dress father's wounds.

For the next three months we lived in a shack instead of a bunker. In the autumn we moved back to the bunker. Then there was another round-up; this time the Germans killed five people who had been hiding in other hide-outs, but they did not find ours.

We moved again to another wood, the 'Black Wood'. Soon afterwards we were attacked by a forester with a group of farmers, obviously wanting to rob us. Fortunately we spotted them soon enough for one of us to take a rifle and shoot at them. That was enough to make the whole gang of cowards run away.

A few days later another of my uncles set off to the village for supplies. The trip was a disaster because at the moment when my uncle had gone into a farmer's house, leaving another man on guard outside with a rifle, someone attacked the guard unexpectedly and took his rifle, and when uncle heard a shout from the yard and ran out of the cottage, he was hit by a bullet from the rifle. He managed to make it back to the woods, however. To be able to dress the wound, my father and one of his sisters set off to the village to get some bandages. This expedition ended tragically for my father. In front of one of the farmhouses he was shot by the bandit who had killed my aunt in the woods. My father was seriously wounded, and an hour later the same bandit put him to death. We even heard the shot that killed him.

Soon afterwards one of the farmers killed that bandit with an axe. I do not know exactly how it came about; we only heard that on Christmas Eve 1943 a farmer had killed the bandit in his sleep, with an axe.

We spent the winter of 1943–44 in the woods. Things were relatively calm; there were no round-ups by the Germans or attacks by the bandits. There were about 30 of us left. In the late spring of 1944 we heard the boom of cannon fire. We knew what that meant, and we took heart. More and more frequently farmers started coming in from the local villages; believe it or not, at times our numbers rose to 10,000. They had run away from the Germans, afraid of repression or of being sent to do forced labour. With us there was even a Soviet prisoner-of-war who had run away from a German camp. It turned out that he was a doctor, and he treated my cousin in the woods when she became ill with typhus. In the late autumn of that year (1944), a Soviet plane circled over the woods. After some time it burst into flames in the air and fell to the ground not far away. I happened to be nearby as I was bringing a sack of potatoes. I had to leave the potatoes in a field because I could see uniformed Germans approaching. The Germans started chasing me, but I managed to run to the wood quicker than them and I hid there.

The Poles, seeing that the front was drawing closer and closer, left the woods, and again there was just a handful of Jews and two Soviet soldiers. The front was now only a kilometre away from the wood. A dozen or so Jews joined us, and there were 62 of us in all.

One day, as the first snow was falling, my uncle and I were sitting near our bunker, the entrance to which was permanently hidden. Then, to our horror, we saw German soldiers a few steps away. We had no time to go and hide in the bunker, and we just crouched under some bushes. For several hours we could not get back to the bunker, as more and more Germans kept arriving and searching the woods. We were told later that on that day several thousand German military police had cordoned off the woods and searched them. They succeeded in capturing 15 Jews, whom they took away and no doubt killed.

On 27 November 1944 all 47 Jews living in the woods set off to cross the front. The adults armed themselves with rifles, revolvers and grenades. When we reached the front line, we came under heavy fire from the Germans. Our patrol, which formed the rearguard, returned the fire with rifles, and in that time we ran towards the Soviet lines, shouting, 'Comrades, do not shoot, we're partisans'. But they obviously did not understand us because they fired at us and even killed one girl, Tyla Hirsch. The Germans killed several of us, including my grandfather, my cousin and Motek Fenek. There were also ten people wounded, seven of whom died in a Soviet hospital. The rest of us were taken to prison, where we were kept for three weeks and, after being questioned, were released. That was in the town of Sędziszów.

From our family, one of my father's brothers, one of his sisters, my own little sister and I had survived.

At present I am living at the Jewish Children's Home in Przemyśl.

(Archive of the CJHC, statement no. 881/II)

15. NUCHIM WERNER

No further details recorded

(*Statement taken by Dr Dawid Haupt, Przemyśl*)

... I was now all alone in the world. I was so unhappy that I wished that they had killed me too, because I was so sad on my own.

But I went on with uncle and his family. We came to Bitków and hid in a haystack in a meadow. We lived there for two months. At night uncle went out to a farmer he knew and brought back supplies. After two months one of the farmers set the Ukrainian police on us; they surrounded the haystack and ordered us to come out. When we did not do what they said, they began shooting. Then all the men came out (there were six of us), and two women and one child stayed inside. As soon as we came out, uncle and I started to run away. The policemen fired at us; they missed me, but uncle was hit in the leg. We ran into the woods. In the woods uncle went berserk; I do not know whether it was the pain of the wound or whether he went insane, but he kept on shouting, and he ran into the village. There they caught him and shot him along with all the other men and the two women and the child, who they had found in the haystack.

I was left on my own in the woods. For three days I wandered about there, eating berries and raw mushrooms.

On the fourth day, I met a gamekeeper who had known my father, and he took me to a hide-out in the woods where lots of Jews from Bitków were hiding. We lived in an underground bunker; the gamekeeper brought us food. A few months later the Banderists attacked us. They surrounded the bunker and spoke to us in Russian, pretending to be Soviets. When we came out of the bunker and saw that it was the Banderists, we started to run away. They opened fire on us and killed about 20 people.

Fourteen people survived, with one boy wounded. From then on the gamekeeper stopped coming and we had to find food ourselves.

At that time a Jewish boy came to us in the woods who the Banderists had caught and tied up and left in a barn. They had been going to torture him the next day to make him tell them where the Jews' bunkers were. In the night the boy cut through the ropes and ran away to us. He told us everything and added that in the barn he had seen two rifles, a revolver and a lot of ammunition which had been hidden there.

The next night he took two of our boys and went with them to get the rifles and ammunition. The boys got into the barn and took the guns and ammunition. Once they had it, they went to the stables and took a cow, which they led back to the woods. Among us there was a butcher; he slaughtered the cow, and we lived on the meat, because we did not have any bread or flour.

From then on we were not short of food, because the boys would take the guns, go to the cowsheds of those farmers whose sons were in the Banderists, and take a cow or a calf. The farmers knew that we were armed and did not dare to leave their cottages, though they could hear that there was someone in the cowshed.

We lived like this till we were liberated by the Soviet army.

(Archive of the CJHC, statement no. 887/II)

16. LEON GEWANDTER

Born 16 August 1932 in Bukaczowce, near Rohatyn; son of Wiktor and Róża Rotstein

(Statement taken by M. Hochberg-Mariańska, Kraków)

Under the Soviets I went to first and second years at school. Father worked as a district vet. When the Germans came, father had to leave his job and another vet, a Pole, came, but he mostly sat in the office, and all the people in the district knew father and trusted him, so they kept coming to him and he continued to work secretly.

As soon as the Germans came, Jews began to be murdered in the villages. The Ukrainians murdered whole families and drowned them in the Dniester. Before the war Bukaczowce had been a village; the Soviets made it into a town. There were no more than about 1,000 Jews, mostly merchants, shopkeepers and butchers.

The first *Aktion* was aimed at cripples and the sick; they took 200 people and transported them out somewhere. At the same time a similar *Aktion* was carried out in Rohatyn. After the first *Aktion* a carpenter we knew who was clever and had lots of good ideas made us a shelter in the cellar, hidden by shelves; on the shelves there were jars and bottles as usual, and behind there was the hiding-place. Then all the doctors were sent to a camp, I do not remember the name, but it was not far away; and they took father. Someone had informed on him that he was still practising even though it was forbidden. Two months later father came back, thanks to the efforts of Limberger, the commissar of the *Liegenschaft* [German land

153

administration]. He was a German who before the war had been *starosta* [head of the village] in Bukaczowce; when the Soviets came he had escaped, and had come back with the Germans. He knew us well and wrote that he needed father. He helped us generally with various matters for as long as he was able to.

Before the second *Aktion* they brought in the Jews from Bursztyn; there were more of them than of the local Jews. The Germans arrived for the *Aktion*, but their trucks stopped at the bridge and the Jewish policemen told us about them. So we went down to our hide-out and waited there for a day and a half till the *Aktion* was over. I do not remember the dates or any details; I know that they transported many people, but it was more the people from Bursztyn than the local Jews. The Jewish police behaved quite well; they did not give anyone away, and they even helped people when they could.

By then father definitely wanted to find somewhere where we could hide, and he made an agreement with a Polish farmer called Stocki. He lived in the meadows on the Dniester, in an isolated cottage. We made ourselves a bunker there, leading from a passage underneath the main room. You lifted up the floorboards in the room and went along a passage as far as the barn. I was there with my parents and my brother and also two Jewish horse-traders. We spent a month there, then things calmed down and we went back to Bukaczowce. To begin with father managed to find work in the *Liegenschaft*, and then there was an *Arbeitseinsatz* and they issued identity cards. But that soon came to an end, and the farmer on the Dniester would not take us back, so we had to go to Rohatyn, because by then they had expelled all the Jews from Bukaczowce.

We had not been there long when the greatest misfortune of all happened. Someone informed on my father. Some people said it was one of the Jews, others that it was the Ukrainian who worked as a receiver of property left by the Jews. Father was accused of not having handed over all his veterinary equipment. The Gestapo came to Rohatyn one evening and took my parents and my brother away. I was at a neighbours' at that time, and that was how I survived. At first no one would tell me anything, but after a while I found out that they had all been shot straightaway. They found a photograph of me and they knew that I also belonged to the family. They searched for me and threatened the *Judenrat* that if I did not turn myself in they would shoot 300 people, but all that time I was hiding at the Jewish carpenter's, the one who specialised in making shelters.

We were expecting the final *Aktion* any day; every night there were sentries posted in order to be able to warn people. Once the *Aktion* began, we stayed in the shelter for a whole week. There were 16 of us there. After a week we left the shelter and split up. I went with the carpenter's family, but then I left them because I wanted to go back to Bukaczowce for my things. It was the Ukrainian Pentecost. There were lots of people about; I hid in the corn, and went to sleep. By then I was very thin and dirty and my clothes were in rags. Someone saw me as I was asleep and they thought I was dead. One Ukrainian farmer came and recognised me. Everyone there in the village knew me because I often went there with father when he had to treat sick cattle. The farmer took me home to his cottage, and let me have a wash and something to eat. From there, I went at night to the Polish farmer who had our things, and he took me in. I stayed in his attic for several months. Then they started round-ups of people from the villages to send to forced labour in Germany; people resisted and would not go, and then the Ukrainians and the Germans would burn their village. My farmer escaped with his family to another village, but he could not take me with him because I did not have any papers, and everyone in the district knew me. There were a lot of Jews hiding in that village; I joined them and we went into the woods. In the woods there were already a lot of Jewish bunkers that were well built, with double entrances. We were in touch with each other, and five of the Jews had rifles. The Germans and the Ukrainians were afraid to enter the woods. Two people knew about our hide-outs: one Pole and one Ukrainian. The Pole always warned us when we were in some danger. The Ukrainian once got drunk and talked about the bunkers; so the Germans dressed him in a uniform and ordered him to take them and show them. But he sobered up and took them to some derelict bunkers where no one was living any more. The Jews made forays at night to properties that were under German administration and brought back all the food we needed. We were not short of anything; the only difficulty we had was with washing clothes, and we all had lice. Several times the Germans tried to organise raids, but they were afraid to go deep into the woods and so they did not harm us.

When the front began to draw closer, they began digging trenches around the woods and setting up artillery, and it became more and more difficult to go out for food. When we saw that the Germans were blowing up the railway tracks we knew that the Russians must be close and a few of us at a time passed through the German positions to the Dniester and the Świerz. By then there were many Poles there who were also hiding from the Ukrainians. At that time the Banderists were murdering Jews and Poles. We waited by the river till the Soviet army arrived.

(Archive of the VJHC in Kraków, statement no. 131)

---

17. FRYDA EINSIEDLER

Born 1935 in Grodzisk, near Łańcut
(Statement taken by Iza Lauer, Kraków)

When the Germans came, they drove us out of Grodzisk across the San. They came to us in the night and told us that by morning we should be gone. Mama left our things with a Catholic lady; she only took her valuables with her, and we set off on foot, a whole group of us, Mama, my two sisters, grandfather and grandmother. Only my father was missing, because he is in America. We walked to Przemyśl. The Germans let us across the San on the ferry, and on the other side the Russians were already there. We spent a year in Przemyśl, and then a year in Brzeżany. Mama asked my father to arrange papers for us.

The war took us by surprise in Brzeżany; there was fighting in the streets. We were afraid that we would be murdered, and we moved to Przemyśl. In Przemyśl the German police searched our flat, but they knew what to look for and where: they asked right away for my coat and my sister's; they unpicked the collars and our money was sewn in there. They turned everything upside down and beat everyone up; the house was cordoned off by the police. We had nothing to eat. Mama met a Polish man from our town and asked him to take me there. Grandmother had already slipped back and she was all right under the Russians there. The man took me, and Mama gave him some money. On the way I called him 'Daddy', pretending to be his daughter. Grandmother was very pleased. She wrote to Mama; the first letter arrived but not the second, because they had already set up the ghetto by then. Three months later my elder sister (one year older) came and joined us. My mother kept my little sister with her.

My mother and sister and the whole family were taken in during the first *Aktion* in Przemyśl and sent to Bełżec.

Where we were they started rounding up Jews. To begin with they only took those who wanted to go, and some people went because it was all the same to them. Grandmother said that she would have gone too if we had not been with her. The Jews who volunteered were not enough for the Germans, and they began rounding people up. Grandmother hid with us in the fields and the woods. At night we went into barns to sleep. We ate beetroots from the fields, and the Poles who had our things sometimes gave us bread or baked potatoes. That was a great luxury, because most of the time we ate beetroot that we baked in a fire, and it was very bitter. How hungry we were! Abandoned, dirty, bitten by lice; it was terrible.

There were piles of branches in the fields; we made ourselves a sort of den and lived there.

We had nothing to drink all day; I was almost dead with
thirst. Grandmother went out and found a marsh. She took
some sandy water in a mug, and when she brought it back we
were so pleased we kissed her hand. Once a boy came past; he
lifted up the branches and saw us. He was going to go straight
to the police, but grandmother bribed him.

Sometimes we sat under the sheaves of corn; it was
autumn and the farmers could have come, but grandmother
said that it was all the same to her, she felt so weak; she
was an old lady, after all; she must have been about 70. And
we no longer cared about anything either; if someone had
found us we would have asked them to shoot us as soon as
possible.

Once we went out very early and we sat in a bush waiting
for the sun to come out, because it was so terribly cold. We
had been waiting such a long time for the sun! Then there was
some movement. A good Polish lady had sent us some hot
baked potatoes. We were really pleased; but although she had
given us a big bowl, it still did not fill us, so we lit a fire and
baked more potatoes ourselves. One woman saw the smoke;
she came up to us, and told us not to be afraid. She arranged
with my grandmother that she would bring some bread under
her clothes. But her brother-in-law's friend, Barzyk, used to
catch Jews; she probably told him that she had seen us, and
grandmother was worried. We moved to Bukorzycka. That
friend came looking for us in the evening; he saw us and
waited for us to come out. We thought our time had come. He
called out: 'Halt! Where are you off to?' He took our bags, and
when he saw that we had some bread, he asked who had
given it to us. We did not want to give the woman away and
we said we had it brought from home. We were crying the
whole time; grandmother called him by his Christian name
and said that we were so young and that we wanted to live,
but he showed no mercy. We refused to go with him. He beat
grandmother terribly. I tried to run away and I was going to

jump in the river, but he caught up with me and dragged me by the ears back to grandmother. We lay on the grass and would not move, for he could not do anything worse to us. He beat us with a big stick. Then he went off and I told my sister that we should run away. My sister would not do it, so I grabbed my things from grandmother because I thought I would need them, and I jumped into the ditch. It was dark, and I heard my grandmother and my sister shouting in the distance. After that I never saw them again.

A Polish lady we knew lived nearby. I met her with a boy; they asked what the shouting had been in the fields. I told them, but they were afraid to put me up for the night. It was already dark; I went to the village and went into the barn of one of the farmers, intending to sleep there, but by chance one of the neighbours came and saw me. He was a good man, but I was afraid he would tell someone I was there, so I went on. I hid in some nettles; I took no notice of the fact that I got stung, and I was so tired that I just fell asleep.

In the morning I did not know where to go. My clothes were all in rags, and everyone stared at me. I decided I would go to the owner of the sawmill; he had bought two cupboards from grandmother and had paid in bread, but he still had not paid everything. I thought that he might help me a bit. The village administrator had our sewing machine, which he also had only half paid for. I thought that in this way I might survive for a while. In fact the sawmill owner's wife did let me change my clothes and told me to go up to the attic. I asked her to find out what had happened to grandmother, but in such a way that no one would guess that I was staying with her.

She found out that my grandmother and sister were no longer alive. That farmer had not been able to take them in, but the next day a woman came to grandmother and talked with her, wanting to help her. Another woman, who had a lot of our things and did not want us to survive and take the things back, had gone straight to the police.

The policemen had been going to take the good woman with

them too. Grandmother begged them to let her go, and they did; my grandmother and sister were taken to the cemetery.

The man kept me a few days and then asked me to go to another village and say that my father had been sent to do forced labour in Germany. But I was afraid that people would ask too many questions, and I did not want to do what he said. As I could not stay with him any more, I went to another lady I knew; she said that she felt very sorry for me, but she was afraid that her children would tell someone, and she sent me to another lady. She kept me for a few days, but people found out in the village and I had to leave. Another woman that I stayed with for some time told me to go and bring all the things that I had left with different people, and then told me to go begging round the other villages. From the time that grandmother had been killed, no one had done me any harm. The village people threw stones and threatened me with the police, but I did not do anything about it, they were not being serious. By now I knew everyone, and I knew who was good and would not do me any wrong.

One day I called in at one farm and the lady there took care of me; I told her who I was. She was a converted Jew, and her husband was a Pole. Her mother-in-law was very religious and very good. They were country people, but intelligent. They washed me, fed me and let me play with their child in the garden. Life was easier for me then. They altered one of grandmother's skirts to make a dress for me.

I slept in the pig shed; they put some straw down and gave me a blanket. They brought me the same food that they ate.

Things were fine for me among the cows and the pigs. Sometimes in the daytime I went out into the garden. Then they sent me to some relatives of theirs; I was going to live part of the time in one place and part in the other. They told me that if ever I had nowhere to go, I could always come back to them. They were so good to me that I shall never forget them; when I go to America I shall repay them. For a long time I went from one neighbour to another. Then one of the women took me to Przemyśl and I found a place in a home. I had been there for four months when the Soviets came.

Now I have already had a letter and a telegram from my father.

(Archive of the VJHC in Kraków, statement no. 458)

18. HELENA ARBEITER

Born 1930 in Baranów, near Lublin

(Statement taken by S. Lewin, Lublin)

The Germans came to us once every two days for money. The money was collected and given to them. They had recently ordered our boys to clean their bicycles and in the restaurant there were 12 Gestapo officers and some Poles. The sentries surrounded the town, and they got drunk and rang a bell for all the Jews to go out onto the street. They drove 4,000 Jews from the Polish district onto one street where the synagogue was. The younger people went; the older ones would not go, saying 'We do not care what will happen'. My parents and I got ready to run away. Grandfather hid in the cellar; he said that he had no desire to live. After a few days he came out of the cellar, and they spotted him at once; they ordered him to be taken to the police, but no one would take him. When he came out of the cellar they searched our house and found a lot of goods. One Pole who had been resettled took him in and kept him for two weeks. Then grandfather came to us because in the other place he had been robbed. We had to run away too, as we were being victimised by Olek Maruszek. We spent the first night in a cowshed. On the same farm there were some other Jews; they heard us talking and came out. They said they could not manage there any more, and they set off for Michow. They were killed on the way, and we were left behind. We were in the woods. We kept meeting more and

161

more Jews; in the end there were 30 of us. We were starving; in the evenings we stole potatoes because we were so hungry. The smoke could be seen; some shepherds noticed it and told everyone in the town that there were Jews in the woods. Maruszek, who was in the *AK* [*Armia Krajowa*, or Home Army, the Polish partisan organisation], came and he shot at us. At first we were frightened and stood still, and then we ran off in different directions. He wounded one of us; he also caught two children, and killed one of them on the way. He tied the other one to the branch of a tree and shot him. Later we saw someone tied to a tree. We thought it was a bandit. When we plucked up courage to go closer, we saw that it was the boy, who had been hanged. We spent several days looking for each other. The wounded were lying in the woods. The next day shots were suddenly heard. We knew that the Germans were in the town so we thought it was them.

Someone fired at us. They chased us for two kilometres. We were completely exhausted. We slept in the woods, each person separately. One woman had to leave her young child in the corn and run away. The following evening we went looking for the child. We looked for each other, and we did not know who had been killed. Then we went to another wood to cook.

In the woods there was a Jewish partisan group that helped us. They had machine guns. Dąbrowski's unit was the only one that accepted Jews. They were part of the Russian partisan movement, but while Dąbrowski was away the partisans gathered the Jews together and started shooting at them. The Jews were armed. One of them ran away and they started to chase him. He fell over and lay as if he were dead, because he was exhausted. Then he got up; everyone had gone. That partisan stayed with us, and while he was with us he went down with typhus. Dąbrowski had given him a place where he could stay in bed, but he had had to run away to us because he was being hunted.

We were living in a marsh in an alder forest. We were always up to our waists in water, because there no one could find us. We built ourselves a shack. Sometimes we nearly drowned in the mud and the swamps. We stole potatoes. And then that bandit found out about us again. He came and was going to kill us all. Wherever we escaped to, he found us. The partisans kept an eye on us. They were constantly forming new partisan units, and these were constantly being knocked out. Things were so bad for us that we wanted to get into the ghetto. We had no water. We went to the ghetto in Adamów near Łuków. The Jews would not let us in because they were afraid of outsiders. The Germans drove up and said that when they caught Jews from outside they killed them. We had to run away from there to escape the transports. It was cold. My mother gave birth in the snow. No one would let us inside. The baby cried terribly. It lived for two weeks. My mother was so weak that she could not walk. We crept into a barn and slept there without the farmer knowing.

Then we went to the ghetto in Końska Wola and there we caught typhus. There were five people to a bed. There was no doctor. We had nothing to eat, and only coffee to drink. My mother died. My sister would not go anywhere; she said she wanted to stay where mother was buried. We wanted to go back to Baranów, but we found out that there was an *Aktion* there. We set off into the country with father. Father went to find some people he knew in a hide-out. They had made a kitchen in a barn. The partisans came to us.

Our hide-out was discovered, and we had to run away. During the round-up my father was badly wounded. They shot at me. Afterwards I heard the farmers who we had asked to hide us arranging to kill him. Father was lying in a barn and was in such dreadful pain that he wanted to hang himself. When I fell asleep for a moment from exhaustion, he started looking for a belt so as to put himself out of his torment. The farmer threw us out. Father could not move; he wanted the Germans to come and put an end to his pain. Then he went out and never returned. I was left alone. I slept for 24 hours solid. In the daytime I stayed in the barn, and at night I went out. The Polish partisans were looking for us. Once I was with a woman. We tried to run away but they caught us. They asked about a partisan called Szymon, who had been witness to the shooting of some Jewish partisans and had got away. They promised that they would not do anything to us if only we told them where Szymon was. They followed us everywhere. Later they threatened to kill us. We were so badly in need of water that we did not feel any need to eat. The farmers closed their barns to stop us getting in. Little children shouted at us 'Jews, Jews'. We ran away back into the woods. We stayed there till the Red Army came.

(Archive of the CJHC, statement no. 272)

19. FRANCISZKA GUTER

Born 9 April 1932 in Kraków; daughter of Edward and Maria Grünes

(*Written account*)

To begin with there were 'only' round-ups, arrests, searches, *Ausweise*, then *Kennkarten* and the ghetto.

In 1941 people began to talk about the ghetto; by 20 March everyone with a *Kennkarte* had to be living in the ghetto. Everyone was hoping for the best. The Germans would not have built those big walls around the ghetto just for a few weeks, and in two months the war would be over.

We were given a flat at 9 Traugutta Street; uncle and his family lived in one room and our family in the other. To begin with things were relatively quiet. You could leave the ghetto if you worked outside or if you had a special pass. Of course, you could not ride on the trams, and you had to wear an armband, but these were trifles compared to what came later – the mass transports to what the Germans called the 'Himmels-Kommando'.

Suddenly, and completely unexpectedly, one day towards the end of May 1942 the Germans began putting stamps in the *Kennkarten* of workers in their firms and of top-rate specialists. A few days later the German military police cordoned off the ghetto. Our windows looked out beyond the ghetto. They had to be blacked out, and it was forbidden to open them. There was a heatwave then. The flats where the windows could not be opened became infested with bed-bugs. That lasted, as far as I remember, nine days. That was the first large-scale *Aktion*. The next day they began to assemble 'unnecessary' people (those who had no stamp); they were to gather in the yards of the apartment houses where they lived. The Germans checked to make sure that no one without a stamp remained. The transport left and when, an hour later, I went out of the building, on the alleyways of Dąbrówka and Janowa Wola, where 60 people had been shot, there was still blood. The caretakers of the buildings swept it up like you sweep up mud after the rain. No one thought anything of it, no one prayed for the victims. People were glad that it was over, that others were still alive, that after such an outburst things would be quiet. But the Germans who had cordoned off the ghetto were still in power. Barely eight days later a new command was issued: since the previous segregation had not been properly carried out, there would be another, and this time it would not be stamps but blue cards. Those designated for the transport were not allowed home but were sent at once under SS escort to the Optima [a former chocolate factory in Kraków, in which during the German occupation Jews worked at various trades]. My parents had not obtained those cards, ownership of which meant that for a while longer you could stay alive. They were kept at the Optima for 24 hours, condemned to death. My father even sent letters to Poles he knew, who we were to go to for help. These letters seemed like a testament to me. As I went to bed at night, I could not imagine that my mother would not come and kiss me goodnight, as she used to every night. The transport was to leave in an hour. Dr Blauówna (who was later shot while carrying out an operation) went several times to Kunde, the Gestapo officer in charge of Jewish affairs, but without success. Perec Selinger, the Jewish policeman, also tried; he had already been twice to Felens of the SS. He tried a third time and got blue cards for my parents. He won them the right to life, and pulled them from the line five minutes before the transport left. When my mother crossed the threshold of our flat she fainted. From that time, there was constant talk of evacuation. No one believed any more that things would be quiet. We knew that it would never be quiet as long as the Germans were there. On 27 October my mother took us (my younger sister and me) out of the ghetto. One of the Polish policemen let us through the gate; on the other side Mr Skarawara, a Polish acquaintance of my father's, was waiting and took us in a *dorozhka* to Mrs Jaśkowa's. We stayed there for a few days. Mrs J. did not want to upset us and so she did not tell us what was happening in the ghetto. Later I found out that an hour after we had left, the ghetto had been cordoned off, and the next day an *Aktion* had been organised. This time they had transported out most of the children, the sick, and many other people, not only those out of work. They took everyone who the Germans did not like. Children were thrown into baskets; all the patients at the epidemiology hospital were shot. My mother witnessed the following scene: when the patients were being shot, a boy of perhaps nine went up to von Malottke, a Gestapo officer infamous for his cruelty, who was carrying out the executions. The boy knelt before him and asked him in good German to spare his life because he was so young and wanted so much to live. The German smiled ironically and said: 'Oh yes, you want to live, of course, you may go then.' And when the boy had taken a few steps, he shot him from behind. This time, by a miracle, my parents survived.

After this 'evacuation' my parents decided not to wait any longer, but to try to arrange 'Aryan' papers and to leave for the country.

Mrs Jaśkowa found a place for us, and on 7 November 1942 we left Kraków with my mother. Father remained in Kraków;

he was working at the airport and for the moment was not in danger.

We lived in a village seven kilometres from Kalwaria, in an unfinished villa. An old lady lived there called Mrs Krzywacka; she was the owner of the villa. To begin with things were completely quiet; we were not registered as residents, but we could walk about the village quite openly. In January 1943 my father and grandmother joined us. They stayed in hiding to begin with. In the summer we rarely went out, as there were a lot of people working in the fields. Finally there came 1 December: Mrs Krzywacka received an anonymous letter that said something like: 'I have found out that you are harbouring Jews; if they do not leave, I shall inform the Gestapo.' We had nowhere to go, so we moved to the cellar. We covered the windows with lime. We slept on beds of straw. The worst thing was that the walls ran with water. The villa still had no tiles on the roof. Twice a day we had to wipe the walls dry. We could air the place only at night. At this time I often thought of Maria Konopnicka's poem 'In the Cellar Vault'. Every Sunday Mrs Jaśkowa came to visit us. She would get up at three in the morning, come to us in the morning and leave in the afternoon. She never neglected us, even a few days after her husband died. She came then, as always. When she was with us I felt completely safe. It seemed to me that if she, our dear guardian angel, was with us, nothing bad could happen to me; and that, since she had looked after us for such a long time, then in the future too nothing bad would come to us under her care. When our money ran out, she continued to pay for us. Another very good woman from the village, Waleria Szkołyk, also knew about us. She brought us water (the well at the villa was broken), and ran various small errands. In January some partisans moved into the villa; there were 21 of them. We did not know them. It was probably one of them who was later responsible for the blackmail.

We thought that things would be quiet now. And then on 27 May 1944 a man came to our landlady and said that he knew she was harbouring Jews. If they gave him 30,000 złotys he would leave them alone; otherwise he would inform the Gestapo. He was going to come back in a week's time to collect the money. At that time we did not have 30,000 złotys; besides, we knew that if that did not do any harm, it certainly would not help us, so we left for Kraków. My mother and sister stayed with the Jasieks on Bronowicka Street, father slept with different friends each night, grandmother was also with friends, and I stayed with the landlady's daughter-in-law.

By then Tarnopol had been taken by the Russians, and I told everyone who saw me there that I had been evacuated from Tarnopol, and that my parents had died on the journey. None of us could stay with Mrs Jaśkowa, as she had a maid who had known us before the war. I was fine in that flat; it was also nice, after the cold and damp in the cellar, to sit in the sun; but missing my family and worrying about them spoiled the joy I had in breathing fresh air. Since we had no other choice, we decided to go back to our old place in Kalwaria. On 6 June 1944 the long-awaited Anglo-American invasion began. This time everyone was convinced that the war would soon be over. They even advised us against leaving for the country. They thought that the train journey was a waste of money, for the war would end any day now. We, however, did not believe that the end of the war would come so quickly, and on 18 June we returned to the villa. This time we lived in the attic. It was very damp there. There were hundreds of mosquitoes, and they bit us mercilessly. Again there were two partisans there, honest lads; they left after a few weeks, and later came back several times. A few of the neighbours knew about us hiding there; they were particularly good and honest people, they were partisans. Mr G. and Mr P. let us know when a pacification was expected. At this time our landlady's son in Kraków was blackmailed on our account, but he came to see us and told us not to leave – that either we would die together, or we would manage to survive. And it was worth taking a risk if it was a question of saving the lives of five people – that was how he expressed himself, though before the war he had not known us. The autumn of 1944 began. There were constant acts of sabotage. The trains no longer ran regularly. The Germans were afraid to cross the village singly. In revenge for blowing up the railway line several times and the beating up of a village official who had co-operated with the Germans, on 6 November there was a pacification of the whole district. At five in the morning, 3,000 Germans cordoned off several villages. Our villa was surrounded by 60 soldiers. Father hid in the cellar, where there was a sloping place under the stairs. While the Germans stayed outside I was terrified, but when they came in I stopped caring what would happen to us; I was prepared for the worst. There were Ukrainians there then; mother just showed them her birth certificate, which was issued in Jarosław. Jarosław was already in Russian hands then. When they asked about my father, mother said he was in prison in Russia. In the villa everything went well. In the village, though, they arrested 60 farmers, including Mr G.; Mr P. managed to get away. A few days later they released 54 people, but not Mr G.; he was kept to begin with in the Montelupich prison in Kraków, and then we heard he was transported out to Gross Rosen. He is probably dead now.

There were constant disturbances in the village. On 26 November another German came to our villa (there were more of them in the village). Father did not have time to hide. It was Sunday. He looked at father's birth certificate and decided he would have to take him in. Father explained that he worked in Kraków and had just come to visit his wife for the Sunday. That did no good. Mama's pleas turned out to have more effect. Perhaps the German also had a wife and children; perhaps his hard heart was moved by a woman's tears. In any case, he left father alone. When my mother said 'God bless you', the German replied bitterly: 'You still believe that God exists?'

He left. Once more we had managed to escape death. Oh! how we longed for a little peace. We no longer even dreamed of an end to the war.

At that time there were soldiers billeted in the village. There also arrived a *Volksdeutsch*, the former organist. He had already put several local activists into the hands of the Germans. The partisans decided to 'put an end' to him. They went to a house that he used to visit, and because no one would let them in, they asked the way to Mrs Krzywacka's; on this pretext they hoped to get into the house. They got in but the man they were after got away and contacted the German police, and a few minutes later we had a visit from the Germans. At the last minute Mama managed to put father onto the roof over the terrace. Since it was dark and the villa was not surrounded, the Germans did not see him. The soldiers searched the place and left. January came. At night there was a glow in the sky. Searchlights shone over Kraków and rockets were continually going off. Once we saw an American plane in flames. For us, the glow and the falling plane were prophecies of approaching freedom.

But even just before the end we were not to know peace. On 10 January 1945 our village was again cordoned off by the Germans. Father hid in his old hiding-place in the cellar. Several Germans came into the villa. Among them were three Silesians. When they found out that we were from Jarosław, they comforted my mother, saying that they would recapture our home town and we would be able to go back there. This declaration was a great comfort to us! This time they searched the cellar very thoroughly. One of them crawled into father's hiding-place, but since it was very dark there and the soldier was in full kit, he made do with exploring the 'terrain' with his rifle. At last they left. Now freedom came towards us in leaps and bounds, preceded by the flight of the German population. How different that disordered retreat was from the triumphant entry of the German forces in 1939. Thousands of Germans on carts and horses, field kitchens, wounded soldiers; that was what was left of the might of Germany. Finally, on 24 January the village was taken by the Russian army. There was no fighting; the 'valiant' Germans had set up their artillery behind the cemetery but, at the sound of shots, they retreated equally 'valiantly', as planned. The next day we set off for Kraków. Leaving the village, I stumbled and fell; it seemed as if all that was bad came to an end with that fall. From now on I had a new life to begin, this time as a free person. A person who may breathe the air like everyone else, who may go out onto the streets. A person equal with all other people.

When we arrived in Kraków the first thing we did was to go and visit Mrs Jaśkowa, the lady who had risked everything that is most dear to a person, her own life, in order to save us.

(Archive of the VJCH in Kraków, statement no. 1153)

---

20. DAWID WULF

Born 23 November 1936 in Kraków; son of Józef and Jenta Dachner

(Statement taken by Maria Holender, Kraków)

Mama found out that there was going to be a ghetto in Kraków. I was very small then and I had no idea what that meant, but I was really glad when instead of going to the ghetto my parents and I moved to Wiśnicz Nowy. We lived with my aunt in a little house. It was springtime and I liked everything there – the woods and fields, lots of space every-where. I played with my cousin and things were fine there. After a few weeks I fell ill. Dr Jabłoński said that it was meningitis, and so we had to go to Bochnia, where there was a hospital. There I was going to be treated by a doctor Mama did not have confidence in, so she took me out of the hospital and took me to my grandmother in Kraków. By then the ghetto was starting to be formed, but grandmother was still living in her old flat. After I got better we moved back to Wiśnicz Nowy. We lived in a beautiful little house on a hill near the prison. Every day I could see the prisoners pushing wheelbarrows. They were going to get bread from the bakery. The Germans often came to see our landlady and I was really frightened of them. I often ran away because I did not want to see them. I was happy in Wiśnicz Nowy; I knew nothing about the war.

After a few months we moved to a Polish lady's. She was friendly towards us. I made friends there with two boys, and as it was summer by then we had a nice time playing in our landlady's garden.

One lady gave me Hebrew lessons.

By then father was in touch with a certain organisation [ŻOB – the Jewish militant organisation]. I was five and I did not really understand what that organisation was, and I did not even know what it was called. But I knew that it was a partisan organisation to which Jews who wanted to fight the Germans belonged. I hated the Germans with all my heart and that was why I liked it and I was glad that something like that existed. We were often visited by Szymek Dranger, his wife Gusta and also Hilek Wodzisławski. They all belonged to the secret organisation and for the while they were working on a farm in Kopaliny. I went there once with father, but I was very small then and it did not interest me at all as I had my own games and pastimes.

Several more months passed like this. Things were very quiet in Wiśnicz Nowy, and the Jews were completely left alone. Then one day we found out that there was going to be an *Aktion*. I knew by then that an *Aktion* meant killing Jews, and I was really frightened of that. But I was most afraid that they would load me onto those terrible goods wagons. The lady we lived with was very kind-hearted; she felt sorry for us and wanted to help us. Father had a rail pass issued by the ŻSS [Żydowska Samopomoc Społeczna – the Jewish self-help organisation] so he was free to travel to Kraków; a Polish workman took my mother in as his wife; and I was taken there by our landlady. I walked all the way from Wiśnicz to Bochnia on foot, by back roads, because the Germans had set up road blocks on the main roads. To begin with I was terribly afraid,

172

but then I calmed down. We finally got to Kraków and I met up with my parents.

We got into the ghetto and we stayed there for a few days, then we had to get away and we went to some people we knew on the Aryan side. From there we went to Bochnia via Prokocim. At the station in Prokocim, the ticket-seller recognised us and was going to hand us over to the *Bahnschutz*, but Mama begged him to let us go and he did. Finally we arrived in Bochnia and after a lot of searching we moved into a house by Solna Góra, where young boys and girls often came to see us. One night Mama and I ran away to Wiśnicz Nowy as there was going to be another *Aktion*. It was a terrible, dark night, and it was pouring with rain; we went on foot. I was very little then but I shall never forget it as long as I live. We hid at the same lady's where we had been before. A few days later father came with several other people from Kraków and the *Ordnungsdienst* arrested many of them, including Mama; father escaped through the window. But they let them all go. Father was hardly ever at home; Mama told me he was in Kraków, but later I found out that he was in a hide-out. I only saw him when Gusta, Wuśka, Halinka, Fisiek and the others came. They were father's comrades.

After the *Aktion* a closed ghetto was organised in Bochnia. The ghetto was divided into Sector A for those with jobs and Sector B for those without. As Solna Góra Street was for people with jobs, we had to move to Sector B. We lived along with other families in a house under which a bunker had been dug out. Often, when I woke up in the night, I could see them digging an underground passage that went from the kitchen all the way to the hide-out. I had a few friends who lived in the same building; we made a few guesses, but we did not know anything in detail as things were kept secret from us. They were probably afraid that we would give something away. One day two informers, Julek Apel and Natan Weissman, got into the bunker. Then they went 'to work' with our boys and gave everyone away. Early the same morning – I remember it was a Saturday – I was woken up by a terrible uproar and commotion. Mama told me to get dressed quickly, because our house had been surrounded by the Polish, Jewish and German police. I was terrified and ran outside the back way. When I went back into the building, the whole place had been turned upside down, and all of the furniture and things had been thrown out onto the street; Mama was very pale and kept running from our room to the bunker and back. I found out that the Germans had thrown stun grenades into the bunker, and when Mama had asked them to stop, they had beaten her up badly. Then everyone had to get out of the bunker and stand facing the wall, and the Germans fired into the air to frighten them and searched the house. In our room there was an oven for baking bread, which was joined to the underground passage. The Germans wanted to search in the oven but they were afraid to so they ordered Mama to take everything out of it. In the end they arrested everyone in the bunker, and took some of the women away somewhere. Among the people arrested was my father. All the children were left for my mother to look after. After the Germans left Mama tried to find out where father was. People said that the whole group had been shot, but that was not true.

On Monday Mama went out and I was playing with Ituś and Mirka in the garden in front of the house. Suddenly we heard loud voices talking. We saw that the Germans had surrounded our house. We ran away to Mirka's aunt's, and they did not notice us. We waited there for a while; in the meantime Mama came back. She realised what was going on, looked for us, guessed where we must be and found us at her friends' house. That time our flat was sealed up and Mama, her brother and I moved into an empty flat where we stayed for a few weeks. Father was in the Montelupich prison in Kraków. Mama did everything she could through people who had influence with the Germans to try to make things easier for father and the others in prison. But the people cheated Mama.

After a few weeks Mama bribed a Jewish policeman and a Polish one and we got out of the ghetto. There were notices saying to take children to the *Kinderheim*, but Mama did not want to be separated from me. I did not want to go there either, because I knew that the Germans would shoot all the children there. All the children said so.

We went on foot to Wiśnicz Nowy, to the same lady that we had lived with before. We went by alleyways and crept across gardens and fields so as not to meet anyone, because everyone knew us. We were about to knock at the lady's door, but we heard a voice we did not know, and we spent the whole night in the lavatory in the garden. There was a terrible storm then, and Mama took off her coat and wrapped it around me. I slept the whole night on her lap. When the lady came out in the morning to milk the goat she saw us and got a terrible shock. We went up the garden to her flat; a lady neighbour saw us and realised what was going on, but at that time we did not know about this. Mrs K. hid us in the attic, but in the evening the neighbour told her that she knew about us, and we had to leave. We went to Mr Łuczyński's, where there was a bunker. Our lady took us there late at night, after the curfew, risking her own life, because that district was controlled by Szmenda, the commandant of the Polish police and the terror of Wiśnicz Nowy and the area. That lady was our good angel, and she helped us many times.

The entrance to the bunker was from Mr Łuczyński's flat, under the bed. You went down a short ladder into the cellar, which before had belonged to Hilek Wodzisławski's family. They had an inn, and the cellar was the cold room. The cellar was divided into two parts: one part belonged to the inn, and the other, well-hidden, was the bunker. Inside, the bunker looked awful – the walls ran with damp and there was an unbearable stink from the cellar. Against the walls there were wooden bunks where we slept, and there was also a table and benches. I felt very bad in the bunker; to begin with I could not understand why there was no daylight or sunlight, which I missed terribly. At night Mama would go out to empty the pot in which we relieved ourselves. When she came back, her clothes smelt of the wind and the fresh air. I used to smell her all over, like a dog. In that bunker, as well as Mama and me, there was also Jochek Wodzisławski, Towa and Hela. Hilek and Fred often used to come to us too.

I was very sad; I was missing father. I knew that he had been put in prison by the Germans, that things were bad for him there and that he was suffering. I dreamed of seeing father again in my life. At that time I fell ill; I had a high temperature, and early in the morning Mama went to our lady's to get some medicine to bring my temperature down, and a little bread, as we were very hungry. I was sick for a long time, I do not remember how many days exactly, but I know that time passed slowly for me, and I thought that it would never end. It was cold in the bunker, even though it was summer.

One night soon after my illness, Fred and Mama and I went to another hide-out. It was a beautiful moonlit night; again we went by the back roads so that no one would see us. We were very much afraid of dogs because they could give us away by their barking. Every time we had to leave one hide-out and look for another, Mama would prepare me for the fact that the Germans might catch us and shoot us. I often talked about this with Mama. I asked if it hurt, and Mama assured me that it only lasts a moment and that it does not hurt at all. If it came to it, I wanted us both to be shot with the same bullet, and I asked Mama if that was possible; and also if it was better to stand facing 'them' or to turn my back and press my face against Mama.

At that time we went to a farmer's and he hid us in his attic. It was much better there than at Mr Łuczyński's. I was seven then, but Mama told him that I was ten and that I knew how to stay hidden. But again, after a few weeks, they were afraid to keep us any longer and we had to move on. A friend of father's, Uszek Weinfeld, was in hiding with us; he looked after us, and we moved on with him. We went to a country woman's where earlier one of father's comrades had built a shelter. It was rectangular and built into the ground, and you went into it through a cubby-hole. It was better there.

Daylight came into the hide-out through a small window. We were bothered a lot by flies, which I used to catch out of boredom. I corresponded with Dranger's nephew, Itus, who was in another hide-out. Hilek used to come and see us and he brought the letters.

One time two men from our bunker set off somewhere with an axe and a saw. I did not know where, but I found out later that they had built a new bunker in the woods. One day, a commotion woke me in the morning. I saw Hilek, with his head wrapped in a blood-stained towel. He lay unconscious on one of the bunks; Mama told me that he had had an accident. Later I learnt that he and some other boys had been to see a Polish woman who had given some Jews away, and he had wanted to take the things that belonged to those Jews. The woman's son had hit Hilek on the head with an axe. He lay in our hide-out the whole day, moaning terribly. Mama kept changing his bandages. Gusta Dranger, who now had Polish papers, also came. From now on the police were looking for us and we had to run away to the bunker that had been built in the woods and was hidden by bushes and trees. Since Hilek could not be left on his own, Szymek Dranger and some of the boys carried him to the woods, where he was going to be left in the care of someone from the ŻOB. I found out later that he died.

Our bunker was built for five people, but there were about 20 of us living in it. It was very cramped and hot, even though we hardly wore any clothes. There was so little room that we took it in turns to sleep. We also had to light a fire in a little tin stove, but only at night, so the smoke would not be seen. Our bunker looked like a robbers' hideaway. Sharp knives were stuck into the beams of the ceiling, and the lads were always cleaning their weapons.

In the meantime the police were rounding up all the Jews in the district. One farmer in particular, Kokoszka, kept trying to find our bunker. I fell ill again; this time it was my stomach. I could not eat anything, and Mama had to go out with me at night for me to get some fresh air. That was very dangerous because Kokoszka used to prowl around at night trying to track us down. Because of this, one day Uszek Weinfeld took us to another hide-out in Rajbród. We went there at night; we stayed in the loft for a few days while they built a new bunker for us under the cattle shed. In the corner of the shed was an underground passage covered with dry leaves that were put down for the cattle. Inside there were two bunks, one over the other, a table and two benches; a carbide lamp was on all day. But the carbide gave off an unpleasant smell which could have given us away, and we started using an oil lamp, which often went out for lack of air. No one knew about us except the mice, who nested there and lived peacefully with us. The owner's wife brought us food every day, which we paid for.

After a few weeks we found out that Łuczyński's bunker had been discovered. Łuczyński and the Jews who were hiding there had been killed, and only three boys had managed to escape. In the new bunker I did not have anything to do; I built bunkers, tanks, cannon and ships out of clay, and in this way the time passed for me. I had already forgotten what the sky and the sun looked like. Out of boredom I read books, but they did not interest me because I did not understand them. I learnt to read German and I learnt Heine's poems by heart. On warmer days in the spring we sometimes crept up to the loft, which I loved doing. And in this way we lived from day to day. The summer came; one day I heard that in the bunker where we had been before, the NSZ [a partisan organisation] had murdered the rest of the Jews who had been hiding there, including Fred, Hela Schneider and Jochek Wodzisławski. In the day we were afraid of the Germans and at night of the NSZ partisans, who were searching for Jews in that area. The worst time was autumn and spring, when the bunker was full of water. We longed for the liberation because we were completely exhausted. I used to comfort Mama by saying that our torment would soon come to an end. One night we heard explosions very close. It is difficult to describe what I felt then. I was terrified that the bunker would collapse because the wood was rotten and the whole place shook with the explosions of bombs and artillery shells; and at the same time I was happy that our liberation was close. The same day the owner's wife told us that the Soviets had entered the village. I came out of the bunker with Mama; I could not walk, and the daylight dazzled me. I was in rags, and my hair was as long as a real caveman's. I was happy that at last I would be free and I would be able to live like other children.

(Archive of the VJHC in Kraków, statement no. 1113)

21. JERZY ALEKSANDROWICZ

Born 7 July 1936 in Kraków; son of Julian and Maria Tislowitz

(*Statement taken by Maria Holender*)

On the day before the last big deportation from the Kraków ghetto, a chimney-sweep we knew built a stove with an alcove at our flat at 25 Krakusa Street. He took out all the parts inside the stove, so that you could hide inside it. But there was only room for me and one other person and I would have to sit on their lap. You got in through the top of the stove; a ladder was needed as it was a very high stove. It was at midnight when Mama and I got into the stove to test it out. I was calm; I did not know anything. I think they had kept it secret from me that there was going to be a deportation. Or perhaps they did not know themselves, I am not sure. At about six in the morning my grandmother woke me up and told me to get dressed; at that time I was in bed with the 'flu. Grandmother said that I could get up now because I was better. I got up, and Mama came from the other part of the flat, where father received his patients. We had to go to the *Ordnungsdienst*. That was like a kind of island; whoever made it there was saved. But on the way people would get arrested. Our building was searched; some German colonel or general searched the building and cordoned it off with soldiers, so we could not get away to the *Ordnungsdienst*. But the colonel treated us well, he gave me some chocolate and left us alone; he just made a thorough search. And then, as father was passing by me he told me that there was going to be a deportation. I was not at all afraid, as I simply did not realise what we had ahead of us. A long time before, father had already made a hiding-place in the kitchen, where five people could hide, but only lying down. There were eight of us in all in our family. But apart from us there were also two people, a mother and a daughter, who were also supposed to fit in that hiding-place. So from the beginning it was planned that two people would hide in the cellar and one in the attic. During the search the stove got smashed so we could no longer hide there.

Aunt Minka and Grandmother Zosia were already hiding in the cellar. When the colonel in charge of the search went down to the cellar, Mama gave me the keys and I took them quickly to the caretaker, who opened the door for aunt and grandmother and led them out onto the street. When the colonel went into the cellar, there was no one there. After the search Mama and I went to the *Ordnungsdienst*, because none of the hiding-places had worked out. We got in, but only thanks to the goodwill of one of the *Ordnungsdienst* we knew, who was a childhood friend of my father. Then father came, and suddenly remembered that he had not put the ladder back against the stove, which he had quickly mended after the search and had put Grandfather Józio inside; and that in the attic where he had put Aunt Minka and Grandmother Zosia and my great-grandparents, he had left open a bottle of potassium cyanide, which gave off vapour and could poison everyone. He was going to run back, but Mama would not let him and made him stay at the *Ordnungsdienst*. We learnt later that Grandmother Zosia had put a cork in the bottle, but a bit too late, because great-grandfather and Aunt Minka had started feeling ill. In the meantime, the deportation had finished. After we got home, father set about examining everyone who had been in the attic. It turned out that although everyone felt weak, no one was actually sick. After that I do not remember much till the final liquidation of the ghetto.

On that day, not knowing what we should do, mother and father and I went out onto the street and saw some people escaping into the sewers. We also jumped down into the sewer. We walked along the main channel on a narrow walkway. Father had a torch and led the way. We walked towards the Vistula, following the direction of the flow. Gradually people left the group, until there was just one man and us. We climbed out at the last minute, because just behind us the German police started shooting. We cleaned ourselves at the house of a factory watchman. We had been walking for three hours, although I had not been aware of it at the time. As we had nowhere to go and hide, we set off walking through the village. On the way we were stopped by two Germans, but they were not on duty and they did not do anything to us, though they guessed who we were. Father remembered a patient of his, a friend of grandfather's. We went to him. On the way we paid a boy 100 złotys to take us there, but he got drunk and gave us away to the Gestapo. The man woke us up because he had found out that the Germans knew about us. We went to spend the night in the fields. There we met a gang of drunks who for 1,000 złotys put us up for the night. From there we got to Podgórze, to the place where Grandmother Rysia and great-grandfather were. They were staying with a man who long ago had promised father that he would hide us. It turned out, though, that he was a Gestapo informer. He set the Gestapo onto us, and the moment they came into our flat, father swallowed some poison, because he did not want them to take him alive. Mother also took poison and she was going to give me some too, but one of the Gestapo grabbed her by the hand and they said something to each other in German. As far as I can remember, after the Gestapo left – mother had bribed them – I handed father the medicine bottles that were on the dresser. Among them was a bottle of oxygenated water. Father pointed at this bottle, his arm stiffening. He drank the bottle, and that weakened the effect of the poison. Then we called an ambulance and went to the St Lazarus Hospital. There father gave the name of Adamski. Some of the nurses there recognised him because he had worked there for several years before the war, but no one gave him away. After having their stomachs pumped, mother and father started to feel better. The next day we went to father's friend, Dr H., who at first promised to conceal us, then at the last minute let us down and refused to help us any more. We found ourselves without a roof over our heads, and Dr H. gave us a few hours to leave his flat. Then father went into town to look for somewhere for us, and he visited the family of one of his patients, the famous artist, Mr W., whose daughter Wicula was happy to take care of us. She found us a flat for a few days, and since we could not go out she brought us food, and cakes for me. We could not stay there long as the flat was located opposite the Gestapo building, and we moved to Starowiślna Street, to Mrs A.'s, who had hidden Jews before, and we stayed there for some time. It was very good there, they were very friendly towards us. But next door was a woman *Volksdeutsch*, and we could not go on living there. We had to find another flat, though from time to time we were able to go back to Mrs A.'s. For a few days at a time we were able to stay on Jana Street with some friends of father's. Their daughter, Miss Helenka, was kind to me and took care of me right through the war, and her parents looked after my grandparents – they took them food and brought us letters from them, and on my birthday they brought a present from grandfather, Korczak's *The Stubborn Boy*.

A friend of father's, Dr Z., arranged a flat for us in Wieliczka. We stayed there for a few months, but the landlady's parents, who lived in the same building, were afraid that we would be discovered and ordered us to leave. I remember that it was November; there was a spell of bad weather, and we could not travel by train, so we rode on a farmer's cart and part of the way we went on foot. We were really afraid on the way as there were patrols. Members of the

Secret Jewish Aid Organisation got us a flat on Sebastiana Street but the flat belonged to a Polish policeman, and mother was afraid to stay there. It turned out later that that policeman was one of the most decent people that Mama met during the war. He probably even belonged to that Jewish Aid Organisation. He knew everything about us and he did not give us away. The whole time we were spied on by one Jew, Ignacy Taubman, who was a Gestapo informer and wanted to give us away.

The policeman we were living with found us a place on Józefińska Street, because the Germans often came to his flat and it was too dangerous for us. There we saw Taubman again, snooping around outside our windows. When there was room at Mrs A.'s, we moved there. When things started to heat up again, we moved back to our old flat in Wieliczka. After a few months (six months), father joined the partisans and we lost contact with him. News reached us that father was dead. The secret organisation did not send us money, as they had promised, but Mrs Marysia brought us an allowance from the Jewish Aid Council. While father was away, his friends from the partisans came to see us, Mr Leon and Mr Stefan and Mrs W. with her little son Oleś, who played with me; they often brought us different sweets and fruit.

After the Warsaw uprising father came back from the partisans, and we were together. At the time the Russians were entering Kraków, we stayed in a shelter. The heaviest fire was directed towards us because there was a German battery nearby. Houses came crashing down right by us. I sometimes had my heart in my mouth when a bomb exploded a few metres from our house and made the whole building shake. I was quite calm most of the time, but at certain moments I was afraid that a bomb would hit the house. After the battle I walked around Wieliczka, but there were no Germans any more, because they had run away. But they were all captured, because Wieliczka was the centre of a big encirclement operation that the Russians had set up as a trap. In the same house where we were living was the billet of the

Russian captain who was interrogating German prisoners-of-war. Behind the shed we found a whole cache of broken rifles and ammunition. After the Russians entered, on 18 January 1945, we returned to Kraków as free, equal people.

(Archive of the VJHC in Kraków, statement no. 1037)

---

22. JÓZEF REICH

Born 2 November 1935 in Kraków; son of Marian and Alicja
(Statement taken by Maria Holender, Kraków)

In Kraków there was going to be a ghetto. Instead of going to the ghetto, I went with my mother to Wola Duchacka, and from there to Niepołomice. Before then no one had paid any attention to the fact that I was Jewish. It was only when the boys in Wola Duchacka started calling me names that I asked my mother about it. She said that we were Jews. I was very upset about my friends calling me names, but I could not do anything about it. The village boys threw stones at me and called me names which at that time I did not understand at all. But I repeated those words at home and, for the first time in my life, I got a terrible hiding. The boys kept bullying me; I was lonely, I had no friends and no one to play with. It was then that I felt painfully what it means to be Jewish.

We lived for a whole year in Niepołomice, with a farmer in his little cottage. After a time some Polish people we knew came for me and took me by train to their flat in Kraków on Słoneczna Street. I did not know that I would not see my mother again for a long time, and I was calm. Mother told me that I was going on my holidays; but I stayed there for a long time. It was very good there; at the beginning I used to go out onto the street, and I was not afraid. I was called Józef Raj. It was only after some time that the lady I was staying with stopped letting me go out onto the street, and from that moment I realised that I had to stay hidden. I was very sad then, but I was not particularly frightened as there were a lot of things I still did not understand. After a few months I found out that mother and father had moved to Warsaw, and that made me even sadder because I felt that it would be a long time before I saw them again. Often, when I was left alone in the flat, I cried for my mother. I stayed there for several months. I could not stay any longer because, in almost every flat, the Germans were coming searching for Jews.

At last a man sent by my father came to take me to Warsaw. I was really happy. And so we set off. I had a comfortable train ride and arrived at that man's flat. There I met my mother and father; I thought they would take me with them, but it was not possible. The man agreed to take me to the country, where he had hired a villa in Radość. To begin with it was good there. Then one day the man's girlfriend told me to stop going out into the garden because the landlady, who was very nosy and talkative, was there. But the next day I went into the garden and played in the sand. The owner of the villa came out of her flat and asked me with a smile what my name was. I got confused; I forgot what name I was registered under, and I gave my old, real surname. The landlady smiled and went away. The next day we had to leave the villa because the landlady threatened that she would inform on us. The man left me with some people he knew in another villa, and he went to Warsaw to tell my mother and father what had happened. I was left on my own for the whole day with people I did not know and I cried because I was afraid that no one would come back for me any more. In the evening the man came back, took me to Warsaw and left me in Grochów, in a tumbledown house with holes in the roof where his girl-friend and her family lived. It was terrible there. I spent the whole day in bed, because there was no hiding-place and I had to hide under the quilt as different people kept coming. My mother did not come until two days later, and when I asked her to take me with her, she said that for the moment it was not possible; she said she was trying to arrange a place for me with some good people, and that for the moment I would just have to manage where I was.

The next day the sister of the man's girlfriend came and took me to her friend's flat. There no one looked after me and I was locked in alone the whole day long. I missed my mother, and mother did not come. A whole week passed like this. Then one day mother came and she was very upset. Fortunately there was no one else at home, and mother said: 'Let's run away quickly; these people are blackmailers.' I did not know what that meant, but I got dressed quickly and we left. Outside the gate a lady was waiting who took me to her flat. She was a tall, elderly lady. I stayed with her for three months. I was called Józef Śniegocki. My new lady introduced me to her neighbours as a relative of hers, and I called her aunt and I thought that she really was my aunt. She was very good to me. I went out into the yard or to the shop, and she sometimes sent me to the market. That lasted a whole month. Then things suddenly got worse. The lady would not let me go out anywhere. Even though I never showed myself, the children playing in the corridor came and stood outside our door and shouted: 'Jew! Jew-boy!' In the flat I was not even allowed to talk loudly; I had to whisper the whole time. The lady kept saying to me: 'You're not here.' She explained that it had to be like that because the neighbours had threatened that they would inform on her that she was hiding a Jew. I did not know what informing meant, but I was beginning to be afraid.

One day the whole building was searched. I hid in a coal-bunker for three hours. From that time on my lady was very nervous and kept saying to me that my mother must come and take me away. And one day mother came and took me to another flat, where I had to call her 'Ma'am'. We stayed together at that man's for one month. And there I also had to talk quietly, and I only went out with mother in the evening. I was so sad; I said to mother: 'Let's go out one day in the day-time, when the sun is shining; why can't I go and play like the other children? Why do I have to go out when it's dark and I can't see anything?' And mother always comforted me and said that we would get by and that when the war was over I would be able to play out like the other children. Sometimes I forgot to call my mother 'Ma'am', and then my mother got very upset. But it was really difficult for me to get used to that, so difficult that sometimes I had to whisper in her ear over and over: 'Mummy, Mummy, Mummy.' And I asked her: 'Mummy, when the war is over, will I be allowed to call you Mummy out loud?'

A month passed and we had to leave that flat. Mother took me to another flat near the ghetto. There was a little room there that was so cluttered with furniture that I could not move in it. Almost all day long I had to sit on the sofa behind the dresser, so that no one would see me. When it got dark I would look out of the window, and every day I could see trams full of Jews travelling to and from work. They were guarded by Germans with machine guns. Mother took me for a walk almost every day. One day as I was looking out of the window I was noticed by a shopkeeper who was talking to our landlady's daughter. When she came back home she said that the shopkeeper had asked who the Jew-boy was in her window. She had replied that it was not her window. Two days later mother came as usual to take me for a walk. When we got back home, our landlady signalled to us through the half-open door not to come in. Despite this mother went into the flat and found out that a moment before the Gestapo had been there looking for me. Because of this, mother had to take me away again. I moved about, changing flats every two weeks. In one place in Żoliborz where I stayed for a longer time, the building was cordoned off. The landlady told me to go out with her young daughter to some friends of theirs, as if we were going for a walk. And thanks to that I survived, because the Germans took in some Jews from the same building. After that search, the landlady left me with a *Volksdeutsch* lady who would not let my mother come to see me. I hid either in the bath or in the wardrobe when visitors came. She often locked me in the flat alone and without food, and did not come back. One day I needed the lavatory so badly that I went in all the flowerpots. But I had to leave that place too; father took me back to mother, and we stayed together till the Warsaw uprising.

One evening we all heard booms, machine gun and cannon fire and grenades exploding. The most terrible thing was the German armoured train which mostly fired at army formations, bunkers and barricades. And we were living in a building occupied by the army. It was very dangerous because we were the target for the shells. Father said right away that it was the uprising, and we were all glad. I was ill at that time, with a temperature of 39°, and I had to stay in the shelter. The doctor said it was scarlet fever. During the uprising, in that army shelter, the Polish soldiers were very kind to us. They often shared their food with us, and when I had a bad cough they gave me some medicine that made it better. When I got better the soldiers showed me their guns and explained how to fire them. That was very interesting. One soldier, who was very nice, sang different songs and cheered us up. Every evening he went up without a gun to take part in the fighting on the streets. When father asked him why, he replied that there were not enough guns for everyone, but that you had to fight. When one of your comrades fell, his gun remained for one of the living to use. The next day a messenger came, a 12-year-old boy who came to us under heavy fire and told us that Topór, the one who used to go out without a gun, had been killed. He had been throwing grenades at the Germans from a certain building, and the Germans had blown up the building.

We had to leave our shelter, because the Germans dropped five bombs on the building and the shelter began to collapse. Partly crawling and partly walking, we quickly sneaked across to the next shelter. As we crossed we came under heavy fire. From that time we had no peace. We wandered from shelter to shelter, from place to place. We wanted to go with the army and get back to the city centre through the sewers. We tried one night; we walked for several nights under fire, and in the end all those who were unarmed were ordered to turn back. There remained only those who were armed and could fight the Germans. The next night we tried again. I was completely exhausted, and I said to my mother: 'Why won't you let me sleep?' I was terrified of losing my mother; I held her hand tightly and we made sure we stayed together. Just as we were about to enter the sewers, we heard the lads screaming: 'Get away, the sewers have been gassed!' And again we turned back. The next day the uprising was over. We all had to leave the shelter with white scarves to show the Germans that we were surrendering because otherwise they threw grenades into the shelters.

From that moment our real wandering began. We went with a crowd of people towards the station. We had no bags because we had lost everything. On the way we saw ruined houses and nothing but rubble everywhere. Near the station the Germans separated us from father, and mother was very worried. We were put on a German electric train to Pruszków. Everywhere, at every step, people were shouting and calling their family and friends. Families were trying to find each other. We spent two days in the camp at Pruszków and we were not allowed to leave. There were huge sheds where they used to repair railway carriages. We were so hungry that we had to ask and beg people for a crust of bread. We had nothing to put coffee in, and once mother brought some in a broken bottle. The next day, as we went through the gate to queue for coffee, by chance we met father, who said that on the way the Germans had robbed him and taken two watches. That was all father had. But we could not enjoy his company for long because in the wagons we were separated again. From then it was a very long time before we saw him again. They left us in some fields, in Petrykozy. For several hours we stayed in the fields, not knowing what to do. Then a Hungarian man helped my mother and led us to a burnt-out building where several people were sleeping on straw laid down on the floor. He gave us some hot coffee and a slice of bread with margarine. I was so hungry that I gobbled it down in an instant. In the morning some carts came and took us to Białaczew. There we lived in a beautiful mansion, the country estate of some aristocrats. We slept on straw and lived only on what we were given by the RGO [Rada Główna Opiekuńcza – the Central Welfare Council, an institution for social care under the occupation]. After some time the Germans ordered us all to leave. On the way, again by chance, we met father, and together we went to a flat that mother had rented in the same village. Later we moved in with a farmer in the village of Żelazowice. After we had been there for three months the front started to move closer. At night trucks full of German soldiers would drive through the village. Some units came back, because it turned out that the Germans had been surrounded. Since they could not get away, they decided to continue their defence, and they filled the whole village with tanks, artillery, lorries and soldiers. That lasted a few hours, and then they finally left the village. It seemed as if the Germans had gone. The next day we went into the woods and collected lots of food and clothing that the Germans in their panic had left behind. On our way back from the woods, we noticed a huge glow in the sky. We went on for a while, and then we saw all the people running away from the village. We joined them and escaped to the next village. We learnt that the Germans had come back and had burned the neighbouring village.

When things were quiet, we went back home. In our yard there was a body, and in the flat the bedding was covered with blood and there was blood everywhere. All our things had been stolen. There were no Germans left at all. The next day, from the early morning, we heard the roar of Russian lorries. The Russians entered the village. I waited for them eagerly because I knew that they would bring me the freedom that I longed for with all my heart.

(Archive of the VJHC in Kraków, statement no. 1117)

23. KRYSTYNA CHIGER

Born 28 October 1935 in Lwów, daughter of Ignacy and Paulina Gold

(*Statement taken by Maria Holender, Kraków*)

Father found out that at midnight the ghetto in Lwów was going to be liquidated. We hid in a cellar which was in a shed. We usually went down there to hide in the afternoon, when mother came back from work, as we were expecting a big *Aktion*. I was seven then and my brother Pawełek was three. From that cellar we went out to the River Pełtew; we kept going straight on till we came to the sewer. In the sewer it was terribly wet and dark; when I went in there I was terrified and I shook with fear. I behaved myself the whole time, I just kept asking father if we still had far to go. In the sewer there were stones with yellow insects crawling on them. We put our things on the stones and sat down on them ourselves. It was really bad for us there; the walls were dripping with water, and there was a horrid, unbearable smell. I could see big red rats running past us like chickens. To begin with I was really afraid, but afterwards I got used to it. And Pawełek was not afraid at all. I lay on mother's lap, and Pawełek on father's. And that lasted for five weeks, day and night. We could not get up or even move. As well as us there were 20 other people. Every day, from the first day, the Polish sewer workers brought us food – black bread and margarine. They were very good to us. Because they were afraid that someone would notice them, they would enter the sewers at various entrances through manhole covers that they opened. I remember their names: Leopold Soda, Stanisław Wróblewski and Jerzy Kowalow. In that sewer there was always light from a carbide lamp that hung on a hook hammered in between the stones. The Poles brought us carbide for the lamp. Father brought water in a can which he carried in his teeth, because he had to walk completely doubled up. It was awful there for me; I was not allowed to talk aloud, all I could do was whisper into

191

Mama's ear. I dreamed of the war ending so I could go out to the outside world. Most of all I missed the sun, the air and the flowers. Once I asked our friends to bring a few wild flowers. I longed to see a dog and a horse, and Pawełek missed the birds. But I did not tell Mama about this because she had lots of other worries.

It was summertime. When it rained the rainwater flowed down to the sewer, and when lavatories were flushed our sewer filled up with water. Then we had to lean low on the stones right by the wall, so the water would not come onto us. Pawełek was very little then, he was only three, and he often cried. Mama got very upset then, because she was afraid that someone would hear and that we would be found out. Once one of the men who were hiding with us got so angry with Pawełek that he even threatened him with a revolver, but it did no good because Pawełek just started crying even louder.

After five weeks we were discovered by some other sewer workers who came down one day to clear the sewers. When they appeared we turned our light out, but one of the men lit a cigarette lighter and they noticed us, so we had to run away. As we were escaping along the main sewer, moving straight ahead and not even knowing where we were going, we suddenly saw the sewer workers who had brought us food. They were very surprised and asked us where we were going. Father told them everything. Then they led us to a side channel and told us to stay there for the night, and they promised that the next day they would find us somewhere else to shelter. In the morning they came back and led us further along the Pełtew by the main sewer; that took almost half a day. On the way I felt a lot better; at last I could walk instead of sitting. And I do not know why, but I felt that a weight had dropped from my heart, and I was so cheerful that I even whistled with happiness. And although the journey was a difficult one – through pipes and holes, with me barefoot in a summer dress and shivering with cold – I was still happy. I got a thorn in my foot, but I took it out myself, as I did not want to hold my mother up. At last we came to a concrete pipe, and we stayed there the whole day. It was unbearably cold there, and there was nowhere we could sleep; the next day our friends came and led us further. We moved aside a board and got into another pipe that was so low that we had to crawl on all fours. There were 11 of us in all; the rest had died because they had gone out of the sewer. My uncle, Kuba Leinwand, had drowned in the Petłew when he went out for water one day and there was a storm. He drowned when the water sucked him in.

It was much better in the new sewer; there was more room, and we slept on bunks that father had built from planks he found in the sewer. There were four bunks. I shared a bunk with father and one other man. It was very cramped and uncomfortable; I was squashed up like a sardine in a tin. Mama slept with Pawełek and another lady. We had one carbide lamp, which shone day and night. The rats used to eat our bread; father would frighten them away with a stick, and then they would run away. Pawełek fed the rats like chickens; he threw them breadcrumbs and boiled potatoes. The rats came right up close and squeaked. And Pawełek was not in the least afraid of them. We had a few bowls and a primus. Everything had been brought by our good sewer workers. One lady cooked soup and coffee and my mother served it out to everyone, so I did not go hungry. Pawełek got used to everything and he stopped crying. One crooked, grey-haired old lady fell ill and died. One lady had a baby, but it died and they threw it into the river. Two young ladies took it in turns to be responsible for keeping things clean. The light was on the whole time; I never knew whether it was day or night. But I guessed that it was daytime when the sewer workers came. When it rained, the rain came into our shelter by a pipe through which you could just barely see a grate and a tiny bit of light. Sometimes I saw a ray of sunlight, but very faintly. Once I climbed into that pipe to look at the outside world, but I did not see anything, I only smelt the fresh air slightly. I missed the sun and the fresh air so much that I cannot describe it. I could hear cars driving up above; I heard people's voices and children laughing as they played. And I often thought that I would be happy if I could play like them. Once I heard a child crying and saying to his mother that he wanted to go to sleep.

I fell seriously ill with measles – that is what Mama said it was – and Pawełek caught it from me, and then he lost his voice. One of the sewer workers brought him some eggs; he had to carry them in his teeth, because in his hand he had a bag of food, and to get to us he had to crawl on all fours.

Once the primus caught alight and a fire broke out. We all took fright; at first someone threw rags onto the primus, but the rags caught fire too. Then we sprinkled used carbide on the fire and put it out. I was really scared, but Pawełek was more afraid than anyone – he ran away to the furthest bunk and hid there. When we had put the fire out we were all black with soot and we looked like scarecrows. Another time, the following summer, there was a flood. After a terrible storm, heavy rain began to fall and started flooding our shelter. Our friends began shovelling the water back with spades and pushing it back into the pipe, so that it began to flow away.

We lived like this for 14 months, and the whole time our sewer workers continued to help us. When we ran out of money, they brought us food for free.

Towards the end of our time there I could hear the wail of sirens and the boom of cannon. I was terrified, though I knew that our liberators, the Russians, were approaching. Finally, one day we heard a loud knocking on the grate of the sewer. It was our sewer workers letting us know that we were free.

We walked for a few minutes along the sewer, and then we pulled off the manhole cover, and the sewer workers pulled us up. We looked so terrible that we did not look like children at all. People took pity on us; one lady brought us some gooseberries. I was so glad to see sunlight, flowers and other people. I was happy; but Pawełek kept crying and wanted to go back into the sewer because he was not used to the light and was afraid of the people.

(Archive of the VJHC in Kraków, statement no. 1155)

Chapter Five
THE RESISTANCE

1. LEON CZERWONKA

Born 1933 in Warsaw

(*Statement taken by Hilda Barberówna, Bielsko*)

... We lived in tents. In front of the tent, especially in the wintertime, we lit fires, mostly to keep warm, and also as a signal to the planes that used to drop food for us. We never ran short of food. My mother was the cook, and she made food for everyone. Father operated the mine-thrower, and I cleaned the guns. Every day the partisans went into the woods or to the railway station to carry out their orders. They often planted bombs and destroyed German property. My father died during one of the operations. We found out that he had accidently stepped on a mine; he never came back to us. I wanted to cry, but mother would not let me; she said that this was not the time to cry.

Apart from me, in that partisan unit there were 50 children aged from nine to 14. My best friend was a boy from Warsaw, Jankiel Goldberg, who was 12. He was very brave. He often played with a pair of binoculars. Once he saw three German lorries. He saw the Germans unloading bicycles and various pieces of equipment for cars. He always carried a rifle. He stood at his post, firing at the trucks. Our partisans came to his assistance and there began an exchange of fire in which about 100 Germans were killed.

In the partisan unit in the forest I was taught to read and write. Before the war I had been in the first form of primary school. We kept things very clean.

The Germans often went on reconnaissance trips to the woods. The moment we sensed that we were in danger, we moved on to a safer place. Some of the farmers spied on us and then informed on us, because they were afraid that the Germans would burn their villages in revenge for harbouring partisans. But there were also many of them who helped us.

One day General Kowpak came to visit us. He is a very nice

man, of medium height with a moustache and a small beard. He even spoke to me. Among other things he asked me: 'What would you do to the Germans?' I answered: 'I'd cut all the Germans into tiny little pieces, and I would not feel a bit guilty about it.'

Then, after we had been liberated by the Red Army, I stayed with all the others in the barracks at Sokoły.

(Archive of the CJHC, statement no. 537/II)

2. HERSZ CUKIER

Born 1931 in Raduń, near Baranowicze

(*Written account*)

In my town, Raduń, there were 1,800 Jews, and they all lived on one street, Żydowska Street [Żydowska is Polish for 'Jewish']. When the ghetto was formed, the street was partitioned off from the rest of the town by a pillar. I remember how one day the Byelorussian militia killed 40 Jews because they had come in from Lida. Jews were not allowed to come in from other towns; they were forbidden to eat meat, butter or eggs. And the authorities threatened that if they caught anyone they would shoot them.

On 7 May 1942 the Byelorussian militia from the Minsk district surrounded the town. For three days they did nothing. They just drove everyone onto one small street. Eighty men were taken in and sent to dig ditches, two kilometres out of the town near the Jewish cemetery. I hid with my uncle on a rubbish tip.

During the digging, one of the Jews suddenly shouted 'Hurrah!' He hit one of the Germans on the head with a spade and wounded him. The Jews started running off towards the woods, and the Germans set off towards the town. But after a moment they realised that the Jews were escaping, and they began firing at them. Five people were killed and 75 got away to the Nacka forest.

We stayed in our hiding-places till the evening. At midnight we set off into the woods. We walked in a straight line for ten kilometres. There were five of us – two women, two men and me. We bought a rifle from the Byelorussians in exchange for four sheepskins. We lived in a dugout and the Byelorussians sold us food. After a while we learnt that they had talked about us a lot, and that we were in danger of being discovered. We joined up with a partisan unit of 150 people, made up of Jews and Soviet prisoners-of-war who had escaped from German captivity. There were about 100 Jews. They had guns. The commander was Yevdokimovich. Their work consisted of blowing up trains. Mines were laid under the rails and a cord was tied to the mine. A train came past once a day. They lay in wait by the woods. They pulled the cord and the mine exploded. After the explosion they ran away at once, as the Germans shot anyone they caught alive.

They were called the Lenin Komsomol. In the winter they stopped operations. They often set traps for German policemen. They wore white overalls so as not to be seen against the snow.

Once 20 partisans ambushed 30 Germans; they killed nine Germans and captured six rifles. That was near Raduń in the winter of 1942. A group of 13 Germans with a machine gun once ran into the partisans. They surrounded the Germans and six Germans were killed. They had been convinced that there were only seven Jews there; they had not expected such a strong partisan unit. At that time I also used a gun. One Jew was killed and another injured. We captured six rifles and six revolvers. I took one of the rifles for myself. In the evening the *razvedka* [Russian for 'intelligence'] reported that the Germans had surrounded us on all sides. A battle developed around Marcinkowice and lasted two hours. In the evening, under cover of darkness, we retreated.

The commander led us 20 kilometres by compass to another forest. We carried the wounded man on a horse. We managed to escape the encirclement. The Germans sent Byelorussians from the villages to reconnoitre. They themselves followed behind. They found a dugout we had abandoned, and threw grenades into it. Our *razvedka* informed us about this. They even left some poisoned bread, thinking that we would go back there. But our civilian *razvedka* told us everything. After the encirclement the commander went off to the Minsk region to look for the chief-of-staff; for a month we did nothing but 'organise' food from the villages. Then we returned to the Nacka forest. The commander came back. Some Byelorussian prisoners-of-war joined us. By then there were about 300 people in our unit. That was in the spring of 1943. At that time we made contact with the staff. In the command there were 10,000 partisans. Our brigade had a wireless set. The work now involved blowing up trains and burning bridges. The bridge near Lida was burned down by nine Jews. They laid down straw and poured petrol over it, and the bridge went up in flames. There were about 100 Jews. New arrivals were not allowed to join if they did not have their own gun. Around the brigade at a distance of one kilometre on all sides there were permanent outposts of two people, each on a 24-hour watch. We had guard-duty once a week. There were ten women, five Jewish and five Byelorussian, who worked in the kitchen.

Every day the commander went on a recce with two of the partisans. Once they found out that the Germans were in all of the villages. Planes were already circling over us. We immediately put out the fire so that the planes would not see it. We were too late, however. The planes spotted our white shirts and started dropping bombs. At the order 'Everyone follow me', we quickly moved away. We moved two kilometres deeper into the woods, and, each of us with a rifle in his hand, we waited for the Germans. For half an hour we crouched in mud up to our knees. The Germans and Lithuanians began shooting. We ran away through the woods, and crossed the river in boats. We already had three casualties. We crossed the Byelorussian–Lithuanian border. There were checkpoints; it was impossible for them not to notice 300 people crossing the border. We waded through waist-deep mud under fire from the border guards. We had the radio with us. We carried our guns so that they would not get wet. Suddenly we heard the rumble of wheels. Carts full of Germans were coming towards us. After a few minutes we realised that the German forces were too great, and we retreated. The Germans fired at us with artillery. We ran back to the border. In the evening we returned for the radio and the other things we had left, but they had all gone. The Germans had waited for us and had lit a fire, but they had given up waiting and had gone; the fire was going out. We wandered from place to place, without anything to eat. The Germans kept searching for us. We went back to our old dugouts from the winter. We ate rotten potatoes. The Germans were still after us. The commander of the brigade suggested that 20 of the Jews and some of the Soviet soldiers should try to make it to headquarters. They walked for a week, because we were 150 kilometres from Minsk. They travelled by night. In the day they slept in the farms. They had a letter addressed to the farmers asking them to help. The commander gave them only rifles, no machine guns.

On 25 August 1943 they were received in the village of Ziemianowice on the Niemen. The chief-of-staff and Brigadier Shubin came to the village. That was the Lenin Brigade. They were attached to the Invincibles Company, which numbered 500 men. Here relations were entirely different. There was a great deal of diversionary work, and army discipline was in force. In each village there was a partisan who was the village commandant. He was the authority designated by the brigade. He organised food for the unit, the delivery of food by cart to the woods and the return of the carts. The farmers had agreed to provide supplies, but had asked that the carts be sent back. The village commandant, usually a Jew, moved freely about the district. There were few Germans in the country. Each unit had its own kitchen. Entry to the kitchen was strictly forbidden as there were instances of poison being found there. There were many spies. I helped in the kitchen and watered the horses. Our company was divided into three sections of 170 men each. Each section gathered food for itself. The brigade was camped across an area of 50 kilometres. It was in contact with Moscow. Once, information was received that arms would be dropped for the brigade, and that for this purpose three bonfires should be lit. Three days later, at night, three planes flew over; they circled overhead and dropped 18 parachutes and three people, one woman and two men, from Moscow. They shouted to us to put the fires out. Soon afterwards German planes from Baranowicze flew over in pursuit of the Soviet planes.

Then, 60,000 Germans moved into the woods. The brigade concentrated in one place. There were 10,000 of us. We stayed in the woods all day long. We did not say a single word. We had four cannon that had been captured by another unit. The Germans were entrenched. We wanted to get through on the main road to Minsk in Russia. On the way three spies, who were in contact with the Germans, split off from the unit. The Germans fired red rockets to try and cut us off. We broke up into small groups of 50 men. For a long time we had no food. We ate grass. We were kept alive by the hope that the Red Army was close. The Germans began to retreat. The commander gave the order to bake dry biscuits, because he expected the liberation to come within a week. The next day lorries drove into the woods. The commander sounded the alert, thinking it was the Germans; we thought they had surrounded us. From our intelligence we learnt that Baranowicze had been liberated. Those were Soviet lorries.

From headquarters I received a certificate and a citation:

Headquarters of the Lenin Partisan Brigade
13 June 1944

CERTIFICATE

This is to certify that comrade Hersz Cukier, son of Abram, of the village of Nacza, Raduń district, Baranowicze region, was a partisan in the Invincibles partisan unit. He joined the unit on 25 August 1943 and was discharged on 12 July 1944 in consequence of the arrival of the Red Army.

Officer of the Lenin
Partisan Brigade
Junior Political
Instructor Shubin

Officer of the Lenin
Partisan Brigade
Battalion Commander Makarov

CITATION

Comrade Hersz Cukier, son of Abram, was in the Invincibles Company of the Lenin Partisan Brigade from 25 August 1943 to 12 July 1944 as a private. He was a well-disciplined soldier. On the orders of the commanding officer he performed duties in the supply section.

Commander of the unit

(Archive of the CJHC, statement no. 638)

3. SAMUEL EISEN

Born 1932 in Tłuste, near Zaleszczyki; son of Majer and Fajga Essig

(*Statement taken by M. Hochberg-Mariańska, Kraków*)

Before the war I completed the fourth form of primary school, but under the Soviets I had to go back a year and be in the fourth form again. Father was the director of the shoemakers' *artel* [workers' guild]. We were comfortably off, though we no longer had the shop. People said various things about the Germans, but we did not believe the stories about the atrocities, so no one tried to escape to Russia when the war with Germany broke out. There were a great number of Jews in Tłuste, though I cannot say exactly how many. When the Germans came, Jews from Buczacz, Zaleszczyki, Jagielnica and Czortków were resettled in our town. Hungarian Jews also came in. There were several thousand of them. They were rich people and the Ukrainians were constantly attacking and robbing them. They hounded them from place to place, and when they tried to get back to Hungary, they were marched out to the Dniester and drowned.

I remember all the *Aktions* against the Jews, though I do not remember the dates. The first was a levy; they went round with a list and picked out the old and the sick. There were 300 people taken and put on a transport. We hid in the fields that time. As well as the brother who is with me now, I had another little brother who was born during the war. In the second *Aktion* they started shooting people on the spot. There were 100 people shot like this, and 1,000 were put on a transport. That time they took my mother and little brother. Everyone was sent to Bełzec. I do not know how people knew that in Bełzec they burned people with electricity. After the third *Aktion* Tłuste was already '*judenrein*'. That time the *Aktion* was organised by the Gestapo, and 7,000 people were murdered in Tłuste. Four huge pits were dug at the 'haystack' (the cemetery). A board was placed across the pit. Ten people

204

stood on it at a time, stripped naked; they were shot by machine gun and fell straight into the pit, and the next ten people were lined up. The executions went on from Thursday till Monday, but only at night. They appointed Jewish *ordners* [Jewish police] to help them; they came out alive, and told people what had been happening there. They had to go down into the pits and arrange the bodies on top of one another, packed tight like sardines to make room for more. Children were thrown into the pit alive and were weighed down with corpses. A German would grab a child by the scruff of the neck and shout: 'Nimm das Dreck und schmeiss herein' ['Take this filth and throw it in']. In the pits the children were soaked in blood. Two little girls crawled out from under the corpses and came back to the town, but they were like lunatics, they would not say anything. All the clothes were taken to the town and stored in warehouses. Later on the Germans transported them out.

Those who were left, only the young and healthy, about 300 of us, were sent to a farm two kilometres outside Tłuste. There were farms like that all over our area. We went there, my father, my brother and me. We lived in barracks and worked very hard in the fields. There were no police and no one guarded us; but in the village and in the town were the Ukrainian police, and if a Jew showed himself outside the farm he was a dead man. The manager was a Pole; he mostly left us alone, but we had to give him 50 złotys a head daily. That was supposedly for food, but we only got a little bread and soup, and we had to buy food from the farmers in the village. Not everyone had money, but the richer people helped the poorer ones a lot, and paid the manager for them too.

We spent six weeks on the farm. People began saying that an *Aktion* would come for us, and we set a watch every night to warn us if something was going to happen. The night they came, I was on duty and everyone else was asleep. It was a beautiful night in the summer of 1943. Right by the farm there was a pond, and in the pond the frogs were croaking; it was warm, and I forgot what I was standing there for, I was just listening to the frogs and feeling good, and my mind was empty. But suddenly I heard someone singing, and I realised that it was not the farmers from our village. I knew their singing. It was the Ukrainian policemen singing. I started shouting and I woke everyone up. But it was already too late because the police were on horseback and a moment later they arrived. The people in the barracks jumped out of bed in their underwear, got out through the window and ran away in a straight line. The policemen fired at them with machine guns and chased them on horseback; I do not know how many of them got away, but it was not many – the next day I saw those who had been killed. My brother and I started to run away with father, but he was hit by a bullet and fell at our feet. We did not stop but ran on; we rushed into the fields and managed to get away. By then it was three in the morning. We slipped into Tłuste and went to a Polish man we knew, Mr Grabowski. He was a religious old man who lived alone with his wife; he hid us in his attic for a day and a night. We had no money, only a gold watch; father had had all the money on him. But father had already been stripped naked along with all the other corpses there; they had taken everything. The manager let us bury father; he gave us spades and my brother and I dug a hole and buried father naked as he lay. We had nothing to dress him in. I know where that grave is, and I shall always be able to find it.

Then we went into the woods. We had no money, but in the village nearby lived a lot of Poles who all knew us and were good to us. They were afraid to hide us but they gave us food. We slept in the woods, and in the evening when things were quiet in the village I would leave my brother and go and get bread. Each day I would get it from a different cottage, and in this way they fed us for two months. We washed our shirts in the river and dried them in the sun. We were only afraid that the Ukrainians would give us away. People told us that 15 kilometres away, in the Czerwonogród woods, there were some 'bandits' in Soviet uniforms who hunted down the

Volksdeutsch and took all sorts of things from the Ukrainians in the villages. We knew by then that they must be Soviet partisans. I wanted to go and join them because I knew we could not live for long like that in the woods, it was getting cold. We set off walking through the woods in that direction. The farmers told me which way to go to find them. I left my brother at a distance and arranged with him that I would give a whistle when I came back; and I went up to the encampment myself. A soldier shouted: 'Stoy! Kto idyot?' [Halt! Who goes there?]. I put my hands up and said: 'A Jew that's escaped from the *Aktions*.' The soldier came up to me, asked who else was with me and sent another soldier with me to get my brother. But my brother was very small then, not quite eight years old, and they told me to take him and leave him somewhere else and to come back alone. I thought that was a good idea. They agreed on the password 'Grisha the Jew' for when I came back, and I took my brother to Tłuste. We got on well with the Poles there; I went to Ignac Wiszniewski, gave him the gold watch and told him that all our things had been buried and that I would give him everything when the war was over if he would hide my brother. And he really did hide him till the end. So after the war we dug everything up and gave it to him, though we did not have anything left ourselves. He kept his word, so I wanted to keep mine.

I left my brother and went back to the woods. They gave me a uniform and everything that I needed. It was a very big army: I do not know how many men there were, but there was cavalry and infantry, tanks and artillery. One company had dogs. Each soldier had a trained alsatian. They could tell from the smell if an outsider was near. They did not bark, but just tugged at the soldier's trousers and led him to the place where the person was. The camp was completely entrenched, and bunkers had been built. I spent a whole year with the partisans. Every day I had lessons in horseriding and shooting. Actually I already knew how to ride a horse, but there you had to do it holding the reins between your teeth in order to have both hands free to load your machine gun. It was very

hard, but I learnt to shoot so well that they took me everywhere with them. Sometimes we rode into the villages at
night and sometimes by day. At night only the cavalry and
infantry moved about, and in the daytime tanks were also
used. We were not afraid of anything. When we found out
that the Ukrainian police were in one of the villages, we went
straight there and captured them, then we hanged them from
trees in the woods. The Germans stayed away from the
woods. Once the Germans came to the village of Nerków to
round up a contingent of people. We did not know about this
and set off there ourselves to collect some cattle. Our patrols
informed us right away that there were Germans in the
village. Very quietly we surrounded the village, and attacked.
It was a real battle. I rode with the reins in my teeth and fired
at the Germans with my machine gun. It was not the police
but the Wehrmacht. Some of the officers escaped; a lot of them
we shot, and we took 150 soldiers prisoner. No one harmed
them. They took away their uniforms and weapons and gave
them civilian clothes with a POW stamp, and they worked for
us the whole time. They were all right; they were given the
same food as everyone, and no one bullied them. We had
meat every day, enough butter, and so much vodka that it
stood in vats. I did not want to drink, but I washed in vodka.
Soviet planes flew in to us and dropped arms and tinned food,
and also leaflets and various orders. When we heard the roar
of aeroplanes in the night, we could always tell from the
sound whether they were ours. Then the rockets went up –
red, white and green – and they knew where to drop the
things.

When the front was close, an order came from a plane to
inform the Germans that if during their retreat they burned
and pillaged, the Soviets would pay them back on their own
territory. As soon as we heard that Soviet tanks were in
Tłuste, we rode to meet them. As I was the youngest, they
gave me a red flag and I rode at the front between two officers.
I had my partisan documents but when I left them I had to
hand them in with my gun. They tried to persuade me to stay

with them, but you could not keep fighting for ever. Besides, my brother was in hiding at Mr Wiszniewski's, and I did not want to leave him on his own. Now we have come to Kraków with a Jew from Rumania who helped us. I just want to go to Palestine and work there. And if I have to fight then I will. This time I shall know what I am fighting for.

(Archive of the VJHC in Kraków, statement no. 87)

Chapter Six
PRISON

1. JOEL LITTMAN

Born 1928 in Kozienice, near Radom
(*Written account*)

On 5 November 1943 the ghetto in Radom was closed down. The leader of our cell tried to make sure that all the Jews got parcels from the Red Cross. I was the only one who did not get any parcels, but everyone in the cell shared their parcels with me. The parcels contained two kilograms of sliced and buttered bread, one kilogram of boiled buckwheat, eggs, an onion and some garlic. The Polish Red Cross sent parcels like these every week. In prison with me there was a prisoner-of-war who had been accused by a Ukrainian of shooting down a German pilot and torturing him. He had been in prison for two years. They had been going to execute him, but he produced witnesses and was given a reprieve. Another was sentenced to six years for having Aryan papers. He defended himself by saying that he did not know that it was forbidden to leave the ghetto. The prosecutor had called for the death sentence, but the judges agreed to a reprieve. Another had been sent to prison for trying to cross illegally into Hungary. We all worked for the 'Bata' firm, making boots and clogs. I escaped execution because my case was with the *Sondergericht*, and, fortunately, I had not fallen into the hands of the Gestapo. I was needed in the case against the bandits who were in prison. The hearing was set for 23 December 1943. I was kept in the prison at Radom for a whole year. On 8 July 1944 I was transferred. At that time, the number of prisoners was about 600. When the front began to draw close all of them were moved. Some were sent to Auschwitz; 12 were killed, including one man from my case. I was sent with two other Jews to Częstochowa. The worst bandit was released. We were loaded onto a goods wagon; we were given a kilogram of bread and 100 grams of lard each. We were escorted by the Polish police, eight policemen, three Polish warders and a German military policeman. They beat us mercilessly on the way.

I made straps for clogs, 35 pairs a day on average. In Częstochowa there was also the Polish police. In the morning I learned that in the Częstochowa prison there were 11 Jews who had been sent there for trying to escape from the ghetto, and tailors who had made clothes for Gestapo officers.

The daily food ration was 250 grams of bread and half a litre of soup. The Jews passed white bread and eggs to me by the guards. Three times a day, at set times, we were allowed to satisfy our bodily needs. We slept on the floor on straw mattresses; the cell was dark. We got up at six in the morning, and muster was at seven. The whole time we got a second dinner from the Red Cross – buckwheat with beans and potatoes.

A week later, on 16 July, I was handcuffed and put on a train. We travelled in passenger carriages. There were 80 Poles and three Jews from Radom; we had to stand and were not allowed to go up to the window. Most of the Poles were in prison for theft or black marketeering. We arrived in Wrocław [Breslau]. We lay on the asphalt floor of a cellar, 80 men to one room. For supper we were given coffee and 100 grams of bread; and in the morning, 150 grams of bread and half a litre of soup. The windows were blacked out and it was very stuffy in the cellar. The German guards bullied us. The Poles were afraid of them. If you failed to bow in the correct way you were beaten and not given any dinner. You were allowed to relieve yourself only once a day. On 23 August 1944 we were given coffee and half a kilogram of bread, and we were handcuffed. They took us to the station – 200 of us. We were put on a prison train, 12 to a cell. We were kept at the station for hours in the sun. The cells were terribly cramped and stuffy. Many people fainted. They were carried out into the corridor and then taken back to their cell. As soon as the train moved off I got across to the window and smashed the pane. Later on, for doing that I was beaten and not given any bread, but in that way we avoided being suffocated. We arrived in Leipzig. The city had been bombed and the station no longer existed. We were taken to a cell. We were not allowed to talk; if anyone spoke they were not given any bread. Since the prison had been bombed, we were housed in wooden barracks. There were 50 people to each hut. It was stuffy. The next day the 200 of us were again taken to a train and transferred to Dessau. This was a small town. We were kept in a barn. We were a bit freer there – there was more room. For two days we were left without food. Then we were each given 100 grams of bread and a little jam.

As well as the guards we were joined by the German criminal police. They began checking the list. They asked me if I was a Pole; I replied that I was 'from Poland'. In this way I did not lie but avoided the dangerous truth. The Poles treated me well; they took pity on me because I was small, and they did not know that I was Jewish. Discipline was strict there. If we met a guard on our way to dinner, we had to turn to the wall and not look at him. Order was kept by one of the guards, who we used to call 'grandad'. The senior of the cell, chosen from among the prisoners, had to report that every-thing was in order. Each prisoner reported 'Prisoner on trial [name] punished for …'. The *Oberinspektor* we called 'Rex', after Rex the Bulldog, whom he resembled. One of the prisoners served as orderly. He kept order in the corridor and gave out dinners; he was a sort of *capo*. Some of these were worse than the guards; they would beat you if they found a speck of dust after you had swept the floor. Bread was called 'hunks', for soup we would say 'water's coming', and parcels were 'grub'.

When someone new joined the cell we always arranged a 'prosecutor'. While he was asleep (at night the window was completely blacked out), the person playing the prosecutor put a blanket over his head and, standing by the door, put a boot close to his mouth to alter his voice and make it sound as if it was coming from the corridor. He called out the 'new boy', who had already been warned by his fellow-prisoners that the prosecutor would come, and who was happy, think-ing that he might be released. The 'prosecutor' ordered the prisoner to get under the table – so that he would not be able to see anything and would not realise that the prosecutor was just one of the other prisoners, and that he was not in the corridor but also in the cell. He was asked: 'What nationality are you?' 'Hungarian.' 'You're lying!' 'I'm not, sir.' 'You will drink three mugs of water as a punishment. Did you have a girlfriend?' 'No.' 'You're lying. I know you did. Do you want to go home?' 'Yes.' 'I heard that you treated people badly, that you used to beat them.' At the end the prosecutor said: 'You'll be released, report tomorrow to the foreman.' Practical jokes like this were constantly being played. The next day the 'new boy', who was convinced that he had been visited by the 'prosecutor', reported to the foreman. The foreman just laughed and told him to run around the exercise yard carrying a plate of food and singing a Hungarian song. One time, by a strange coincidence, the next day the 'new boy' really was released and was sent to Skarżysko.

We called habitual criminals 'recids'; the military police were the 'Passover', and guards were known as 'grandad'. One bad guard was nicknamed 'Red Alex', and another '*Der stryj mit dem Besem*' [the uncle with the broom]; we referred to Hitler as '*zwei zweierlei und vierer-Führer*' [two-times-two and four-Führer (a play on words)] or '*Hutelmacher*' [hatmaker]. The Jewish police were called 'dachshunds' because they were always toadying; the Polish guards used to swear at the prisoners, calling them 'bloody thieves'.

The prisoners used to sing this song:

> Enough of this torment and these alarms
> This endless lack of sleep and food
> Far from the police and the handcuffs
> To cross to another world
>
> Life cheated me
> Life pushed me in the can
> It brought everything down upon me
> And now it pretends not to know me
>
> Who will hear me today
> As I sing in the prison silence
> That my heart weeps with pain

Prison

Do you know this prison
Do you know these grey clothes:
These are the prisoners behind bars

A tiny winged friend
Flew in through the bars
He looked at my prison rags
And flew off far away

They used to frighten me with hell
That it is somewhere else, not here
Now they have put me in hell
What would God say?

I remember the names of the Polish guards from Radom:
Kraśnicki, Jagodziński, Monela, Bochenko (a Ukrainian),
Małecki.

Dessau was taken over by the German police. The Polish
guards were transferred to Wrocław. The list was read again.
The police were wearing helmets. They did not suspect that
there were any Jews among the prisoners. When the name
Littman was read out, one of them shouted: 'What, a Jew is
still here?', and tried to kick me, but I dodged him. As they
took me to the train they kept their eye on me and said, 'Jews
should be killed off'. They kept beating me and telling me
that I was not walking properly. We were transferred to
Magdeburg in a prison train, with 15 to a cell. They had a top-
security prison there with double bars. We got 150 grams of
bread for the whole day, and we were lined up in the corridor
facing the wall. We stood like this for three hours. Then 200
people were put into one cell. Later we were taken to Hanover
and split up: 80 people were sent to the courthouse prison,
and 120 to the police prison. In the courthouse prison the food
was not bad, 400 grams of bread. They did not know there
that I was Jewish. In the police prison they only gave 200
grams of bread; and there every 'grandad' had a rubber
truncheon. The prisoners had to stand up straight, facing the
wall. If anyone turned round they were beaten terribly. We
were badly underfed, we were weak with hunger. The soup

there was just water with cabbages in; in the morning they served coffee, and in the evening nothing.

On 29 August 1944 we were transferred to Hameln, the Jews separately. All our watches and things were taken away and put in storage. We lay on straw in the corridor. Then they gave us a change of clothing and put us into cells, three to a cell. We did not know how to adapt to the rules in that place. The orderly told us to scrub the asphalt floor till it shone, and to polish the bucket and bowl with a brick. We did not know how to do this. One of the guards, called 'the Tiger', came to check things; he said that it was dirty, and he beat us. I shared a cell with a German gypsy and a German who had been sent to prison for political reasons. Later they put me in a separate cell. I spent the whole day gluing bags. When we went out for exercise, everyone had to stand by the door of the cell, facing the wall. When we met a guard, we had to turn our head towards him and salute with our head. During the exercise we had to run round the yard till we were gasping for breath. As I was severely weakened, I begged the guard, 'the Pug', to let me sweep the yard instead. After I begged and begged he eventually agreed. Even though people knew I was Jewish they were good to me. They made me wear a star so that everyone would know I was a Jew. The guard used to hit us in the face; he was always checking the grilles and the window bars. If your bed was not properly made he would beat you about the face. The Poles and the Germans were treated the same, the Jews worse. A 20-minute walk every day; muster at seven o'clock, then breakfast, then sticking paper boxes and bags in the cell, and, at 12 o'clock, dinner: buckwheat, potatoes, beans. At seven in the evening, supper: 200 grams of bread, 50 grams of jam. You had to make 300 bags a day, that was the quota. The orderly, who was also a prisoner but was responsible for order in the corridors, had a quota of 150 bags. Usually I did his quota too, and for that I got more soup. Sometimes we were given propaganda books in the cells. Satires on Churchill and Chamberlain, the glorification of the German army and so on. In the next cell there was a blind Pole. 'The Tiger' used to beat him with a length of rubber because he did not understand what people said to him. I had rheumatism in my legs and I could not run. 'The Pug', an 80-year-old guard, could not walk, but he could beat people. If anyone went up to him and did not take off his cap, he would beat him. The sick used to go running along a short corridor, the healthy along a big one. Although I had rheumatism and felt ill, the German doctor, who was also a prisoner, would not give me a sick note; he was a political prisoner and he used to say: 'All Jews are cheats.'

The 'grandads' were changed every two weeks. A new guard was called a 'bandit'. One of the guards was nicknamed 'Fajwek'. In April 1945, when the front was drawing close, they ordered us out onto the yard; they confiscated our things and let us go back to our cells. We lived through the English air raids. We expected to be evacuated at any moment. The window panes kept being smashed in the cells. The guards would not let us go out for a walk; they were constantly in a rage, and beat people for no reason. Other guards assured us that we would be able to go home. The next day, almost all the Germans were granted an amnesty. Out of 1,000 prisoners, 400 were left in the cells. On 2 April we were assembled in the yard. We were given two days' supply of bread. We were to be taken to Hamburg – Poles, Czechs, Frenchmen imprisoned for sabotage, and one Jew. After six days we arrived in Schwerin. We had eaten all the bread at the beginning of the journey and for six days we had had nothing to eat. Some Germans had thrown some raw potatoes into the carriages. In the course of those six days 220 people died of starvation. In Schwerin the strongest men fainted from hunger. We were each given 200 grams of bread. The next morning we arrived in Butzow. We were kept at the station for half a day without food. About 100 of us were sick, the other 80 were barely able to walk. It took us three hours to walk three kilometres. The sick were put onto carts.

We were housed in a prison barracks with bars on the windows. We were given three-quarters of a litre of soup. We lay there, utterly exhausted with hunger. We were filthy, we had not been allowed to wash. They did not know that I was Jewish because I had pulled the star off. The guard used to give us socks to darn, and for that I got an extra hunk of bread. The guard was afraid to let me do the darning in the barracks as there were lice there, so he let me do it in the yard. For that I would get double helpings of soup. One of the prisoners who knew me noticed this, and said: 'This is a Jew.' They started asking me where my star was. I gave the excuse that I had lost my old jacket with the star on, and that I had been given a new one; I said I was only half-Jewish. 'You're lying', the guard shouted at me. Knowing that there were no papers in Butzow, I told him to check. The guard threatened that if I did not tell him where my star was he would throw me in the dark cell. There they only gave you bread and water. The front was getting closer, but we remembered that Hitler had said that even if he lost at 12 o'clock, at five minutes to 12 he would kill all the Jews. One Pole and I decided to escape. He began digging a hole in the barracks. The German orderly found out about it and told the guards. They assembled us in the yard and ordered the person who had done it to own up. The German pointed to that Pole and they took him to the dark cell. I kept on thinking about escaping. The situation with food was very bad – 180 grams of bread a day, three-quarters of a litre of soup (water and turnip without salt); we had no work, and we were guarded very closely. From January to May we did not once have a bath or change our clothes. On 2 May we learnt that Hitler was dead. Dysentery broke out; 120 people became ill with it. There were no doctors, and all we had were some powders and some charcoal. We slept on straw in the stables where horses had once been kept. There were Czechs, Poles and German Nazis who had been sentenced for theft; these used to threaten me, saying 'So many Germans are dead, why should that Jew stay alive? Kill him'. But they did not have the courage. We were so hungry we ate raw nettles and grass. The Germans did not allow this, because they were afraid of an epidemic. When we were finally liberated, 90 of us were sick in bed, and 30 had to be held up, as they were so weak they could barely stand.

(Archive of the CJHC, statement no. 637)

2. JAN KULBINGER

Born 13 May 1930 in Drohobycz; son of Tadeusz and Jetti Lieberman

(Statement taken by M. Hochberg-Mariańska, Kraków)

There is nothing special that I have to tell about the Soviet period; the most important thing was that during that time my father and sister died. There remained my two older sisters, my little baby brother and my Mama, and, of course, me. Straight after the Germans entered there was the first pogrom, organised by the Ukrainians. The Germans gave the Ukrainians one free day in which they could murder Jews. At that time the Poles were still helping the Ukrainians. Later they stopped helping them. We were hidden by a lady neighbour, who later became a *Volksdeutsch*. I did not stay locked inside because I do not look Jewish at all; I walked around the town and no one stopped me. I saw Ukrainians beating Jews with spades, whips, hammers and knives. They took the victims to the cemetery and there they shot them. People hid for three days because, although it was supposed to be only one day, afterwards, when they caught someone, they would not let them go.

Later they formed a *Judenrat* and a Jewish police. They ordered the *Judenrat* to provide people for labour. The people in the *Judenrat* knew perfectly well that it was not for labour, because they sent their own families into hiding straightaway. Others had to report in, and at that time thousands were transported out. In Drohobycz there was a closed camp where Jews worked making roof-tiles; both my sisters were sent

221

there. Mother was taken away during one of the *Aktions*; I was left alone with my little brother and one sister. She had fallen ill and so had been sent back home from the camp. When there was an *Aktion* we stayed in the attic, often for days on end, without food. The neighbours stole all of the things from our flat, so we had nothing left. We went to various people for meals. In the second *Aktion* we again managed to stay hidden. That time people were sent to Bełżec, and a lot of people were shot in the Bronicki woods. Then they made the ghetto, but I still went all over buying and selling things, because otherwise I would have starved to death. I traded wherever I could. No one was afraid of the death sentence.

The third *Aktion* lasted four weeks. They went poking about and searching in all the hiding-places, and the Jewish police helped them. We were in a walled hide-out, where there were about 40 people; the Jewish police gave us away. It was possible to buy your way out with money, but we did not have any. They took us, me, my sister and my brother, to the Sammelstelle, but all three of us escaped at night through the window of the lavatory. But that did no good, the *Aktion* was still going on and they took us back to the court, where Jews were being assembled for a transport, and from there we could no longer escape. They drove us to the station like cattle. The wagons were big, and they packed 400 people into each one. I could not stay there, I had to get away. My brother and sister did not want to run away – once they had been caught they lost the desire to escape. But not me. We went about 30 kilometres further and people cut a hole in the wagon. I said goodbye to my sister and brother and I jumped out. I was lucky, I did not even hurt myself. My cousin, Józek Rabach, also jumped out; I met up with him when I got back to Drohobycz and from then on we stayed together the whole time.

We sold newspapers in the Aryan district and traded in anything we could. He also looked Aryan, even more so than me. I found out that my sister in the camp had been put on a transport along with everyone else.

In the spring of 1943 the ghetto was completely closed down. Józek and I hid in the fields for a few days, but we knew there was nothing for it but that we would have to move away, because everyone in the area knew us. We got on a train to Lwów. In the train with us there was a Polish lady from Drohobycz. We did not know her, but she knew us and straightaway she started complaining about the Jews, saying that they were running away, that they wanted to stay alive, but that they would not succeed – they had been alive for long enough. We heard all this and we could not leave the carriage, because by then everyone was looking at us and watching our every move. The moment the train stopped in Lwów, they called the *Bahnschutz*. They took us at once to the *Schutzpolizei* and, without asking us any questions, transferred us directly to the ghetto. At that time the ghetto was being closed down. We stood on the square with all the others. I saw people taking poison, mothers giving poison to their children and grown-ups giving it to their elderly parents. I was wondering how we might save ourselves, but for the moment nothing could be done. Only when they had driven us to the tram, on the way to the Janowska camp, did we try to escape. But they caught us straightaway and set about us with their rifle butts. I began telling them that we were not Jews, that we were not from Lwów; but no one paid any attention to me. As soon as they got us there they locked us in the Jewish bunker by the camp gate. There they kept Jews who had passed themselves off as Aryans. The Gestapo beat people up. When it was proved that someone was Jewish, they beat them so savagely that you could not bear to watch. I was only concerned that Józek should get through and not confess. One of the Gestapo came up and looked at us. He asked who we were. I told him we had come from Drohobycz; we had been passing by when the trams came in, two Jews had escaped and they had arrested us instead of them and sent us here. He hit me and started shouting: 'Who do you think you are, coming from Drohobycz to loot the ghetto? You just wait, I'll show you!' Let it be looting; I was not going to deny that.

We spent one day in the bunker, then they transferred us to an 'Aryan' bunker, and there we finally got fed. I said that we were called Jan and Józef Bandrowski, that our father had died and that we had a stepmother in Drohobycz. I said we had run away to look for work because our stepmother beat us and did not feed us. We had come to Lwów, and we were walking past the ghetto when they arrested us instead of two Jews who had escaped from the tram. They wrote everything down and sent us to the *Sicherheitspolizei* [security police] on Łąckiego Street. When we got there and saw that a doctor was examining men and segregating them, I thought: 'That's the end of that, then.' But the doctor, a man in glasses who looked like a Jew, examined us and said: 'Aryans.' They put us together in a cell. There were 60 people in there; we slept on the floor. They were mostly thieves and bandits. There was one old man, Mr Winiarski, who had been put in prison for harbouring Jews. He predicted that we would be released in seven days. At that time it was Pentecost and the Polish Committee sent us some good soup and bread. The criminals forced us to let them put tattoos on our hands – I had a sailor and Józek an anchor.

After a week they called us out by name and took us downstairs for more questioning. All the children from the prison were there, six of us including one little nine-year-old girl. She was Jewish; she would not admit it, so the Gestapo officer said that if she confessed they would not do anything to her, and if she did not they would beat her. And he spoke so sweetly to her, telling her not to be afraid, that they would not do anything to her, and that she would be all right, that the stupid girl believed him and said that yes, she was Jewish. We had to give yet another statement, and then we were made to stand facing the wall and wait till all the others had been questioned. Then the Gestapo officer said that he was going to make a telephone call in connection with our case. I thought that that would be it, that he would contact Drohobycz and find out that none of it was true. But he telephoned the Polish Committee to ask them to come and take two boys away. And he typed out a certificate to say that the *Sicherheitspolizei* was handing over Jan and Józef Bandrowski into the care of the Polish Committee. I knew that this paper was the best document there could be for us, better even than a forged birth certificate, because it was really issued by those gangsters. During the final interrogations I had been very much on edge because I was afraid that Józek would let something slip – he is younger than me and I looked after him the whole time. But he just repeated exactly what I said.

A car came from the Committee and took us to the Home. There were nuns there. Right away they said: 'Children, you must go to confession, because you've just come from prison and you must have a lot of sins on your conscience.' This was a new fix we were in. I managed to get out of going to confession, but Józek had to go because the other children of his age were also going to their first communion. He went and just tried to copy the other children, and everything went well.

A few weeks later a farmer who had a farm in Nowy Lwów on the outskirts of the city came looking for a suitable boy to tend his cows. I volunteered at once because I was so bored just being in the Home; and the farmer liked the look of me. Then Józek was taken on by another farmer and we both had jobs, though we were quite far from each other, and we could see each other only on Sundays. Józek was not happy there and I tried to find him another job closer to me. Where I was there was a lot of hard work. Tending cows is not bad work but it is boring. I also had to muck out the stables, help with the digging when it was needed and generally do whatever the farmer needed doing. Once some guests came and they talked a lot about the Jews; the farmer asked: 'Look at him, don't you think he might be a Jew?' He was not making a joke. He had asked me before, and I told him to go to the Committee and they would show him the certificate. But the guests laughed and said that it was not possible, and the farmer's daughter-in-law, whose husband was in the criminal police, said: 'Don't worry, if he's been with the Gestapo and they've examined him, they wouldn't have let him go.'

In the end we became tired of working as cowherds because they kept giving us more and more hard work, and we were walking around in rags because they did not give us any money apart from just enough to buy food. A couple of times I went to the German army – there was an anti-aircraft battery stationed nearby. We started work there and stayed till the end, till the Germans retreated. No one suspected us. We had great shocks of blond hair and they thought we were Ukrainians. In the summer of 1944, when the Germans fled, we wandered around the countryside for several days. After the Soviet army arrived we met up with our uncle, who is a doctor, and he looked after us and brought us to Kraków.

(Archive of the VJHC in Kraków, statement no. 140)

Chapter Seven

ADULTS ON CHILDREN

1. JÓZEF GITLER-BARSKI

General Secretary of Joint in Poland
(Report of interview with Noe Grüss)

Care of children in the Warsaw ghetto

The work of Centos, the organisation uniting charitable organisations caring for Jewish orphans, covered Warsaw and the suburban clinics. A child health care department was set up within the Jewish self-help organisation in Kraków to cover the whole country. Gitler-Barski and Dr A. Berman, a member of parliament, were the directors of Centos in Warsaw.

As the general population of the Warsaw ghetto grew and the Jews concentrated in one place, the number of children also rose – in 1941–42 there were about 50,000 of them.

The well-to-do classes did not tend to have many children, while the poor who came in from the provinces had large families. Many children were alone after their parents had been taken to the so-called work camps, from which they did not return because of the high mortality rate, caused by an outbreak of typhus among the adults. The children's situation was tragic. They were crammed into the narrow alleyways of the ghetto. Many of them were from the provinces, child vagrants who, swollen and starving, waited in vain to be saved by the grown-ups. In the face of these conditions, Centos began a campaign to save the children. The political and social circles of the ghetto were mobilised, industrialists, businessmen and the general public, and they demonstrated great generosity. In less than a year there arose a network of institutions under Centos: children's homes, hostels, day-centres, children's canteens, and even playgrounds and summer camps on the outskirts of the ghetto.

More than 5,000 children found shelter in the long-term institutions, which were set up thanks to great public support, and of which there were about 20. Centos organised hostels in conjunction with tradesmen's guilds such as the bakers and the brushmakers, each of which gave millions to set up a particular hostel. About 30,000 children attended the day-centres and the canteens.

The children's canteens were actually secret Jewish schools run by educational organisations (Tarbut [Hebrew school], Ciszo [schooling with Yiddish as the language of instruction], religious education) which Centos brought together in a 'Children's Food Committee'. The canteens were located in the school buildings of the above-named organisations, and the waiters and other staff were schoolteachers who taught classes after hours. Today the Ministry of Education recognises this secret education and honours the certificates issued then. Children's choirs were organised in the canteen schools, along with general educational activities. About 60 per cent of the children living in the ghetto attended these schools.

Centos also operated 'detention centres' where children found begging on the streets were taken and kept in quarantine for a certain period before being transferred to a hostel.

Centos employed about 1,000 paid staff, and there were about 2,000 volunteer workers.

Despite the scope of their work there were still many vagrant children. This state of affairs continued until July 1942 when the *Aktion* to evacuate people from the Warsaw ghetto began. The Jewish disciplinary services were forced to hand over to the Germans 'contingents' to be put on transports. Centos obtained an exemption from these contingents. After eight to ten days the Germans took charge of the contingents themselves, and then one institution after another went to the Umschlagplatz. It must be stressed that the teachers displayed great heroism, selflessly accompanying the children even when they had the opportunity to go into hiding. A well-known example of this selflessness is that of Dr Janusz Korczak accompanying the children. Another example was that of the hostel on Dzielna Street. Mrs Janowska, the manageress of the hostel, assembled the staff and announced that she had noticed that many teachers were going into hiding. She demanded that the staff take a resolution not to

230

abandon the children. Anyone who was not prepared to go with the children should leave at once. No one left, and during the next blockade the staff carried out their duties till the very end.

The liquidation of the children was carried out with great deceitfulness by the Germans. They assured the children that they were taking them to another place, and recommended that they take blankets, knapsacks and so on.

The first phase of the liquidation came to an end in mid-September 1942. At this time they closed down the institutions in Otwock and elsewhere in the Warsaw area. In proportion to the number of adults, not many children remained. Children were hidden in stoves, in cupboards, and in various other hiding-places. It seemed that Centos's role was over.

Dr Berman began resistance work on the Aryan side. Gitler-Barski stayed in the ghetto. In fact, there were still many Jewish children in Warsaw. They began to emerge from bunkers, recesses and hiding-places on the Aryan side. The police and the Germans organised hunts for them and sent them to the small ghetto. About 1,200 children remained there, and new institutions were set up to care for them, including day-centres and small hostels for a few dozen orphans. The provision of care for these children was supervised by Dawid Guzik, a director of Joint. [Guzik died in an air crash in Prague in March 1946.]

A great deal of energy was devoted to efforts to save the children from the Umschlagplatz. On one occasion Mrs Maria, the manageress of the hostel in Twarda Street, sent a short letter with an appeal to rescue 60 young girls from the Umschlagplatz. Gitler-Barski went there, and after extensive efforts and negotiations with Schmerling, the commandant of the militia, he succeeded in saving the children.

At that time it would have been possible to take even more children away, but Schmerling would not agree to this. It was incredible that even the small five- or six-year-old children realised at once what was going on and held up their identity cards which entitled them, as children of parents with the necessary *Ausweise* [identity card], to leave the Umschlagplatz. Over a dozen children were saved in this manner.

The work of Centos continued until 18 January 1943. During the *Aktion* of 18 January the Germans also closed down the day-centres. Józef Gitler-Barski describes one scene from this *Aktion*:

> In the night of 18–19 January I went to 56 Zamenhofa Street to see how the children were. The rooms looked as though a massacre had taken place there. The furnishings were destroyed, utensils were smashed, feathers from mattresses were flying in the air and there were bullet holes in the walls. There were no lights. In the furthest room I noticed a blanket rolled up into a bundle. In the bundle there was a five-year-old boy who showed faint signs of life. I thought he had frozen to death. Suddenly, without opening his eyes, he said quietly but clearly: *'Ich will nicht sterben'* ('I do not want to die'). He lost consciousness. I took him to a shelter, and nursed him back to life. Unfortunately, that boy died later.

After 18 January, there was no more work for Centos. Apart from isolated individuals, there were no more Jewish children in the ghetto.

(Material of the CJHC)

2. SARA MUNK

Teacher

(*Written memoir*)

Food stations in the Warsaw ghetto

Immediately after the Germans entered Warsaw, the provision of care for the Jewish children became an urgent problem. Many Jewish families that until now had been well-off found themselves in dire material need. In view of the shortages of foodstuffs, and their high cost where they were available, feeding the children became an important concern. This concern was addressed by the TOZ and by Centos. Children's canteens were set up and later converted into 'food stations', staffed by teachers from the Jewish schools. Since the German authorities did not allow schools for Jewish children, the teachers decided to organise lessons in the canteens, of course under the pretence of providing food. The children registered at the canteens were divided into groups corresponding to the various classes. The lack of teaching materials, schoolbooks and exercise books caused considerable difficulties; but the children were keen to learn. They showed great enterprise in various subjects, and drew or cut out pictures to decorate the dining rooms.

As well as the lessons in the canteens, there were also study groups. These were attended by the better-off children. The groups met at the flat of a different pupil each day, so as not to attract the attention of the German authorities.

We received foodstuffs for the children's canteens directly from the TOZ. Through the first months of 1941 supplies were plentiful. For the Easter of that year we even received matzos, fat and eggs.

In autumn 1941 the Warsaw ghetto was created. Confining the Jews to a tiny area, cutting them off from the rest of the world with walls and barbed wire, and transporting in Jews

233

from the small towns, all had a disastrous influence on the Jewish community, and especially on its children.

Forced to live in impossibly cramped flats, left to fend for themselves in view of the general predicament, they had to manage on their own, and often were the only breadwinners for their entire family. The children who 'looked right' slipped through the barbed wire or through holes in the wall and crossed to the Aryan side. There they bought food and brought it back to the ghetto. Many children fell victim to the bullets of the German military police as they crawled through the barbed wire. Great skill and courage were needed to 'get the goods'. Little seven- or eight-year-old boys and girls, thin as rakes, would slip like rats through cracks in the wall. They would throw the goods, bread or potatoes, over the ghetto wall, where there was usually someone waiting to pick them up, and they themselves squeezed through a hole. Other children made money by trading in the ghetto itself. They sold cigarettes, sweets or toffees; still others, who were less enterprising, went out onto the streets to beg.

At this time attendance at the canteens increased significantly, while at the same time the number of children remaining afterwards to take lessons dropped. Children who up till now had studied regularly would eat their meal and then explain, often with tears in their eyes, that they did not have time for classes because they had to help their parents and go and make money. These were often the children of resettled families who, after selling everything that could be sold, had found themselves in an impossible situation. This was a time when huge numbers of Jews were being evacuated from the small towns to the Warsaw ghetto. So-called resettlement stations were set up. In these places, mostly flats attached to the synagogues, the resettled families were housed. The level of hygiene in the flats was appalling. Adults and children lay on straw mattresses in terribly cramped conditions. Very often there was only one stove in the room that was supposed to serve several families for their cooking. The children from these stations came *en masse* to the canteens for dinner; often the hot soup was their only cooked meal of the day. As winter approached, fewer and fewer children came to the canteens, because of lack of clothing and footwear. There began the undesirable practice of adults taking food home for children, a practice which we resisted without success.

The parents' explanations of why the child could not come – lack of clothes or shoes, or sickness – were quite plausible, but not always true. Parents often took soup for three or four children in order to feed the entire family. Meals were served from 12 till three o'clock. The children were divided into groups according to age: 6–8 years old, 8–10, 10–12 and 12–14. Each group came at a set time. In theory, all children had identity cards which gave their group and the time at which they were supposed to come. Often, however, children did not come on time, explaining the fact that they were late by saying that they had no watches, for these had either been sold or confiscated by the Germans. This made the work much more difficult, for we could not deprive children of a meal just because they had not come on time.

During the meals the children chatted about various things, depending on the group. We tried to introduce topics that were far from the horrors of reality. All the terrifying experiences left their mark on the children's minds. Smiles were hardly ever seen on their apathetic faces. There were those, however, especially our 'smugglers', who, filled with a sense of rebellion against the restrictions on their freedom, longed to avenge the wrongs they had suffered. The dreadful conditions caused the children to age prematurely. The children of the ghetto left their carefree childhood outside the walls; in the cramped cage where they had been imprisoned, they lost the sunny, carefree smile of a child and in most cases bore their fate with the resignation of old men. Yet they participated actively in the discussions, nearly all of them: little Henio, with his suitcase of cigarettes; Marek, who had just run in from the Aryan side, exhausted, with a sack of potatoes; Hanka, the beggar girl from Leszno Street; and many others. There was great interest in Ilyin's book *100,000 Whys*, and the children discussed each chapter after reading it. At the food stations, gymnastics, games and choirs were also organised. In the games the children could burn off some of their energy. Each game caused such delight, and there was always a joyful hum of voices.

In the winter of 1941 Centos organised a course in puppetry for the teachers and supervisors, to help them put on shows for the children and to provide the necessary materials for these shows. Centos itself also mounted a series of splendid puppet shows for the children.

In the summer of 1941 a typhus epidemic broke out. Appalling living conditions, lack of hygiene, hunger and shortage of medical supplies all contributed to the high mortality rate; and when, in the autumn, a number of streets were cut off from the ghetto, the life of the Jewish community became truly hellish. The question of maintaining standards of hygiene was constantly being brought up at the food stations. Doctors and hygienists conducted examinations of the children. A huge percentage of the children had lice. They did all they could to remedy this, but cramped living quarters and the lack of clothing and soap hardly made matters easy. Nor did frequent visits to the bathhouse help.

The streets became full of starving vagrants in rags. I should also mention the 'chapers' (from the Yiddish word *chapn*, to snatch). These were young boys, dirty and ragged, who would lie in wait against a wall or loiter in the street. They would observe passers-by carefully. They were particularly common near confectioners' and grocers' shops. When they identified a potential victim with a parcel, they would snatch it from them, sink their teeth into it and try to run away. As they ran, they would try to stuff as much of the food as possible into their mouths and to swallow it. In the end they would be caught by other passers-by and severely beaten. The streets were also full of children begging, with thin bodies and swollen legs and faces. They would sit or lie by the wall. Many of them lined the walls of the court building on Leszno Street, sitting next to one another. Every one was a skeleton dressed in rags. These pitiful spectres were known as the 'flowerpots of the ghetto'. From those flowerpots nothing would grow any more.

The Jewish community was by no means indifferent to the plight of the Jewish children. Efforts were made to care for the children and to save them; and yet the means were unequal to the numbers who needed help. Several boarding-houses and day-rooms were established. In apartment buildings, house committees set up so-called 'children's corners' in each house. The committee would rent a room from one of the tenants where the children from that house could gather under the care of a supervisor to spend a few hours of classes and games. The poorer children were also given meals in the flats of the better-off tenants. But there were also houses, and these were in the majority, where all of the children were in need of support. The house committees of the wealthier groups attempted to help with money or by sending dinners. Alas, the means were insufficient. The products supplied to the canteens were of worse and worse quality; the number of children in need of meals kept growing; and hunger spread from day to day. Children who until recently had looked healthy now resembled skeletons. Their appearance could be seen to change daily, until one day they would stop coming to the canteen, and a grown-up would come to collect their meals. A week or two later we would receive news that the child had died. Many of our colleagues fell victim to typhus at that time, the summer of 1941.

Despite the fact that the children were given frequent baths, they continued to be infested with lice, and the mortality rate was very high. Fewer and fewer children stayed for classes. Those who were able, however, studied keenly. The children were unusually mature. Taught by the bitter experience of a terrible reality, they lost the trustfulness and faith of the child. It was hard to find answers to their searching questions. Their favourite subject was to ask each other what they would do after the war. A typical reply was: 'I'll buy a huge lot of bread and I'll eat till I'm completely full.' The children demonstrated great enterprise in organising various events, such as cleanliness week, a spring festival and other things. In this work they let off steam, and found an outlet for their creative energy; and, above all, it allowed them to forget the horrors of the reality around them. How many children's talents found expression and release! The children, often dressed in rags and with sunken cheeks, changed completely under the influence of the dance. Whoever saw little eight-year-old Halinka whirling around to the rhythm of a song sung by the children around her, or Szulimek dancing the *cracovienne*, or little Henoch, recounting with words, mime and gestures how he crawled through to the Aryan side and how he escaped from a sentries' hut after being arrested – whoever saw these things could never forget them. The children went wild with delight, and smiles appeared on even the most apathetic faces.

It was not only to eat soup that the children came to the canteens. Of course, the amount and quality of the meal were of the greatest importance to the hungry child. And yet we had many indications that the children came to escape, if only for a moment, from reality and to share their cares and worries, to play a while, read, talk and seek advice. I remember nine-year-old Basia asking for advice about what to do. She had the opportunity to stay on the Aryan side with a Polish lady she knew. But should she leave her parents in the ghetto? Should she save herself? I encountered this dilemma many times. A child, being the only breadwinner for the whole family, gave up the chance to stay on the Aryan side so as not to abandon his or her family to its fate. These and many other requests for advice, testify to the trust the children placed in the teachers at the food stations.

In the spring of 1942 two children's playgrounds were opened. The Jewish children had never had such a place to play in even before the war. Equipped with up-to-date gymnastic apparatus, it was an ideal place for rest and recreation. It truly was an oasis in the hell of the ghetto. Each day a different group of children would come to the playground. The place rang with singing and the joyful noise of children's voices. Here they forgot about the terrors of everyday reality, about the hunger, the poverty, the round-ups and executions. Here there was peace, there was sunlight, there was freedom. Long-forgotten, happy moments of childhood returned for a brief time and brought forgetfulness. The boarding-houses were also happy places for the children. Torn from the lowest depths of human destitution in the resettlement stations, dressed in clean clothes and fed properly, in the care of the supervisors they quickly entered the spirit of a children's home. They forgot about their terrible experiences. In the spring an exhibition was arranged in the children's home on Dzielna Street. Beautiful drawings, different everyday utensils made of wood, various toys, beautiful plasticine models, clothes, lovely slippers made of scraps of material and pieces of cord, and outstanding pieces of schoolwork such as essays and reports: all of this showed what could be achieved given the necessary encouragement.

The Jewish community strove to save the children. The profits from all kinds of events were donated to help them. Alas, neither playgrounds, nor homes, nor food stations, nor children's corners could save the Jewish children; they were doomed to be exterminated. In July the liquidation of the ghetto began. The first *Aktion* was aimed at the sick, the elderly and the children. An assurance by the German authorities that certificates issued by Centos and the TOZ would be honoured turned out to be a lie. The children's canteens continued their work until the very last moment; until the last moment the teachers remained at their posts, until they were led with the children to the wagons and to destruction. I witnessed the moment when the children were led out with Dr Korczak. He walked at the front of the column of children and went to die with them.

(Material of the CJHC)

3. SABINA MIROWSKA

Kraków

(Statement taken by Maria Holender, Kraków)

The Kraków Orphans' Home under the German occupation

On the day war broke out between Poland and Germany the Jewish Orphans' Home at 64 Dietla Street found itself without supervision. In the prevailing chaos, the members of the management left Kraków. There remained only the director of the Home, Anna Feuerstein, who had occupied her post for 17 years. At that time there were about 200 children in the Home. There was also a staff consisting of supervisors and domestic servants. In the first days of the war, during the bombardment, there was great panic among the children. They stayed in the shelter and ate food from the Home's reserves. After the Germans entered Kraków on 6 September 1939, the Home slowly returned to its regular routine. After a time the Germans visited the Home; they were very impressed by how tidy and clean it was, and thanks to this the Home was in their good graces. Evidence of this was the allocation of food that came in for the Home via the Jewish community authorities from the *Stadthauptmann* of Kraków.

This state of affairs lasted till August 1940. Since some of the Jewish population of Kraków were issued *Ausweise* [identity cards] permitting them to remain in Kraków, the management of the Home also began efforts to obtain such documents. At this time Schmidt, the *Stadthauptmann*, issued permission for the Children's Home to remain in Kraków. This, however, did not last long, for in the first few days of March 1941 an order was issued to establish a Jewish district in Podgórze. All the Jews in Kraków were ordered to take all their belongings and move to the Jewish district, the ghetto, by 20 March 1941. The Children's Home, thanks to the intervention of the Jewish community authorities, was given an extension till 1 April.

Moving the entire contents of a five-storey house presented

240

enormous difficulties. Moreover, the building at 64 Dietla
Street was suited to the needs of an orphanage (large
dormitories, a dining-room, a gymnasium equipped with
apparatus), and it was difficult to find a suitable building in
the ghetto. In the end they chose the Wasserberg Foundation
building at 8 Krakusa Street. It contained small rooms and it
was difficult to place all the children.

I worked in the Children's Home from May 1940, as a
secretary. I was in constant contact with the children; I was
responsible for their records, and I knew about every little
happening in their lives. Owing to the shortage of staff, older
girls in the Home looked after the younger children. The
children were reasonably well-dressed, though the lack of
stockings in particular made itself felt. The children were
given a religious upbringing: before each meal they prayed,
and the boys wore caps at table. For the festival of Hanukkah
in 1940 a great celebration was organised on Dietla Street,
where the children played blithely, not sensing the tragedy
that awaited them. At this time in the Home there was an
8-year-old boy called Juliusz Propst who was mentally handicapped. He was not able to live with other children and so the
Home for the Mentally Handicapped in Iwonicz, run by the
Order of St John of God, agreed to take him in for a fee of 90
złotys a month. He lived there for almost two years, until
Stadthauptmann Rodler issued a decree that all Jewish
children currently living in Christian full-time care institutions – nurseries, homes for the mentally handicapped and
others – were to be transferred to Jewish Orphans' Homes. To
add to the anxieties of the staff, one day a priest from Iwonicz
brought Propst back to the Home, which by then was already
situated in the ghetto.

As a result of this decree yet another surprise awaited the
Home. We received notice from the Christian nursery in
Koletek Street in Kraków that we were to take from them ten
children supposedly of Jewish origin. When we went to
collect them, not only did the children know nothing about
being Jewish, but they had been brought up as Christians.

When they were brought to our Home and placed among children brought up in the Jewish faith, for a long time they greeted each other with 'Christ be praised'. Most of these children did not have surnames; they were foundlings, and it was very difficult to establish their origins.

At Krakusa Street the management of the Home made efforts to ensure that the children had at least a basic diet. Collections were constantly being taken among the Jews, and this helped to support the budget of the Home for some time. A brushmakers' workshop was set up where the older children could work and earn money for the Home. On 1, 4 and 8 June transports left the ghetto for Bełżec. Several thousand Jews were evacuated. By then the Orphans' Home was also in danger of evacuation, and it was only thanks to the efforts of the Jewish community administration that, for a while, it escaped this fate. This was not official news, but I found out about it in confidence in the offices of the administration. After the evacuations the ghetto was reduced in size and the Orphans' Home was moved yet again to an even smaller building at 31 Józefińska Street.

It was here that the true Gehenna of the Jewish children began. Both children and adults were gripped with fear of evacuation; they lived in constant terror and uncertainty of what tomorrow would bring. The supervisors tried to find manual work in the various military units, in order to obtain protection in the event of an *Aktion*. This was naturally to the detriment of the children, for this work took up most of the day.

In August 1942 there were evacuations from the villages and small towns around Kraków. Outside the gates of the ghetto stood Jewish children who had either run away themselves from the *Aktions* or who had been brought in by Poles. These children were taken to the Orphans' Home at the order and on the recommendation of the head of the Jewish police, Symche Spira. In this fashion the number of children in the Home doubled. The management of the Home was in despair: there was nowhere to put the children. The problem was solved by sleeping two or three children to a bed. In many cases these children, unwashed after a journey of several days, had scabies, and by sleeping with the other children they infected almost everyone in the Home. It became clear later that the Germans had so graciously agreed that we should take the children in as a trap that had been planned from the beginning.

One day I was sent to the *OD* [the Jewish police] where a seven-year-old girl was handed over to me to be taken to the Orphans' Home. She was a German child, the daughter of an SS officer and a mother supposedly of Jewish origin. Her father had been at the front and her mother had been arrested. The girl had been in Berlin and later in an NSDAP home in Zakopane. Naturally, she could not speak any Polish; she wore a swastika on her coat and explained to me that this was a sign that only Germans could wear. As I crossed the street with her she noticed a German officer. She pointed at him and told me that her father wore the same kind of uniform. She sang Nazi songs, '*Wir fahren nach England*' and so on. It was difficult for her to get on with the other children because they could not understand each other. She kept her distance; she felt herself to be a German and, subconsciously, she thought she was superior. She met the same fate as the other children.

At the beginning of September 1942 the building at 31 Józefińska Street was requisitioned by the Germans as a furniture warehouse. Two buildings away, at 29 Józefińska Street, was the tradesmen's hostel, run by Matylda Schenkerowa, where boys over the age of 14 lived. Because of the lack of a building for the Orphans' Home, the two institutions were joined together. And this was the beginning of the end. There was no longer any hope of order or tidiness. Special three-tiered bunk beds were built for the children, as otherwise it would not have been possible to find room for them all. More and more children kept arriving, and it was only a single-storey building. The children were totally subdued, as if they sensed what lay before them. Work was found for ten of the older girls as nursing aides at the Jewish Hospital for

Epidemic Diseases, to protect them from evacuation; but alas, nothing came of this.

On 27 October 1942, that is, the day before the general evacuation, people in the ghetto already knew that there was something ominous in the offing. I was in the Home till ten in the evening; everyone there was very anxious. In spite of this, everyone still had a glimmer of hope that this time the Orphans' Home would be passed over. On 28 October 1942, in the early morning hours we learned that all those in work were to line up according to their place of work outside the *Arbeitsamt*. When I left home in the morning and set off towards the Orphans' Home, I discovered that the Home had been cordoned off by the police and that no one was allowed to enter or leave. Those of the staff who lived at the Home but were also employed elsewhere were not allowed to go to the *Arbeitsamt* with the other workers. For the same reason, the girls who worked at the hospital were unable to get out. At about midday the children and staff were led out into Zgody Square to be put on the transport. The youngest children, who could not walk by themselves, were thrown into baskets, loaded onto lorries and driven out of the ghetto. I learned later that they were taken outside the city and shot. The older children and the staff were taken from Zgody Square to the station at Płaszów and from there to Bełżec, where they were executed.

I also want to recount an incident that took place in Zgody Square. The Jewish militia offered to release the director of the Home, Anna Feuerstein, and her husband; but she refused, saying that she had been with the children for over 20 years and was not going to leave them at a moment like this. At this time they released the manager of the hostel, Entenberg, who told me about this. A number of boys from the hostel saved themselves by leaving the building by the roof in the early morning. In this tragic fashion the story of the Kraków Orphans' Home came to an end. The day after the children were taken away, the Home was a chilling sight. Scattered about were single stockings, little shoes and various items of

244

clothing that the children had left behind when they were taken away in such a rush; and the building, which shortly before had been so full of movement and life, stood empty, silent and ominous.

A few days later, I was informed that at 17 Krakusa Street a *Tagesheim*, or day-care home, was being opened for children who by some miracle had survived the general evacuation. These children had lost their parents and had no one to look after them. The *Tagesheim* was set up on the orders of the Germans, and was organised by the head of the Jewish police, Symche Spira, and the president of the Jewish community administration, Dawid Gutter. They gave assurances that, as long as they were there, nothing would happen to the children, and that what had happened to the Orphans' Home had been beyond their control. I did not work at the *Tagesheim*, though I helped out there from time to time. I did not believe the assurances of those men, and I realised that this was another trap for the children. It made my heart ache when I saw beautiful little children handed over voluntarily by their mothers, who had to work in the ghetto or were being sent to the newly established camp at Płaszów. The *Tagesheim* was housed in what used to be Dr Kranz's hospital. As more and more children came, and mothers were transferred *en masse* to Płaszów, the need arose to expand the *Tagesheim* and find a permanent place for the children. At this time the institution was moved to a much larger building at 17 Krakusa Street.

On 13 March 1943 the ghetto was cordoned off by the Germans and all those in work were ordered to transfer to Płaszów within a few hours. The sick and elderly and the children were to move to Ghetto B. We were aware of what lay ahead for these people. The *Tagesheim* was full to bursting. Leaving the ghetto, mothers risked their lives in trying to smuggle children out in knapsacks or in the ranks into the camp. The Germans tore children from their mothers and brought them to the *Tagesheim*. The despair of mother and child was boundless. Many a mother was prepared to die with her child, but the Germans did not allow the mothers to leave the ranks. The desperate mothers asked what would become of their children, and were told by Goeth and the *Judenrat* that they did not need to worry because the children would be taken to the camp the next day. Once again, this proved to be a deliberate deception. I learned what had happened to the children from the *Tagesheim* in Ghetto B only later, when I had already been in the camp for a number of days. The children had all been shot on 14 March 1943 and the bodies had been taken to a mass grave in Płaszów. The clothes that the children had been wearing were taken to be stored in the clothing warehouses at Płaszów, and many of the mothers recognised among those clothes the dresses or coats of their own children.

By a miracle, a handful of children made it into the camp at Płaszów, and remained there in appalling conditions till 14 May 1944, when there took place the tragic transfer of children, the sick and the elderly from the camp to the crematoria at Auschwitz.

(Archive of the VHJC in Kraków, statement no. 1079)

4. REGINA NELKEN

Kraków
(*Memoir*)

Children in the Kraków ghetto

Even before the war, Jewish orphans were sent to the Orphans' Home on Dietla Street, while boys over the age of 12 who were learning a trade lived on Krakowska Street at Craftsmen's Hostel No. 1, which was set up and run by Matylda Schenkerowa, and in Hostel No. 2 on Miodowa Street, established by Aleksandrowicz. When they were moved to the ghetto, the two hostels were joined together

246

and were located in the shelter on Józefińska Street. Mrs Schenkerowa continued to act as director, while the manager was the former manager of Hostel No. 2, Entenberg. The hostel was run in exemplary fashion; the children were found apprenticeships in various trades, anything to prove to the authorities that things were working. In the evenings, classes were organised.

During the first evacuation these children were left alone. Due to financial problems, or possibly on the recommendation of Spira [a Gestapo informer], at that time commandant of the OD [Jewish police], the Jewish Orphans' Home on Krakusa Street and the Hostel were joined together and the former was moved to the Hostel building; from this time the two institutions went through a common hell.

The head of the hostel section was still Matylda Schenkerowa, and of the Orphans' Home, its president, Marek Biberstein. The two institutions had their best time in the summer months of 1942. Various educational events and entertainments were put on in the hall of the hostel, bringing in relatively large amounts of income to cover the increasing costs. There were more and more children. Children were transported in from the outlying towns and villages, and others who had been in the care of Aryans were often found outside the gates of the ghetto. Children were also brought in by the Gestapo after having been caught out in the city, including some of half-Jewish origin. There was one 10-year-old girl whose mother was Jewish and whose father had been serving in the German army. Seeking to protect the child, the father had put her in a home in Zakopane. The father died in action; after his death the 'non-Aryan' origins of the girl came to light and she was sent to the Jewish Orphans' Home in the ghetto.

The workers in the various factories began to be moved into barracks; at this time, desperate mothers foisted their children on us, begging us to take pity on them, and the children, silently reproachful and afraid, were for a long time unable to ease the pain they felt.

On 28 October the children from the hostel were evacuated. Only five or six boys managed to save themselves. In the night they had noticed that the *Sonderdienst* [the Special Service] were cordoning off the shelter; they got up into the loft and hid in some cubby-hole there. The evacuation took place in the morning, unhurriedly. The children were formed into fives and led out onto Zgody Square. The manager of the hostel, Entenberg, who lived in the building, and Feuerstein, the manageress of the Orphans' Home, were also taken in; but Entenberg and his wife were taken off the square by SS officer Kunde.

Even though people knew the terrible consequences of gathering children in one place, the Jewish community administration was forced to set up something else in place of the Orphans' Home, which this time was called a *Tagesheim*, because it was supposed to be an institution that looked after the children during the day; in the evening, after work, the parents were supposed to take them home. Hundreds of children, whose parents had been evacuated, were left with no one to care for them and even without a roof over their heads because immediately after the evacuation the ghetto had been reduced in size by cutting off a large number of streets, and the remaining people had rushed to occupy empty flats, regardless of whether any children were in hiding there.

To begin with the *Tagesheim* was located on Limanowskiego Street in Dr Kranz's Hospital for Epidemic Diseases, which had been completely closed down after the evacuation. A staff of supervisors and teachers was rapidly organised under the direction of President Biberstein, and the *Tagesheim* quickly filled up.

After some time the management was forced to expand the *Tagesheim*. It was moved to the building on the corner of Józefińska and Krakusa, where it was run on a large scale. There were bedrooms and play-rooms, and a large dining room. There was a separate section for babies. And more and more children were joining the Home, because every day new work-places – the airport, the cable works – were moving their workers into barracks; a 'Julag I' was formed and took hundreds of people to the Ostbahn. The victims, unable to take their children with them, were forced to leave them at the *Tagesheim*, in which few had any faith after the previous bitter experiences. Despite careful supervision by the management and the nurses and even with the relatively good food, the children wasted away. A longing ate into the little ones' hearts; the nurses reported that the children cried at night, calling for their parents. Eventually they fell into a state of apathy, and waited indifferently for what the future had in store.

Children also came in from the Aryan side, of unknown origins. There was one Aryan girl called Janka Tarlińska or Tarłowska, whose parents lived on Dietla Street; when they were arrested, she was sent to the *Tagesheim*. It was a terrifying experience for her; she kept trying to get back to her home. In the evenings after work I had to take her home with me; only then would she calm down. Unfortunately she caught measles just before the liquidation of the ghetto, and I was unable to save her, even though she gave me the address of a Protestant minister living on Grodzka Street next to the courts. If her parents are still alive, it will have remained a mystery to them where their child perished.

The children in the *Tagesheim* played strange games. They did not laugh but they shouted, did not play but fought each other, gave orders, evacuated, hanged or robbed each other; almost always these games ended with an adult having to intervene.

Someone spread a false report that children with jobs would be treated as adults, and so in the event of an evacuation they would be saved. This was a signal for all those children who till now had still been in the care of their parents to be handed over to the *Tagesheim*, where a 'stationery department' was set up making envelopes. At bottom, it was probably just a method of organising a registration of all children to see how many innocent victims were still in the ghetto.

And the children worked till they dropped. They would return home with their heads aching, sad, exhausted and resigned. There were some children whom it was impossible to persuade to work; at any opportunity they would run out into the yard, so as to be able for a moment to play at being children: playing tag, swinging on boards and so on. Others ran away back home and declared categorically that they would not go to work. Their mothers were in despair. Some of the privileged children already proudly wore the 'R' sign.

At this time, too, various events were put on to raise funds for the *Tagesheim*. Mr Spira proved after all to have a 'Jewish heart'; at these events he often wept bitter tears, while his wife and daughter brought various gifts for the children. He willingly gave permission for events to benefit the children: different singers appearing in Förster's club, an evening of *Gebirtig* sung by the Grüner brothers, and other things. Just before the October evacuation, a splendid hall in the Optima was set up exclusively for such events, and a number of high-class artistic performances were given – piano concerts by Rysiek Lustgarten, the Martens singers from Germany, the Luksówna children's ballet and other events.

In the meantime there were rumours about the final liquidation of the ghetto, and people knew that something terrible was about to happen. And so came the day of 13 March 1943. That morning I was in the *Tagesheim*, not suspecting anything, when at 9 o'clock the tragic news was spread. Mothers and fathers came with their children; some said goodbye to them, others had gone completely crazy and just abandoned the children and fled; heart-rending scenes took place. The children were assembled in the main hall. Some were crying; others sat quietly, afraid, round-eyed, their faces pale, grey and tragic. At some point the President came in, very upset, from the community administration and ordered us, the so-called 'workforce', to go home; he remained and left the *Tagesheim* only at the last minute.

A small handful of children from the *Tagesheim* survived by hiding at the *OD*; in the evening they were taken to the camp, to have their life prolonged by another year. The next morning word went round the camp that lorries full of children were outside the camp gates. Some people even heard them shouting and crying. Those children were brought to the camp at the promise of Commandant Goeth, so that they might have their final resting-place there.

The time in the camp constitutes a separate chapter in the tragedy of the Jewish children. Here, too, they had to be either in hiding or counted among the adults and so sent to work in the *Gemeinschaften* [work places]. Every day they had to get up for the musters, which were often long and exhausting; the adults constantly had to conceal them from the authorities, while the children themselves, prematurely old and aware of what awaited them, were little more than a bundle of nerves, and bore no resemblance to the laughing, carefree children we had known before. And once again a *Kinderheim* was set up, when various survivors of other ghettos brought their children to the camp. The liquidation took place in May 1944 as part of the liquidation of a group chosen by what was called 'health selection'.

This was organised in a most refined manner. While the adults were assembled on the *Appellplatz* [assembly ground], the children were left in the *Kinderheim*. At some point, in the Neue Gelände in the distance, we noticed trucks full of children, surrounded by a cordon of troops armed with rifles. We could see the children waving their arms, and we could hear them shouting, all to the accompaniment of songs played over the loudspeakers. The songs, such as 'Mother waits beside the cradle', tore at the hearts of the mothers, and Goeth, seeing the crowd going wild, ordered everyone to sit with their back to the assembly ground and assured us that the children were being taken to a better camp.

Some children saved themselves by hiding down the pit in the latrines.

(Archive of the VJHC in Kraków, statement no. 1078)

5. WILHELM KRANZ

Kraków

(*Statement taken by Maria Holender, Kraków*)

Jewish children in the prison of the Kraków–Płaszów concentration camp

I was a prison guard in the camp at Płaszów, in the *'Krantzówka'* [named after the guard] and in the 'Grey House', from 15 August 1943 to 14 October 1944. The *Krantzówka* was situated inside the camp; it was a barracks walled off with barbed wire that housed camp inmates convicted of minor offences. In the Grey House there were five communal cells, a dark cell and 20 standing cells, each measuring 40 by 50 centimetres and two metres high. This prison was located in the cellars of the Grey House. Only the standing cells were for camp inmates; the other cells were for prisoners brought in on the instructions of the Gestapo, the *SD* [Special Service] or the *Kripo* [criminal police]. These prisoners were entirely at their disposal; they were not on the camp roll, and only received prison food. The inmates were punished for stealing from the barracks for trading, or for smoking in the barracks or during roll-call.

During the final liquidation of the ghetto on 14 December 1943, Gitla Katzowa, née Landau, and her four children were transferred from the *OD* prison to the Grey House. Her seven-year-old daughter Billi, with her light blond hair, was a delightful child. She was always well-behaved, solemn and obedient, and at the same time uncommonly sensible. Eight-year-old Runia Landau was Katzowa's niece, the daughter of Landau of Skawina. She had dark brown hair and large, dark, dreamy eyes, and was exceptionally intelligent. Józio Katz, a six-month-old baby, and his five-year-old sister, Haneczka, who had flaxen hair and beautiful blue eyes, were the grand-children of Kornitzer, a well-known Kraków rabbi. Gitla passed all these children off as her own (she had Hungarian

252

nationality; at this time her husband was in the Montelupich prison). The eldest child, Runia, looked after the younger ones. She washed them, combed their hair and played with them. Every morning Runia would say her morning prayers out loud, and the other children would repeat the words after her. The same happened in the evening before bedtime. In addition to this the children learned Hebrew from a prayer-book that Gitla had brought to the prison with her. The children were sensible beyond words. They were fully aware of the situation in which they found themselves; they were sorrowful and serious. They lived in perpetual fear. Twice a week I would accompany the Germans on an inspection of the prison. I watched those poor, frightened children holding their breath, stiff with fear. At these times they would run to Gitla Katzowa, clinging on to her as if they were afraid to part with her. Subconsciously, they were aware that any visit by the Germans could bring something bad. I stroked their heads and reassured them, telling them that nothing would happen. These children had already experienced many segregations in such prison cells, and it was not so easy to comfort them. A desperate, eternal fear could be seen on their troubled faces. They knew that whoever the Germans took from the cell would never come back again. Through the bars of the cell they could hear the frequent shootings from the 'hill of death' that was not far from the Grey House, and the desperate cries of the victims. I tried to cheer the children up by whatever means I could. Every day I would take a different child for a walk on the pretext of going to the doctor. I trained them so well that whenever we met a German who asked where we were going, the child would explain: *'Zahnschmerzen, Bauchschmerzen'* (toothache, stomach-ache). These walks usually lasted for three hours, as I would use the opportunity to run errands round the camp. The inmates used to give the children sweets and other confectionery. The children received food secretly from the *Kinderheim*; this was sent by Mala Hofsteter Mandelbaumowa. Dr Weichert, director of the JUS [Jüdischer Unterstützungsstelle – the Jewish Support

Centre], allotted special funds for the children in the prison, with which Dr Aleksander Bieberstein, the camp doctor, bought extra food. Once a week I took the children all together for a bath; I tried to make sure that they were clean and had a change of underwear.

In these conditions the children survived until 15 July 1944, when at four in the morning they were driven out by road to the French border to be taken to a concentration camp for Hungarian citizens. A few days after the liberation they returned to Poland and are currently living with Runia Landau's father in Cieszyn.

At the beginning of March 1944, an eight-year-old girl, Niusia Całusińska, was brought to the Grey House. She had been caught with Aryan papers at Tola Wróbel's. I asked her several times whether she was a Jew or a Catholic. She insisted that she was a Catholic, and I was completely unable to get the truth out of her. In my presence she would kneel and say her prayers. Finally, after some time, she confessed that her real name was Schlang and that she was from Kraków. I knew her parents, who at that time were in the camp at Płaszów. The next day I told Niusia that she could see her mother. She was delighted and could not believe her good fortune. I managed to bring Niusia and her mother together. The meeting was to take place in the OD guardhouse, in the presence of Chilowicz, the head of the OD. I brought the girl out of the prison so that after a separation of several years she could see her mother again. I was astonished when the girl, who recognised her mother instantly (as she later admitted to me), refused to acknowledge her. To my question as to whether she knew this lady, she replied with a shake of the head, displaying no other movement or emotion. The cause of this was the presence of Chilowicz, who was dressed in a leather coat and a Tyrolean cap and was holding a riding crop. The girl was afraid that he was a German, and she did not want to confess; even at this moment, for all her eight years, she was able to keep a grip on herself and behave like an adult. At this point I explained to her that this man was not a

German but a Jew; at this she threw herself at her mother and began hugging and kissing her. I put Niusia into the communal cell where Katzowa's children lived.

On 5 May, at nine o'clock in the morning, a car carrying prisoners from the Montelupich prison drove up to the Grey House and the Gestapo led Niusia out of the prison. She said goodbye to the children; she did not cry at all, even though she knew she was going to her death. Her final words before she left the cell were to ask me to send her love to her parents and to comfort them. The same day, when I took Katzowa's children their dinner, I noticed that their breakfasts had not been touched. Runia, Billi and Haneczka were sitting quietly in a row on the bench, not saying a word to each other. When I asked why they had not eaten their breakfast, Runia replied: 'Today we're having a day of expiation for Niusia.'

One day in the summer, a seven-year-old girl called Marlena Reiner was brought to the Grey House from the Criminal Police on Szlak Street. She had been on Aryan papers in the Salwator district of Kraków, and she had been playing in the garden when, by a terrible accident [during a round-up by German police in connection with the discovery of a secret printing-house], she was arrested and taken to the police station. Here she was kept in a dark cell for three days, without food or heating, in order to make her reveal the whereabouts of her mother. The German who brought her to the camp prison, a Silesian, told me how bravely the little girl had behaved. When asked where her mother was, the little girl replied that she knew but would not tell, even if she were to die. She was promised a bar of chocolate, sweets and toys, but the girl not only did not give her mother away, but, in the presence of the Germans in the office and the head of the *Kripo*, she had the courage to say aloud in Polish: 'I know you, you bandits, murderers, thugs. I know that no one's ever got out of your clutches alive. You can put me on the ground and cut me with a knife, I'll still not tell you where Mama is.' I could not believe this when the German told me about it, but Marlena repeated the same thing to me in prison, when the

German had gone. I still found it hard to believe how heroic the child was. It was only when I saw with my own eyes how she behaved on the day of her execution that I realised she really was an extraordinary child. After six weeks in prison she went to her death with the grown-ups. She walked in front, her head held high; it almost seemed as if she had a smile on her lips. Her last words were: ' ... but I didn't give Mama away.'

(Archive of the VJHC in Kraków, statement no. 1224)

6. ESTERA PINAJ-RECHTERMANOWA

Excerpt from a memorandum to the Łódź Judenrat

(*Translated from German*)

... We should like here to bring up an issue which everyone will admit is an urgent one, and to say something about a problem the solution of which can no longer be deferred. We refer to the problem of child beggars on the streets of the Jewish quarter. Each of us knows these children, each of us encounters them daily, and passes them by with a painful sense of helplessness.

Dressed in rags, they sit or lie, dirty and lice-ridden, with an unpleasant smell, rotting while they are still alive; singly or in groups, they line both sides of the street. For hours they wail in tired, tearful voices; they twist their sorry little bodies painfully, so as to evoke more pity.

They know how to pretend to be unconscious or dead; or how to seize up in artificial convulsions. Then, after a few hours their 'guardians' appear, check their 'work' and collect the 'takings'. And there are takings. Passers-by often take pity on them and give them something; one grosz follows another, sometimes a generous hand will even throw down half a zloty. These compassionate people do not realise that with their offerings they are supporting the most shameful of occupations: the exploitation of children for professional begging. They do not see that they are accustoming the children to a lifetime of begging, and are helping to push them to the very depths of physical and moral degradation. The older and stronger of the children are the terror of the bakeries and shops; they steal where they can and what they can, snatch parcels from the hands of passers-by, and form organised gangs of young criminals ...

(From the files of the Łódź ghetto)

---

7. DR GOLDFAJNÓWNA

(*Excerpts from a memoir*)

Experiences of the Jewish children in Prużany

The children were terrified of the Germans. Whenever a Jewish child saw a German, the child would run home crying and rush to his mother, shouting: 'Mama, hide me, a German is coming!' It was no good trying to convince him that the German had already gone and would not come back any more. The child would not stop crying and begging his mother to take him to the attic, the cellar, the sty – anything to avoid the German. We had a mayor by the name of Schumacher who was a Nazi; he wore a swastika on his sleeve and on his cap. Twice a week he would come to the ghetto with a great riding-whip in his hand and beat people unconscious, especially children. He had a Byelorussian lover. We asked her to use her influence to stop him going to the ghetto and beating children. She answered by saying that firstly, here in the provinces this was the only recreation he had and, secondly, this task had been entrusted to him by the party. When, on the first chance I had, I asked him why he beat Jewish children, he justified himself by saying: 'I beat them a couple of times a week, but I also give them bread, even though there's an order to starve Jewish children to death.'

The children suffered from a lack of vitamins; they were pale, exhausted and fearful. They never asked their mothers for food, but from the early morning they would ask: 'Mama, will the Germans come to the ghetto today?' They were content with a slice of black bread, what was known as *Judenbrot*, and they were happy if they were given a little *Magermilch* [skimmed milk]. How jealous they were when they looked through the barbed wire surrounding the ghetto and saw the Aryan children, who would go up to the wire and slide their fingers across their throats: '*Jude kaput.*' The Jewish children would hide in the furthest part of the ghetto, so as not to feel jealous. They would cry and curse Hitler, saying that he had no children himself and yet was merciless to other children. The children understood the situation they were in and did all the jobs that fell to them.

In our town there was a brewery that the Germans had demolished; where the ice-cellar had been there was a huge pit, which looked as if it had been made by a massive bomb. The owner of the brewery said that when they were laying the foundations for the cellar, 3,000 cartloads of earth had been removed. This was the pit that children up to the age of 12 were ordered to fill in. The poor children got up at five in the morning (the mayor would go round checking the houses of all the Jews at five o'clock, and woe betide any child he found still in bed). Mothers woke their children, and the children went to work sleepy and hungry. They carried earth in little baskets and in aprons. It took them two months to fill in the pit; afterwards, they planted flowers there to appease the mayor, whose bloated belly was big enough to take a dinner tray and service for six people.

In the ghetto there was a boy who was a violinist, a real virtuoso. Before the war he had performed at the Warsaw

Philharmonia in children's concerts. Now he spent all day going round with some brushes and cleaning the Germans' shoes. In payment he would receive a clip on the ear. In the evening, when the ghetto was locked and all the workers had returned home, he would take his violin and play mournful songs. The Austrians would often come up to the barbed wire to listen to him play. Sometimes they would cry, and throw him a roll or some chocolate. The called him the '*Wunderkind*'. When they started transporting the Jews to their deaths, some of the Aryans thought that the boy should be saved, because whoever kept him now would become rich in the future. But before they could reach a decision the boy perished.

I had a pretty 12-year-old niece called Jadzia Chajkin. She sang and danced like a real artist, and spoke good Polish, Russian and Byelorussian. I wanted to take her out of the wagon, but she announced proudly: 'I'm too young to be a witness, I want to share the same fate as my sister and my parents.' I was surrounded by children who clung to me, sensing my attachment to them. They studied my face, and whenever they spotted a smile they would smile too and say: 'Dr Goldfajnówna, everything will be all right and the enemy will break their necks.'

The children helped us in everything. When the Germans marched into the ghetto and demanded a ton of coffee, or they would shoot all the members of the *Judenrat*, the children, without asking anyone, all went to their various homes and with tears in their eyes asked: 'Give me some coffee for the Germans, or they'll shoot the *Judenrat*.' When I had to leave the ghetto to go to the Aryan side on business connected with the *Judenrat*, the children would say: 'Good luck with softening up our jackals.' And the little ones would accompany me to the gate and ask me to bring them an egg or a carrot back. I would tell them when I was coming back, and the children would already be waiting for me. Straightaway they would grab my bag, and jump for joy if they found an egg, a carrot, a few apples or some 'Aryan' bread. We had no cattle, in the ghetto one never saw poultry or dogs (there were special posters up about this). We were allowed only cats and rats. When I returned from the Aryan side, the children would shower me with questions about whether I had seen cows or ducks, and they would longingly remember past times.

It is difficult to imagine children without smiles, songs or games. But that is how it was in the ghetto. I recall one incident. One day, when I was on my way to the hospital, avoiding the busier streets so as not to meet any Germans, I came upon a large group of boys who had made weapons out of wood and were singing an anti-Hitler song. In the song they called him the 'old bachelor', or 'three groszy and one grosz is together a Führer' [a play on words: Führer sounds like Vierer, which in Yiddish means a four-grosz coin]. I told them off, saying that today, when we expect death at any moment, it was not right to sing. The children showed me their wooden weapons, with a nail fixed at the end, and told me that they were not afraid of death, and that in the battle they would put all the Germans' eyes out with those weapons.

Even small children realised what was happening; they did not sulk or get upset, but were quiet and well-behaved. They listened to every conversation, and bore their lot without complaining. For example, on 10 December for some unknown reason the head of the Gestapo had the idea of getting all the Jews onto the streets and counting them. At 7 o'clock in the morning, in a 15–18° frost, we were driven out onto the street. Some 12,000 Jews were assembled. We were made to stand in rows to make it easier for the Germans to count us. The adults were convinced that there was going to be an execution; seven people died of heart attacks. But the children stood quietly from seven in the morning till two in the afternoon.

On the last night, 27–28 January 1943, the small children did not sleep, they begged their parents not to abandon them but to let them die together. The children knew that sometimes mothers abandoned their own children, and that later the Germans dealt with the children. It is hard to imagine what our children went through. Mothers strangled their children with their own hands, or threw them out of third- or fourth-storey windows. In the night, when we took poison, each doctor injected his or her own child with the poison. The following scene took place at the flat of my friends, Dr Rozenkranc and Dr Pik. Rozenkranc injected first himself, then his son with a fatal dose of morphine. He took his son in his arms and, smiling, said: 'What good fortune it is to die of poison, and not at the hands of the barbarous Nazis.' Dr Pik first administered the injection to himself, then to his beloved son; then he lay at my feet, weeping and accusing himself: 'What kind of father am I that I could kill my very own child!' As sleep overtook me, I could still hear his words. Mrs Adelson's grown-up son refused to take poison; all night he cursed his mother and reproached her, saying: 'What sort of a mother are you that you want to poison your only son?' Then he began to beat her and call her a Nazi. My niece, Nickin, had had three operations in order to have a child. Alas, the child was a healthy one, and everyone liked her. I could not kill that child. I administered all the injections, to myself first of all of course. After ten or 15 minutes I lay on the sofa and fell into a deep sleep. My niece was terrified; she tried to wake me, shouting: 'Aunt, for the love of God, get up and give my son an injection, as his aunt you must save him from the Nazi torturers!' I was unable to lift my arm, and my legs felt as if they were paralysed; I heard Dr Pik crying, and told her to ask him.

I did not die from the poison. Even on the train I saw the precision and brutality with which the Germans killed our children. I saw them breaking open skulls and tearing out brains, lifting children on bayonets, smashing two children's heads together. When I am alone, I hear the moaning of the earth and the voices of our Jewish children as they call out for vengeance for the shedding of innocent blood.

(Archive of the CJHC, statement no. 138c)

8. L. BRENER

(Statement taken by Noe Grüss)

Jewish children in Częstochowa

In October 1939, a month after Częstochowa was taken by the Germans, the TOZ [a society for Jewish health-care] began to operate on a larger scale than before; it needed to fill the gap left after other institutions, especially schools, had ceased to function. From January 1940, as well as providing meals, a day-room was set up where children were given regular classes. About 2,000 children took part in these classes.

From March of the same year the day-rooms were open all day long. The children were given three meals. Before dinner they had lessons and afterwards they worked. They made shopping bags, slippers, handbags and so on, sales from which went towards the upkeep of the day-room. There were three day-rooms of this kind.

The day-rooms were managed by Liber Brener, currently president of the Jewish Commission in Częstochowa. There were few qualified teachers; but thanks to the generosity of young adults who completed practical courses and subsequently worked devotedly for the good of the Jewish children, high standards of teaching and education were achieved. Every month the children put on performances that brought in money. Their repertoire included a children's opera called 'The Dolls'. There was also a theatre group and a 60-strong adult choir, which gave its profits to the children. These shows were an essential source of money, since from 1941 funding from TOZ headquarters in Warsaw and from Joint stopped.

In the ghetto there was also a clinic for mothers, the 'Drop of Milk'; a canteen for babies; and a children's dispensary run by the TOZ. Independently of the TOZ, the 'Charity' society led by lawyer Hansfeld maintained an orphanage that cared for 150 children.

After the evacuation, on 22 September 1942 we succeeded in concealing 73 children and their mothers in a bunker that had been prepared earlier in the grounds of the Möbellager factory; they remained here for six weeks, right up to the transfer to the small ghetto.

Here four bunkers were built, two of them especially for children, who were taken there in sacks and knapsacks and by similar means. If the children began to cry as they were being transported in this way, the workers would begin to sing loudly to drown out the tell-tale noise. These groups of workers were led by Mechel Birencwajg; he would lead a cart loaded with packages, and while the Gestapo inspected the packages, the workers carrying the children would pass by.

To begin with the military police did not react to the presence of the children in the ghetto. This encouraged us to open a school for 120 children. When the police found out about this, they visited the school; they behaved decently while they were there, and gave an order that the children should be given some jam.

In January 1943 the ghetto was cordoned off. The administration realised what was going on in time and broke up the school. In this way many children were saved.

After the liquidation of the ghetto in June 1943, a number of children were found places in Aryan homes.

In July 1943 they executed the children who had until then been legally employed in the Hasag [Hugo Schneider Aktion Gesellschaft – a munitions factory] camp. About 40 children survived through till the liberation.

(Material of the CJHC)

---

9. THE LIQUIDATION OF THE JEWISH ORPHANAGE IN LUBLIN

Compiled by B. Lewin, Lublin, from the testimonies of witnesses

Right on the outskirts of Lublin, towards the main road to Warsaw, there is a village called Tatary. At number 122, set back from the road a little, is a farm where the farmer, Karol Mulak, an old man who can still remember tsarist times, lives a quiet life with his family. From Mulak's barn there is a broad view across the fields. From here the old farmer saw things which were supposed to be kept carefully concealed from human eyes: the crime of a mass murder in which the victims were children in swaddling clothes ...

... It was in the early spring of 1942. I remember that the earth was still frozen, when one Saturday (I do not know the exact date, but it was in March or April), prisoners were brought in to dig pits. It was on the land of a man named Morawski, about 50–100 metres away from my farm. For the whole of Saturday and half of Sunday the prisoners worked without a break, struggling with the partly frozen ground. Despite a strict ban and the presence of *SD* guards, I observed these strange preparations from my barn. The pit was about five metres long and 1.8–2 metres deep. When they had finished work the prisoners were marched off. A dull silence rose over the fields, full of forebodings ... even the sky covered over with dark blue-grey clouds. I waited ... At around two in the afternoon my daughter rushed in frightened, telling us that traffic had been stopped on the main road, both for civilian pedestrians and for military vehicles. There were Gestapo officers in tall caps moving around. They were cursing, and fired warning shots at onlookers; they were even ordering Wehrmacht soldiers staying at the nearby hospital to move out of the way. One officer took up a position on a nearby mound, threatening to open fire with a machine gun on people in the steel mill if they should start to take too much of an interest in the events that were about to take place. Suddenly, on the road there appeared a huge lorry covered tightly with a black tarpaulin. It drove into the field, about 100 metres from the main road, where the pit had been dug. The lorry backed up to the very edge of the pit, and when the tarpaulin was taken off there appeared tiny children, most of them wearing nappies. Among them there were also two grown men. The Ukrainians lined the children up on the pile of sand; a Gestapo officer shot them with a machine gun, then one of the men threw them down into the pit, while the other stood in the pit and laid the children down, still in their nappies, half-alive and shaking, in rows across each other so as to take up as little room as possible ...

The men's hands were soaked in blood; they moved about the field like emissaries from the underworld. Another Gestapo officer opened fire with a machine gun on the dying bodies in the pit in an effort to silence the terrible groans that were coming from inside. The groans grew quieter but did not stop; they took on bizarre tones, as if the earth were shuddering, rocked by sighs.

The monstrous work was coming to an end; they left the pit open and drove off for a new transport.

After perhaps an hour the lorry returned. This time it brought older children. They went to their deaths in fours, holding each other by the hand. They stood over the pit; a German shot them with a revolver, so that they fell into the pit at once ...

(Archive of the CJHC, statement no. 636)

The Children Accuse

10. HELENA WOLKENBERG

Teacher

(Statement taken by M. Turek, Białystok)

The fate of the children from the Białystok ghetto

The final liquidation of the Białystok ghetto began on 15 August 1943. In accordance with the decree issued by the treacherous German executioners, in the early hours of 16 August all the Jews had to leave their flats and gather at a pre-arranged place (between Jurowiecka and Fabryczna Streets); anyone found still in their flats would be shot.

At around noon of that day the Jews, formed into fours, began to be led out under a heavy escort. They were all assembled in a field outside the city, about 30,000 of them. It was a hot August day, and the sun burned down mercilessly; the cordon of bandits forced that huge mass of people at bayonet point into a tiny area. For several days on end they were not allowed a drop of water; anyone who dared ask for a little water for a crying child was answered with bullets from one of the members of the *Herrenvolk*.

The following morning, 17 August, the Jewish *Ordnungsdienst* announced that the Germans had decided to send all the children back to the ghetto, where they were to be well looked after in one of the boarding houses. The treacherous Germans explained this move by saying that all the adults were being sent to do temporary work, and so until they returned the children would remain in the ghetto.

Some of the mothers were completely resigned and handed their children over voluntarily; in most cases, however, the children were taken from their parents by force. About 1,200 children were taken away. Along with the children, about 40 adults left the field, doctors, teachers and nurses; I was among them. We were led back to the ghetto, and were housed in the building at 10 Fabryczna Street. We stayed there with the children for about a week; the conditions were relatively acceptable. On 22 August, after all the Jews of Białystok had been transported out, the children's turn came. The Gestapo appeared, accompanied by the Ukrainians, and headed by Friedl, the notorious ringleader of the whole operation; they announced that the children were being sent abroad, where they would be exchanged for German prisoners-of-war.

They took us to the railway station where a special train had been prepared and stood waiting. We got in; they handed out bread for everyone, and the train moved off. After travelling for two days we arrived in Theresienstadt. There the children remained in the carriages. The adults were transferred to another train on the pretext that we were going somewhere to set up a camp for the children. They took us to Auschwitz. There were three women with us who had foreign passports (one of them was a lady called Suchodolska who had a five-year-old child with her). A selection took place on the spot, and those three women, and the other women who had children with them, were sent to the gas chambers. I was sent along with 17 other women and four men to work in the camp. A few days later word reached us that the children from Białystok who had been separated from us had been brought to Auschwitz, where they had been gassed and burned.

(Archive of the CJHC, statement no. 552/2)

11. ANNA MAAS

(Statement taken by Dr Dawid Haupt, Przemyśl)

The shelter in Przemyśl

I was in the Przemyśl ghetto until 2 September 1942. At first I worked in the shelter, and then, after the final liquidation of the shelter in November 1942, in the hospital. The shelter, which also contained an old people's home, was located in the barracks on Czarneckiego Street. The manageress of the shelter was Mrs N. Rebenowa, and subsequently Mrs Naglerowa. Hela Reich, Fryda Seifert and Sabina Laub also worked there.

The story of the shelter is perhaps the most terrible episode in the tragic history of the ghetto. There was not a single *Aktion* that did not constitute above all a blow aimed at the shelter.

In the first period of its existence, about 300 children lived there, including babies. At that time, the old people's home cared for 40 elderly men and women. After the end of the first *Aktion* in August 1942 the number of children in the shelter rose to 400. This happened simply because during the *Aktion* mothers seeking to save their children would at the last minute bring them into the shelter, and when there was not even time for that they would abandon them, hoping that someone would bring them to the shelter. Repeated incidents of this kind, where mothers going to their deaths would abandon their children, were perhaps the most tragic moments in the history of the ghetto.

Twenty-five children and all 40 old people were taken during the August *Aktion*. On the orders of the Gestapo, we led both the children and the old folk straight out onto the square. We received the order directly from Gestapo officers Benewitz, Stegeman and Reisner; they instructed us to include the oldest children in the group of 25.

The *Aktion* of September 1942 closed down the shelter completely. This time, on the orders of the Gestapo, all the children were led out onto the square. We had to carry the babies to the point where they were to be put on the train. All that is known of the fate of those children is that they were put on the train together with the other people who had been evacuated, and that they were transported out of Przemyśl.

After that *Aktion* the shelter was completely deserted. It was a terrible sight when, upon returning from the square, we found the shelter abandoned, and in it a single child who had been left behind by mistake and who in this way survived for a little while longer. The next day the Gestapo appeared and took away all the shelter's linen. They were helped in this by Ukrainian youths, who took the opportunity to grab for themselves anything they could find of any value.

Three weeks later they began to set up a new shelter. About 50 children were housed there; but it was not to last for long. Soon the building where the shelter was located was cleared out on the instructions of the head of the NSDAP, *Stadthauptmann* Gieselman. On his orders, the children from the shelter were given into the care of various families. It is worth noting that Gieselman issued his instructions to close the place down on the day after he had visited it and had expressed his admiration for the organisation and management of the shelter.

After the building on Czarneckiego Street was abandoned, the shelter was moved to new premises in the Jewish hospital, where it was allotted only one room and a kitchen. According to the instructions issued by the Gestapo, the new shelter was to hold no more than 25 children. In fact, at the beginning of November 1942 there were 50 children, though not all of them were listed on the official records.

In accordance with the recommendations of the then president of the shelter, Dr J. Rawicz, all the children who came to the shelter were taken in, in spite of the Gestapo's instructions. During the *Aktion* of November 1942 the Gestapo loaded the children onto lorries, drove them out to the cemetery at Grochowice and executed them there.

(Archive of the CJHC, statement no. 690)

269

12. CHAWA WOSKOBOJNIK, L. LIDOWSKI

The murder of Jewish children in Równe and Nowogródek

Równe: In the summer of 1942, 250 Jewish children aged ten and under were assembled in the sheds on Perłowa Street. All around stood a cordon of Gestapo and police. They were kept there for seven days; no one was allowed in. The shouting and crying could be heard all along the street. Afterwards, from the stories told by the Gestapo, it was learned that the children were not allowed to leave the sheds even to relieve themselves; they were given nothing to eat or drink. The Gestapo and the Ukrainian police tortured them. They held feasts in the presence of the children; they stuffed themselves with food, and when one of the children asked for something to eat, they killed that child. One Gestapo officer boasted that he had taught the children not to ask for anything. At the Gestapo council meeting at General Koch's it was decided: (1) to form the children into fives; (2) to place a sign on each child's chest saying in German and Ukrainian: 'We are going to Stalin so he will feed us'; (3) to give each child a bottle of milk on a string and a hunk of bread, though they would be forbidden to eat or drink any of this; (4) to lead them through the town to the 'yellow street' and to kill them there.

All this the Gestapo carried out meticulously. The children died in terrible suffering.

Nowogródek: The Gestapo pulled in about 6,000 Jews from the entire region and locked them in the courthouse building. A promise was made to send them out to work. For four days they were kept there and tortured. Children up to the age of seven were taken from their parents and led to a square outside the town where a long, deep grave had been dug. A total of 300 children, tied together with rope, were marched to the place of execution. On the way they were beaten savagely. On the square they were killed with pitchforks, staves, and knives, and then were thrown into the grave. The children who had been killed and the children tied to them who were still alive were all thrown into the grave; inhuman cries came from inside. The Gestapo stood around the edge of the grave with revolvers, aiming at the heads of children who were still alive. Then, when cries could still be heard, the mothers were brought to the grave to collect their children.

Most of the mothers lost their minds. They were killed and buried together with their children.

(Archive of the CJHC, statement no. 753)

---

13. JERZY ROS

Warsaw

(*Excerpts from testimony*)

The road of death

... At that moment, through the gates of death comes a tall, handsome man with dark, fiery eyes and a black Hungarian-style moustache. On his back he is carrying a bulging sack with his belongings. His face clearly shows the strain. Like the others, he receives a hefty kick in the small of the back. He is directed to the right, to the road of life. This one still has some work in him.

At this point, something has taken the interest of one of the generals. He beckons the *Oberscharführer*, who is dressed in the style of a colonial officer, and points to the sack. Who knows what treasures the Jew has concealed inside it, since he is bearing his property with such care. The SS officer acts quickly and deftly (his superiors are watching; there is a chance of promotion, a fur for Greta, a bicycle for Fritz). He runs up, wrenches the sack from the hands of the Jew and tips it upside down.

And out of the sack, to everyone's surprise, falls a small, soft, black-haired girl of six, maybe seven. Her dazed eyes, wide as her fear, look about her. Her mouth curves down, ready to cry. The daylight dazzles the girl, and it takes her a moment to recognise her father standing next to her; she clings onto his leg, burying her face in his trousers. And him? This tall, strong man stands helpless, looking now at the soldier standing before him, now at the staff of generals, now at the tiny creature desperately holding onto him. At the blood of his blood, bone of his bone. In nature everything seems to have gone still. The breeze has stopped blowing, as if it wanted to follow this scene more carefully. Only the chattering sparrows continue their unending disputes some-where under the eaves. A sign from one of the mighty, a movement of a hand dressed in an elegant glove; the child is torn from her father and pushed to the left. To the left, towards Stawki, Małkinia and further, on the road of death.

In despair, the father turns towards the lorry. He wrings his hands. He runs after the little girl. The SS officer pushes him back, striking him across the back of the neck with the handle of his riding-whip. There is another gesture from one of the mighty. The father is allowed through to the child! He flings his arms around her. He kisses her face, wet with tears. The little girl throws her pink arms around him, and clings onto him trustingly. They walk off together towards Stawki and Małkinia, and further, further on the road of death.

From the black rim of the Gestapo cap, the skull looks down with unseeing eyes. The generals whisper amongst them-selves. It was good that there arose an opportunity to show their subordinates that, even during an *Aktion*, there is room for mercy in the heart of a German soldier.

If, that is, it is in accordance with the national interest.

(Materials of the VJHC in Warsaw)

14. EUGENIA GURFINKEL

Warsaw

(*Statement taken by Maria Hochberg-Mariańska*)

Testimony of a mother: excerpts

My husband and I had a grocer's shop; when people in the ghetto began signing up for the workshops, the *Schoppen*, we managed to get out of it somehow – partly by paying people, partly by concealment – and we continued to run the shop. We did well out of it; and above all we cared for the children. I had two beautiful little daughters; one was six, the other not quite two. Children in the ghetto were growing swollen and dying, but my two girls were always so fresh and healthy. I gave them everything I could. And if only there was enough, I would help the other children too. I never turned a hungry child away from our door. I thought that God would allow me to save my children. My husband was a good and able man who looked after the children just as much as I did. We simply lived for those children. In the first evacuation of 22 July 1942, we hid with the children and somehow got through. In those days people still had no idea of what might happen. We were happy thinking that maybe things would be all right now.

On 18 January 1943 another evacuation began. I knew that something was going on downstairs, because my husband was on edge, but he calmed me down, saying that they were transporting prisoners from the Pawiak [a Warsaw prison]. In the end he had to tell me to take the children and hide. I hid with the others, while he went out to see what was happening. He left, and never came back again. I waited a whole day and night, and then another day, but then people told me that there was no sense in waiting any longer. I was shattered. He was such a good husband and a good man; what was I supposed to do with the children? I cried all day, and begged to be allowed to die. But the other women shouted at me, saying that I was a mother, that it was wrong even to talk like that; I

273

had two sweet, lovely children and I had to live for their sake. I had to go on trying to save the children. By then they were really frightened, and so sensible, too much so. The elder one kept saying to me: 'Mama, let's build a shelter.' She knew that other people would not take you into their shelter if you had children: children were children, they could shout or start crying and give things away in no time. At that time I had money, and I had a shelter built in our flat, on the fourth floor. At that time I lived on Zamenhofa Street. In that shelter I had food for a whole year; my mother-in-law was with me there. The children were frightened the whole time. They did not want to sleep in the flat at all, but in the shelter; they would not allow anyone to undress them at night, or even take off their shoes. Even the little one understood and cried when I tried to undress her.

In April 1943, when the *Aktion* began and we were in the shelter, the children were so good that they did not make a sound; the younger one even hushed the older one. She kept saying 'Quiet – there's a German coming'. But she was so frightened that I had to carry her day and night, and I even had to go to the lavatory with her. It was exhausting with those children then; but I thought that that ordeal would save my children. I cared for them constantly, and kept them as clean as I could. I knew that I was one mother in a thousand who could give her children decent food.

After a few days people began to knock and tell us to come out, because there was a fire. The uprising had begun in the ghetto, and the houses had begun to burn one after another. At 44 Zamenhofa Street there was a warehouse full of furniture that had belonged to some Jews; a fire broke out there, and from that our building also caught fire. The stairs were already burning, and I had to leave the shelter. The Germans were already taking everyone in one by one. The Jews were standing in the courtyard, looking wild. One man carrying a child wanted to go and look for a hiding-place. But there was nowhere to go. I had always tried to stay together with all the other Jews. I said: 'Listen everyone, we have nowhere to hide any more, let's go with everyone else. The time has come for us to go where our brothers and sisters have gone.' Under an escort of Ukrainians we were taken to the Umschlagplatz. Terrible things went on there. People threw themselves from windows, took poison, and went crazy. I still had my children with me; I was alive. But we had no water for those three days; the children did not want to eat anything, but day and night they kept asking: 'Please can we have some water, Mama, please?' I bought a mouthful of water for each of the children for 100 złotys from one of the policemen. After three days we were marched off to the trains. It was hard everywhere with the children. People were always getting angry because the children were crying; they said the Germans would hear and would come and beat everyone. On the way to the train we had to walk down a corridor formed by policemen who stood there and beat everyone on the head with their truncheons. I saw this from far away and I was terrified for my child, the one I was carrying. I held her close, covering her head with my coat, and I managed to get through safely so that the policemen did not hit her. I was so glad about this that I cheered up right away: maybe I would save my children. When we got to the wagons, people started crowding in, and they were being driven on; I thought the children would be crushed. Then a Gestapo officer shouted at the people to help me, saying could they not see that there were children there. At this point he seemed like an angel to me for helping my children. In the train people were crying, cursing or praying. Some said we were going to live; others, that we were being taken to our deaths. This went on the whole time. I still had my children with me and I believed that it was my fate to suffer on their account and to save them. I could not feel my arms any more, as I was still carrying the little one, but I gave that no thought.

In Lublin we were taken off the train and they began to sort us into groups. Skilled labourers went off to work in Poniatów and Trawnik. But I had no trade and I still had my children; they would not accept me anywhere. I remained with the

largest group; there were women and children there, and I
thought that it would be better like that. They loaded us back
onto the train. In the evening we got off; the men were
separated from the women and we were marched off on foot.
It grew dark. I had no idea where I was or where I was going.
The Germans marched on either side of us, carrying electric
lamps. I led one child by the hand; the other was so heavy that
I kept thinking I could not go on, that I would just sit down
there with the children, not caring about what would happen.
But then I would remember that I must not give up, that I had
two good, dear children and that I must save them. My
mother-in-law was with us, but she was an old woman and
she could not help at all. In the camp at night we met the men
again and mixed in with them. The women looked for their
husbands; they cried, happy to be together again, and happy
that they would live now, for this was a work camp. But it was
Majdanek. When it grew light I saw how dirty and shabby the
children were, and I cried for them. I was so terribly tired that
I did not have the strength to fight for a little water. I did not
know what was happening to me. They began segregating us
again. Young people to one side, children and elderly to the
other. At this time I stayed alive only because of my mother-
in-law, because when I refused to hand the children over, she
took them; the children knew her and did not try to stay with
me. I did not even have time to think what this might mean
before I was already on the other side and they were marching
us to the bathhouse.

At that time I still did not and could not believe that they
killed children. All the other women and I reassured each
other, saying that we were probably going to be sent to work
and that the children would be kept separately. But I was
trembling with anxiety to see them and find out where they
were. As we were going to the bathhouse there was a fat
German in civilian clothes standing there and all the mothers
began calling out to him: 'Where are our children?' He gave a
gentle smile and said: 'Don't be afraid, the children are in
good hands, nothing will happen to them; they'll get milk and

everything they need.' And at that time we were stupid enough to believe what he said; but that same day, when we went to work in the garden, some Poles who were working there said to us: 'What? You stupid women, you've come to Majdanek and you do not know they have ovens here? They've already burned all the children and the old folks!'

I am a simple woman; I cannot express what I felt then, I do not have the words. I had taken such care of those children, I had been through so much with them and all the time I had kept on believing that they would be saved. I cried and wailed to God, but I felt as if I had turned to stone; I was so tired I could not think, and I did not have the strength to take my own life. In the throng I felt like cattle; I just kept going on and on, staying alive ...

(Archive of the VJHC, statement no. 139)

---

15. KAROLINA SAPETOWA

Kraków

(Statement taken by Róża Bauminger, Kraków)

Jewish children saved

The Hochweiser family consisted of the parents and three children. Samuś was the youngest, then there was a girl called Salusia and the eldest boy, Iziu. I was the children's nanny. In the first year of the war the father was shot. When all the Jews were moved to the ghetto, I left them. Every day I went to the ghetto and took what I could; I missed the children very much, I thought of them as my own.

Whenever things grew unsettled in the ghetto, the children would come and stay with me. They felt at home in my house. In March 1943 the ghetto was liquidated. The youngest boy was already staying with me in the country. On that day I went up to the gates of the ghetto, which were surrounded on all sides by the SS and the Ukrainians. People were rushing around like lunatics; a crowd of mothers and children was moving helplessly towards the gates. Suddenly I noticed Salusia and Iziu with their mother. She spotted me too, and whispered to her daughter: 'Go to Karolcia.' Without much reflection, Salusia slipped like a mouse between the heavy boots of the Ukrainians, who by some miracle failed to notice her. With her hands stretched out imploringly, she ran to me. All numb, I set off with Salusia and my aunt to walk to my village, Witanowice, near Wadowice.

Iziu and his mother were transported out and I never heard from them again. It was a hard life; it can only have been by a miracle that those children survived. To begin with the children used to go out of the house, but when relations grew more difficult, I had to hide them indoors. However, that did not help either. The local people knew that I was harbouring Jewish children, and there began harassment and threats from all sides to get me to hand the children over to the Gestapo, because otherwise they might burn the whole village, massacre us or something. The village administrator was well-disposed towards me and that often put my mind at rest. The more insistent or aggressive neighbours I would calm with a telling-off; sometimes I bribed people. But this did not last for long.

The SS were constantly sniffing around, and once again arguments began, until one day the farmers declared that we must get rid of the children, and they hatched a plan to take the children to the barn and cut their heads off with an axe as they slept.

I walked around like a madwoman; my old father was deeply concerned. What could we do? What should be done? The poor children knew everything, and before they went to bed they would say to us: 'Karolcia, do not kill us just today!' I could feel myself going numb; I took a decision that I would not hand the children over at any price.

I had an idea that saved the situation. I put the children on the cart and told everyone that I was taking them outside the village to drown them. I drove through the whole village and everyone saw, and believed me; then, when night fell I brought the children back and hid them in my neighbour's attic. It was a hot July; the children lay curled up on a half-metre-thick layer of dust. The poor things: larger and larger spots appeared on their bodies; and their fingernails and toe-nails began to fall out. They began to stink. I felt that I could not keep it up. But I struggled on; I had to make money so that at least the children would not go short of food. I also had to pay for that awful hiding-place in the attic.

In this way, those unfortunate children suffered for three months; then I somehow managed to heal the ulcers on their little bodies, but the children were deathly pale, especially the girl. Fear could always be seen in her face; the little boy was somehow tougher and more vivacious.

My money ran out and I could not keep up the payments, so I had to take the children back and put them in the cattle-shed. There was nothing else I could do. One day there was a search and an SS officer went into the shed. We were all convinced that the end had come, that everything was over. But Samuś behaved really smartly: he ran to get some straw and started laying it out for the cow to lie on. We were all amazed that the child had had such a clever idea. Salusia stood in the corner, all pale. The danger passed and the children were saved.

From that time on things were quiet until the Red Army came; the children were happy and I was even happier than them. I shall never part from them again, and even if they were to go to the far ends of the earth, I would go with them. They are like my own children; I love them more than any-thing in the world, and I would do anything for them.

(Archive of the VJHC, statement no. 170)